The World Was My Garden, Too

Other Books by Sam Pickering

The World Was My Garden, Too

Sam Pickering

Lake Dallas, Texas

FIRST EDITION

Requests for permission to reprint material from this work
should be sent to:

Permissions
Madville Publishing
P.O. Box 358
Lake Dallas, TX 75065

Acknowledgements:

The author and publisher gratefully acknowledge the *Georgia
Review* in which selections from these essays first appeared.

Author Photograph: Vicki Pickering
Cover Design: Nancy Parsons
Cover Art: Childe Hassam, *The Island Garden*, 1892, watercolor
on paper, Smithsonian American Art Museum, Gift of John
Gellatly, 1929.6.64

ISBN: 978-1-948692-14-4 paperback, 978-1-948692-15-1 ebook
Library of Congress Control Number: 2018968032

Dedication

For Vicki who tolerated a few leaf spots and a little rust but who kept days green and free from canker and blight.

Table of Contents

Preface, or the World Was
My Garden, Too.   ix

Rummaging   1

Re-Reading *Nicholas Nickleby*   30

Uncommercial Traveller   47

Jogging   69

My Study Window   95

As the World Turns Us   118

As the World Turns Us, II   135

Eureka I   161

Eureka II   186

Allergies   234

Breakdown Years   251

About the Author   269

Preface, or
The World Was My Garden, Too.

In January I pruned my study. Afterward I donated eight cartons of books to the annual sale at the Mansfield Library. In thinning my shelves, I discovered several volumes that I hadn't read and forgot that I owned. Among the books was *The World Was My Garden*, David Fairchild's account of his travels as a "Plant Explorer." At the end of the 19th and through the first third of the 20th century, Fairchild was responsible for introducing thousands of plants into the United States. He traveled the out-of-the-way globe sending back flowers and shrubs, trees, grasses, ferns, and agricultural crops—varieties of wheat, cherries, bamboo, and soybeans, among greenhouses of others. He introduced Americans to kale, avocados, and quinoa, this last a grain I ate for the first time three years ago. The biographies of generals and presidents with a few reformers tossed in as social leavening usually dominate textbook accounts of American history. But, to my mind, Fairchild did more to shape this country than any of the "great men" celebrated as fathers of the nation.

The World was published in 1938. My volume appeared in 1945 and had belonged to my grandfather, Mother's father. He wrote his name and the date inside the front cover on the first free end page: "John L. Ratcliffe 1946." A stroke killed him two years later when I was seven years old. I don't know how the book ended on my shelves, but I suspect Mother saved it for me, seeing or hoping to discover aspects of her father in me. Grandfather himself was a plant man, a florist with several stores who owned extensive nurseries in which he grew and experimented with flowers. Every spring his thoughts turned to flowers, and he went to Italy to welcome the season. I spent childhood summers on Cabin Hill, his farm in Hanover, Virginia. Every night in the middle of the dining room table a magnolia sat in a basin. When I went upstairs to go to bed, I always found a water lily on a platter on my bedside table. Surrounding the house and along the drive were orchards of flowering trees: magnolia, persimmon, pecan, cherry, and dogwood. Looking like green hems, rows of boxwood stretched through fields above cattle pastures, twenty-five thousand, Mother once told me, "every variety that grows in Virginia." Mother was prescient. Grandfather's loves flow through my sapwood, and if he had lived until I was twenty, I would have spent more time outside than inside houses, my arms not laden with books but bursting with flowers and bouquets of my other outdoor loves, insects and reptiles.

On the desk in my study now are a pair of hyacinths, the flowers on one purple, those on the other pink. Above and behind them loom two pots of Easter lilies. At dusk the fragrance of their blossoms fills the room, clotting the air like sweet cream. Spring hasn't arrived in Connecticut, but it is close. Two days ago, a Cooper's hawk landed near the wood pile in the back yard. After standing motionless for a moment it ran through leaves scampering like a pigeon. Next it hopped atop a log and froze, ignoring gray squirrels that foraged nearby and instead scanning the ground for young chipmunks breaking hibernation and leaving burrows. Last week a skunk sprayed the side of the garage, the perfume evoking memories of happy, blooming country nights. All seasons are gardens. Most of my plants are weedy and not cultivated, in winter, for example: braids of spore sacs beading the stalks of sensitive fern, the fruits of virgin's bower balding and breaking into feathers, and then the split follicles of milkweed, each half the keel of a rowboat, salty and storm-wracked, beached and eroding out of sight into sand. Like racks of small soiled neckties, leaves crinkle around mugwort. Atop the rosettes of spotted wintergreen white veins slice razor-edged across leaves, and wedging themselves into and between mullein's empty seed capsules, insects spin tents around themselves.

The World Was My Garden awakened nostalgia for a life I didn't live—a feeling or perhaps a fever common to oldsters, especially to the retired no longer incessantly distracted by the forgettable and who have the leisure to imagine. Happily, fevers break. Although I envied Fairchild's explorations, my meanderings to Canada, the Caribbean, Arkansas, and around Storrs that I describe in this book satisfy me. I write about long-discovered, recognizable trees and flowers and then a great deal about people. Fairchild appears to have known every important person in the botanical world. Explorers, thinkers, inventors, and the upper crusts of social movers and shakers became his friends. I spent my life in universities surrounded by decent, admirable people. However, few escaped the classroom long enough to morph into characters. No one was called Doodlebug, Hangnail, or Mole Eye. At the Community Center no one groans after exercising or sings in the shower. Nobody is the subject of fond, entertaining gossip. Still a locker-room remark occasionally startles me into an exclamation. "I reduced my blood pressure by eating beets," a mathematician told me after I mentioned a recent visit to a cardiologist. "I eat beets at breakfast, lunch, and dinner. Before flicking my light off at night I go to the kitchen and for a bedtime snack treat myself to a platter of sliced beets. I sprinkle vinaigrette on them. A couple of times I doused them with Miracle Whip but that wasn't so good."

"Never again will I make a left turn when driving," a French professor informed me in December. "They cause too much stress. You'd be surprised how easy and tension-free it is to reach your destination by turning right,

right, right, and right." "Last week I received an email from the widow of my thesis advisor," a man sitting next to me in the locker room recounted. "When our marriage was bad, you sided with him not me," the woman wrote, "and when you ate dinner with us, you laughed at his jokes and not at mine." "I didn't know they were having marital difficulties," the man said, "and I ate dinner with them only once. That was in 1973, forty-five years ago, a day before I received my Ph.D. I left Ireland right after getting the degree. I haven't seen, heard, or thought about the woman since then. Insofar as jokes go, not only do I find false jocularity unappealing, but I can never remember any." The man paused then continued sounding both mystified and exasperated. "Yesterday I received a second email. The woman wrote only three sentences, 'There's another thing. My jokes were better than yours. Yours weren't funny at all.'"

In *Plain Talks on Familiar Subjects* first published in the late 1860s, Josiah Holland criticized "college-made men." They "hold principles subject to precedents" and "blindly worship words and phrases." "Pure scholarship is always conservative," he wrote. It timidly resists change, clings to "dominant institutions," and "swims easily along the current of peaceful life, but shrinks from emergencies, and shirks the work of revolutions." I am more teaching than college made. Only in the pool at the Community Center do I make a splash, and when I doze on the daybed in my study, revolutionary thoughts do not disturb my peace of mind. I don't worship words, but in these pages, I toy with words and, honestly, why not? What I write about phrases won't make me diabetic although a few sentimentalists have called me a sweetheart. I was an ordinary teacher. I am not wealthy or poor enough to be a curiosity. I'm not important, and I'm indifferent to opinions of me. No one is proud of me. No one envies me and seeks my acquaintance. Living without hope doesn't make me unhappy. At my death, Vicki has promised that obsequies will be muted and private. I am the invisible neighbor. I've never been guilty of peculation, and only rarely have I been the subject of conversation and speculation. I am not the Seventh Son of a Seventh Son. I am the First and Only Son of a First Son who worked for the Traveler's Insurance Company for forty-five years. My index finger does not possess magical healing properties, but my writing hand is limber. Holland would probably think me dull and lay my books aside without reading them. That would be a mistake. A writer's life is a duplicitous guide to his books. Pickering, a cousinly critic once wrote, "minces along until suddenly he puts on Seven-League Boots and bounds into strange worlds."

The moods and follies of men and women interest me. The circle of people I know is a dot compared to Fairchild's ring of acquaintances. Still, I write much about people. Many of them are tourists. Of course, people are tourists every day of their lives. I don't differentiate between people created out of whole cloth and men and women molded out of dust and ribs. In fact, individuals whose conceptions are fibrous appeal strongly to me. Moreover, they are easier to control than characters whose beginnings are corporeal. If a fictitious character strays beyond the hem of a paragraph, I snip the wayward thread. Furthermore, because all people eventually slip the shackles of blood and bone and become imaginary, I think it better for them to start as fictional beings and develop as pages are turned. Characters who populate my books are aware of my predilection for puns, and if one tries to butter me up with a pat of spoiled wordplay, I can quickly sweep it into the disposal—a pun like I heard an archdeacon make last week. He said missionaries sent to Borneo in the late 18th century deserved praise for giving local cannibals their first taste of Christianity. Would that the divine had gone further and noted that missionaries were especially toothsome if caught young, preferably between sixteen and eighteen. At that age they were tolerant and palatable. They were latitudinarian, and their beliefs had not hardened into indigestible doctrine. Insofar as the Lords of the Church were concerned, simony spoiled their gastronomic appeal. While bloating their personal vestries, greed ran rancid through their corpses turning them into fly bait useful only to butchers making oleaginous sausages.

In 1828 appeared *The Man of Two Lives*. Although written by the man "Himself," for propriety's and convention's sakes, the book was attributed to James Boaden. The narrator was named Frederic Werner and died initially in Frankford on the Main when he was forty-five years old. "I distinctly remember the last expressions that I used, as life was ebbing fast away," he recounted. After surveying his misspent existence, Werner clasped his hands together and "exclaimed with convulsive energy," "O, that I could return again into the womb of my mother, and spring once more into a world in which I have trifled with time and abused the blessings of my condition! I have suffered much and deserved to suffer; never having promoted the happiness of others, I of necessity poisoned my own." At that agonizing moment, he questioned, "did I fancy a voice of more than human sweetness, or did really some immortal spirit speak to my mind, rather than to an ear stiffening into clay" and say, "UNHAPPY MIND, THY WISH IS GRANTED; THOU SHALT ONCE MORE ANIMATE A HUMAN FORM."

On returning to consciousness the narrator discovered that he had become Edward, the infant son of George Sydenham, Esq. and his wife Sophia. In retrospect it was a blessing that not all Frederic's pleas were granted. His previous mother Mrs. Werner had aged beyond childbearing years and bounding from her womb shrieking and kicking would have caused serious, probably fatal, damage to her organs of generation. Moreover, having to be reborn in order to experience a different life seems inelegant and inefficient. Only the imaginatively-impoverished experience just two lives. With this in mind, readers should be aware that matters usually labeled inconsistencies mark signatures of my pages. As people shuffle though their years, they lead many lives. Personalities and interests change like cards flipped out of a pack. The old man is not the boy he once was or the youth he became. The accomplishments of his middle years differ, to use one of Vicki's favorite words, from the assholery of his geriatric decades. Consistency cannot be foolish, as Emerson declares, because consistency is an impossibility.

My Garden, Too is nonfiction. Approaching truth, however, is a roundabout process best accomplished by creeping toward it camouflaged by lying. In *The Art of Fiction*, Walter Besant opined that the modern English novel "almost always starts with a conscious moral purpose." I don't place the palm of my right hand on my forehead and bow down to high idiosyncratic purpose. I admire benevolence, but I don't inculcate morals. Novels depend upon plots and uncertainty. I planned this book. It contains stories, but it does not have a plot and doesn't create or depend upon uncertainty. Most of the stories are silly. I think them healthy. They reduce tension and lower blood pressure elevated by a diet heavy with zeal and ambition. They don't upset. They tickle for a moment then are forgotten. Many are old standbys, and gnat-straining cannot make them meaningful. In Missouri after a judge fined a countryman fifty dollars for purloining chickens, he questioned the man. "How in the world did you do it?" the judge asked. "The coop was near the house, and two vicious dogs roamed the yard." "Judge, it wouldn't do you no use if I was to tell you," the man answered. "If you went after those chickens, you'd get half your backside chawed off and the rest filled with buckshot. You best hunker down right here and confine your rascality to the courtroom where you knows your way around."

I also quote poetry. None of the verse is engraved in hieroglyphics and reading it won't strain the mind and precipitate a poetic fit. In 1913 an emended version of the arachnophobic "Miss Muffet" appeared in *The Southern Planter*: "Fleshy Miss Muffet / Sat down on Tuffet, / A very good dog in his way; / When she saw what she'd done, / She started to run— / And Tuffet was buried next day." As I intimated earlier, morals are often mysterious and difficult to live by. The moral appended to this Plump rather than "Little Miss Muffet" was at first glance straightforward: "There is no dog in a dog biscuit." On the other hand, what the statement implies about the culinary use of Tuffet's corpse is best left to literary critics.

Understandable poetry helps digestion, and I read a soupcon before every meal. Yesterday's lunchtime digestive came from Charles Heber Clark's *Out of the Hurly-Burly*. Colonel Mortimer J. Bangs, the editor of *The Morning Argus*, decided that a dash of the poetic would increase sales of the newspaper. To this end he hired Mr. Slimmer, a poet to enliven the paper's obituaries by composing a few lines describing each of the deceased. "Lighten the gloom. Do not mourn over the departed, but rather take a joyous view of death which after all," Bangs instructed, "is, as it were, but the entrance to a better life." "The death-angel smote Alexander McGlue," Slimmer wrote typically. "And gave him protracted repose; / He wore a checked shirt and a Number Nine shoe, / And he had a pink wart on his nose. / No doubt he is happier dwelling in space / Over there on the evergreen shore. / His friends are informed that his funeral takes place / Precisely at quarter-past four." McGlue's family had not attended college and were not poetry aficionados. "My late brother had no wart on his nose," McGlue's surviving sibling stated calling the obituary slanderous. "He had upon his nose neither a pink wart, nor a green wart, nor a cream-colored wart, nor a wart of any other color."

In this book, on several occasions the alert reader may hear the sepulchral notes of the Last Roll Call. Twice a year I telephone Ida, a distant cousin. We reminisce about childhood and describe the doings of our offspring. Last week I telephoned Ida. She answered immediately. She was her usual ebullient self. I told her a couple of humorous stories, and she laughed appreciatively. "Sam," she then said, "I'm sorry, but I have to cut this conversation short. Call back next week. Johnny died last night, and I have a thousand things to do before the funeral. Tonight, twenty-two family members are coming to the house for dinner." Johnny was Ida's husband. He'd been ill for a year, but he had not been expected to sprout wings any time soon. "Twenty-two people for dinner!" Vicki exclaimed. "That's awfully hard on Ida. I hope the meal is catered. Do you suppose she'll serve cold cuts?"

"The Magic of Sport predominates in most lives in one way or another," Nat Gould wrote, adding, "it will be a bad day for England, or any other country, when sports decay and maudlin sentimentality obtains the upper hand." A hundred-and-ten years have passed since Gould's *The Magic of Sport* appeared. Much has changed. Sports have not decayed. They have flourished and themselves have become the object of abject sentimentality. In this book I do not discuss sport. I believe their magic has devolved into black magic — witchery that damages and corrupts both individuals and countries. Neither do I write about violence. Recently I read James Hain Friswell's *Varia: Readings from Rare Books* published in the middle of the nineteenth century. A chapter "Howell The Traveller," focused on letters James Howell wrote in the seventeenth century describing his experiences on the continent.

Howell first left England in 1619. On being appointed steward of a London glass factory, he went abroad "to perfect his knowledge and engage 'gentlemen workmen.'" In subsequent years he traveled in various capacities eventually going to Copenhagen as Secretary to the British Ambassador. In one of his letters Howell recounted what an eyewitness told him about the torture of Francoise Ravaillac who stabbed and killed King Henry IV of France in 1610. Ravaillac's "body was pull'd between four horses, that one might hear his bones crack, and after dislocation they were set again," Howell wrote. Next Ravaillac was transported "half naked with a torch in that hand which had committed the murder." At the spot where the king was killed, Ravaillac's hand "was cut off, and a Gauntlet of hot Oyl was clapped on the place to staunch the blood." Ravaillac "gave a doleful shriek; then was he brought upon a stage, when a new pair of boots was provided for him, half filled with boyling Oyl." Afterward, Howell continued, "his Body was pincered, and hot Oyl poured into the holes." "In all the extremity of this torture he scarce shewed any sense of pain but when the gauntlet was clap'd upon his arm to staunch the flux, at which time of reaking blood he gave a shriek only," Howell concluded. "He bore up against all these torments for about three hours before he died." Howell's letter nauseated me, and his portrayal of Ravaillac's death is the single example of man's inhumanity to man that appears in this book. As people age, they develop cultural allergies. I refuse to watch violent movies and television shows. I will not read descriptions of, much less write about, such horrors. Self-conscious blinkering distorts reality and promotes illusions, but a day devoid of illusion would be unbearable.

This being *My Garden,Too*, I write about the domestic — little things experienced by most people. Teased out of ordinary hours they seem insubstantial when in reality they are the warp and weft of happy days. When Vicki comes to bed at night, she doesn't immediately fall asleep. Instead she rumpuses about waving her legs in the air and spinning her feet doing three exercises she dubs "Tumbleweed, Clothespin, and Wind Farm." Furthermore, once she knows I am awake and consequently am grumpy, she welcomes them, saying, "Here come Tumbleweed and Clothespin. Watch out for Wind Farm." For my part when a dream jars me out of sleep I get my own back by waking Vicki and describing the dream — the more nonsensical the better. Last week

I dreamed that I was training twenty-two race horses. All were owned by dentists struggling to break addictions to golf. I remembered the names of several horses: Here Today — Pulled Tomorrow, Bicuspid, Pick, Amalgam, and Root Canal. "But that's only five. What are the names of the other horses?" I asked Vicki. "Be quiet. Let me sleep," Vicki said. "No," I answered. "Those aren't good names. Think of some more." "Go to Hell," Vicki said. "Ah," I said; "that's better. Give me a couple more names." "Oh, Lord," Vicki said. "Oh, yes, now you're cooking," I replied. "You're on the Nomenclature Track. Its turf is faster even than that of Churchill Downs." "God, you think you're clever," Vicki said thoroughly awake. "You are so tedious." I didn't answer because I had begun trotting back to Slumber Land. In any case good husbands do not linger in the Winner's Circle.

Only infrequently do I write about strident controversies roiling the moment. However, I prefer gentrification to genderfication, and recently Vicki and I spoke about the language used by lady preachers. I don't like hearing female divines rant, stamp their high heels, and bellow *F* and *S*-words, in fact the whole alphabet of naughties. When I mentioned my disapproval, Vicki became thin-lipped and accused me of stereotyping. "There are no male preserves in the dictionary," she said, "and women can and should use the same language as men." Such conversation usually ends here. Sometimes I mutter *prostate* and limp away. Often, I deflect the conversation by requesting the dinner menu. To keep words on the railed track between knife and fork, I toss out a quotation, typically a remark by Myrtle Reed, say, "the complexities in man's personal equation are caused by variants of three emotions: a mutable fondness for women, according to temperament and opportunity, a more uniform feeling toward money, and the universal devastating desire — the old, old passion for food."

Let me add that in this book I do not discuss sexual congress. I have no hobbies of my own, and the private hobbies of strangers bore me. Still, nowadays troops of university-educated people seem to be behaving irrationally. The retrospective anxiety about intimate matters has affected my friend Josh. Last week before swimming he complained that females began harassing him when he was young. "They took advantage of my youth," he said, "and forced unsought intimacies upon me, resulting in my becoming addicted to carnality. The only way I knew to allay the infelicitous cravings was to marry. Imagine the life I might have led had I remained single — explorer, adventurer, not a man about town, but a man about deserts and jungles. The possibilities were endless." Giving advice is presumptuous, but I discouraged Josh from airing his grievances. Clearly age had jostled his equilibrium and unbalanced him. Josh once taught Shakespeare, so I told him, "Don't bemoan your yellow leaves and ruined choirs. You've enjoyed an easy, comfortable life. Don't become vulgar and resentful. Spring is approaching. Birdsong will whistle through the air. Forsythia will burst into yellow, and violets break white and blue through the gray grass. Memories will glow; you'll shake off this ill humor and forgetting meaningless significances order Polly to put the kettle on so you and I can have tea."

In my essays I ponder age. How could I do otherwise? Soon I will be eighty, and books written by boys and girls playing in intellectual sandboxes inevitably strike me as jejune. The young men I see on television bore me. They are so muscular and so addicted to mindless strutting that they seem parodies of masculinity and more queenly than kingly. Among William Hale White's *Pages from a Journal* was a sketch of an old tree. "An aged tree, whose companions had gone, having still a little sap in its bark and a few leaves which grew therefrom, prayed it might see yet another spring," White wrote. "Its prayer was granted: and spring came but the old tree had no leaves save one or two near the ground, and a great fungus fixed itself on its trunk. It had a dull life in its roots, but not enough to know that its moss and fungus were not foliage. It stood there, an unlovely mass of decay, when the young trees were all bursting. 'That rotten thing,' said the master, 'ought to have been cut down long ago.'" In breasting the lachrymose tide that washes over the elderly and patronizingly celebrates their trembling doings, White saw himself as a truth-teller and the voice of reason. Nevertheless, there was much that White did not see: black racers living underground amid the tree's roots, chipmunks in their burrows, and squirrels nesting high in the branches. Because he did not examine the trunk, he ignored the nests of bluebirds, nuthatches, chickadees, flickers and pileated woodpeckers, phoebes, screech and barred owls, tree swallows, and house and winter wrens, among an aviary of other birds. Neither did he notice beetles, among borers alone: shothole, flatheaded, roundheaded, American plum, lilac, dogwood, willow, birch, and root-feeding. Old trees are godparents to life. Like a moral at the end of a fable, an old tree should hang over every garden. Its crumbling presence is a visual lesson. It teaches gardeners that if they want their plots to be vital places and their worlds and days to be gardens, they should avoid mowing and pruning, hedging life into sterile regularity.

Although White's sketch of old age made me wince, what galls is the generic uplift of the sort voiced by Arthur St. John Adcock in his "The Art of Keeping Young." "Self-forgetfulness, a sympathetic interest in lives outside our own, the cultivation of a quiet mind, and a habit of making the best of things," Adcock wrote, "these will keep a man's heart from growing old, and so long as his heart is young, the age of his bones is comparatively unimportant." Adcock's prescription for prolonging adolescence is poppycock. Adcock is oblivious to the heart-regulating pleasures of melancholy. Furthermore, relatives of the man who forgets himself and his pills will shortly thereafter be visiting his bones in Skeleton Park. Additionally, as a person ages his sympathies contract. Self-interest warns that in expanding concerns to include lives beyond his own, a man multiplies worries and responsibilities thus guaranteeing the impossibility of achieving a quiet mind. Also, a crowd of friends so drains the sympathies that to protect themselves from physical and emotional collapse, aging people often retreat into contraceptive surliness. Lastly, instead of straining to make the best out of bad things, the wise man jettisons the bad and devotes his failing energy to enjoying the good.

Illness has not yet locked me into mental inflexibility. As a result, my thoughts about age and many other subjects vary not only from day to day but also from paragraph to paragraph. "Who can answer for the mood of tomorrow?" Holme Lee asked in *In the Silver Age*. "Who knows whether we shall be traversing a broad plat of monotony, or going through a deep-brooding glen, or climbing a hard ascent into light and fresh air or 'sitting down by the wayside aweary' and putting our burden off?" In "New Year's Eve," Charles Lamb testified, "I am in love with this green earth; the face of town and country; the unspeakable rural solitudes, and the sweet security of streets. I would set up my tabernacle here. I am content to stand still at the age to which I am arrived; I, and my friends; to be no younger, no richer, no handsomer." Lamb said that he did not want to be "weaned by age" or drop "like mellow fruit" into the grave. Lamb's essay is beguiling and seductive. It turns the reader into a lotus-eater making him fancy curbing time and embracing quiet unending contentment. Lamb was forty-six in 1821 when "New Year's Eve" appeared. I have had three decades more experiences than Lamb and despite loving the green earth and rural solitude, I do not want time to stop. In the morning when I push myself out of bed, pain radiates through me like a spider web jittering in a cold wind, and I imagine the warm ripeness of dropping like mellow fruit. Moods change, but the Great Expectation remains—not Dickens's secular expectations most of which lose appeal as people age but expectation of

The End. If willing suspension of disbelief comes so easily that a person accepts a plethora of religious faiths, I suppose he might have great expectations. Certainly, people's fantasies are carnivalesque. A lady preacher in Monroe, Louisiana inspired by distilled spirits told her congregation that after the Resurrection the sanctified played calliopes not harps. The remark intrigued but did not upset her congregation. The preacher was a Christian, but she lost her pulpit when she insisted that God resembled an Alligator Gar. "To say that Man was created in the image of God," she declared, "is a viperous narcissistic perversity." "If the earth as imbeciles think," she continued shutting her *Bible* and striding away from the pulpit, "was created for Man then what damnable ingrates you recipients have proved to be."

I'm bookish, and reading my essays, a reviewer once wrote, was "like walking through the stacks of a library and after plucking dusty volumes from the shelves sitting down on the floor and reading them." True enough, I wander libraries and read old books, many of them dusty and rarely checked out. But I don't sit on the floor. I sit in a chair at a desk and take notes. For someone my age getting up from the floor is difficult and inelegant. Recently I finished a volume remarkably suitable for my age: John Kendrick Bangs's *The Autobiography of Methuselah* composed by George W. Methuselah and published in 2348 B.C. Methuselah lived in Ararat Corners, one of the few places on the globe that Fairchild doesn't seem to have explored. If Fairchild had been there, doubtless he would have unearthed the tablets on which Methuselah wrote the account of his life.

In the beginning of the autobiography, Methuselah assured readers that he was going to tell the truth. He was aware, he stated, that a few of the tales might seem extravagant exaggerations, "especially those having to do with Prehistoric Animals, or Antediluvians as I believe the scientists call them." Methuselah valued the truth even more than I do. If, he testified, "I tell the story of a Pterodactyl that after being swallowed whole by a Discosaurus, successfully gnaws his way through the walls of the latter's stomach to freedom, I make no claim that all Pterodactyls could do the same, but that in his particular case the Pterodactyl to which I refer did it."

Reading specialists determine the holdings of school libraries. They select books deemed age-appropriate and prune volumes judged unbefitting. They focus on beginning readers, that is children in elementary and middle schools. They devote little attention to advanced readers—adults my age. "That is because," a theorist in a Department of Curriculum and Instruction explained to me, "the reading proclivities of septuagenarians are firmly established. The young are malleable and adapt easily to change. For the elderly, habits, and this includes reading habits, are crutches. Knock away a habit and the person may fall down so hard that not even a healer can pray him to his feet again." I am not sure the theorist is correct. What is true is that age influences a person's reading. For example, few octogenarian women purchase handbooks which teach natural childbirth. In contrast writings about senescence have a magnetic effect upon the elderly. Especially popular are articles offering retirement advice or suggesting how to avoid dementia and prolong life. In January while in the library I skimmed through last year's Sunday numbers of the *Nashville Tennessean*. I read rapidly. Athletics bore me, and most of my Tennessee friends have fallen off the perch or into desuetude. Only one article slowed my page-turning. The Bozeman Institute of Health and Wellness announced it was suspending "development of its Ponce de Leon gamma globulin injection," this after two decades and a gold mine of research money. When perfected, the injection would ideally strip thirty-five years off a person's life. Eligibility was limited to people over seventy-five in good physical and mental health. Thus, a successful inoculation would transform an eighty-year-old into someone aged forty-five. The Institute walked away from the project not because of obvious problems that would accompany success of the injection, such matters, as familial relationships, that, for example, between the newly-minted forty-five-year old and her older middle-aged daughter. What difficulties, one wonders, would arise stemming from intellectual change? Would a forty-something have the wisdom and attitude of an octogenarian and perhaps suffer from early onset curmudgeonism? And, surely, the theological perturbations associated with being literally born again would be more difficult to master than the Ten Commandments. No, as could be expected in a capitalist society the Institute mothballed the project because of financial concerns. Once a person "revisited" his forties he would lose his Social Security and be forced to give up his pension and its healthcare benefits. Only someone whose upper story had begun to collapse would trade comfortably settled old age in for the anxieties associated with a new model, one that would likely break down leaving him a penniless and homeless hitchhiker lost amid the by-ways of an unfamiliar suburb. "Only in the unlikely occurrence that millions of geezers invested in the injection would returns from the enterprise match the investment. As much as pure science appeals to me personally," the chairman of the Institute's board of directors, testified, "we are trustees of institutional and average citizens' money. We serve others and must not allow personal desires to determine company policy. We owe it to our stock holders to insert a plug into the program before the cash flow becomes a torrent and washes away the dividends that shore up savings, awaken hope, provide comfort, and underwrite wars."

In the poem "Words," Julia Young said that some of her words dashed and leaped. In contrast a few lingered "like a funeral train." While others whirled "in a breezy sweep," many lagged sluggish, sober, and plain. Like my life most of my words are plain. No policeman has given me a ticket, not even a parking ticket, and no grammarian has arrested me for bad usage. To add a little exoticism to life, I occasionally stick an unfamiliar word or expression into a sentence, for example, calling a bobolink a reed bird or saying that writing a poem was courting the nine, these last being the muses. Learned people often mistake obscurity for profundity, so using words that drive readers to the dictionary, especially a dictionary published before the nineteenth century, will increase admiration for my writing and respect for my mind. Certainly, the experience of the main character in George Ade's "The Preacher Who Flew His Kite" verifies this assumption. The preacher was not a big hit with his congregation, several pews of which slept through his sermons. He realized that if he wanted people to believe "he was a Nobby and Boss Minister he would have to hand out a little Guff." To accomplish this, he stripped meaning out of his sermons and converted them into pastiches of quotations from well-known nonexistent celebrities, among them, "the great Icelandic Poet, Ikon Naurojke," the "Great Poet" Amebius the Greek, Polenta the Italian, and the renown Persian theologian Ramtazuk. The allusions resuscitated the preacher's reputation. The congregation was proud of his learning and from henceforth thought him "HOT STUFF."

As nonfiction often proves inadequate to expressing truths, so conventional language fails to reflect thought and feelings. Consequently, people invent words. For years members of my family have seasoned dinners by discussing language, not simply matters like the pronunciation of forehead or the illiterate transformation of *I* into an objective pronoun but also arguing about words we ourselves fashioned. I mastermined ghormanhydras, but Eliza has had the effrontery to correct my pronunciation, insisting that the word is properly ghormanhygas. At this lexiconic moment we agree that the definition of the word is mysterious. In the future, alas, one of us may compile a meaning or meanings and thus upset the glossarial equipoise. Since retiring, I have not kept abreast of the doings of English departments. Of course,

I've noticed that cutting-edge departments now teach less literature and bales more politics and sociology. Such changes do not arouse my ire or concern. Long ago I called universities "post-adolescent day-care centers." What is taught in classrooms is incidental to real education which is personal and self-generated.

Because I write, I have pondered the increasing prominence of composition in literature departments or, as writing laboratory assistants call it, Composition Studies. In his *Medical Essays*, Oliver Wendell Holmes reflected on the popularity of homeopathy. "Homeopathy," he wrote, "has proved lucrative, and so long as it continues to be so will surely exist, — as surely as astrology, palmistry, and other methods of getting a living out of the weakness and credulity of mankind and womankind." The most efficient method of learning to write is to shut the door to one's room and, sitting down alone, write and write and write. During breaks a person should read. Teachers can correct errors in traditional grammar, but there are no Metallic Tractors, Ozella's Lozenges, or Powders of Dobb that can transform an inept writer into a skilled wordsmith overnight. As can be expected in a corporate society, shelves of optimistic pharmacological textbooks have been compounded offering hope and instruction to disconsolate would-be scribblers. The will to hope is powerful. Intention may induce a student to buy a handbook, but it doesn't write essays.

Composition courses themselves are the miraculous Tar Water in which English curricula float. If Tar Water lakes dried, what I wonder would happen to English Departments, Colleges of Arts and Sciences, and to Universities themselves? That won't occur. Composition like homeopathy is a money-maker. Hosts of practitioners, theorists, and administrators prop up Composition Studies, and themselves, by celebrating the curative powers of writing. Their pronouncements smack of advertisements pasted to bottles of patent medicine. As impurities disappear from a person's prose, so the argument runs, they also vanish from his mind, enabling him to think clearer and better while simultaneously freeing him to become a more admirable person. The individual whose sentences no longer suffer from erysipelas will himself not be plagued by hysterical and scurvy thoughts. The perennially-unanswered question is how important outside the college classroom is writing well. Put simply it's not important. Rarely does success or the version of success called happiness hinge on a person's ability to compose intelligible declarative sentences.

Well, that's enough run-on thinking even if the sentences read nicely and are correctly punctuated. In *Wildflowers of the Pacific Coast*, Emma Thayer lamented that "often you will see a most beautiful specimen growing just beyond your reach on some rugged point." "I once saw," she continued, "a whole bed of fine bell-shaped flowers on a point above me, impossible to reach. They grew wondrously beautiful while I gazed, and I imagined that they grew larger and larger until they looked like a whole chime of bells ringing out a dirge to my disappointed ambition." Literary gardeners know that thoughts frequently resemble wildflowers. Many grow out of reach. Even if a person has a blue-black writing thumb and moves a promising specimen to a familiar plot, fertilizes rigorously, and revises carefully, often the idea doesn't thrive. I haven't expressed my concerns about the medicinal place of Composition in English very well. Like Thayer's campanulas, they bloomed beyond my grasp. However, I have weathered the temptations of ambition, and inability does not ring a dirge and make me melancholy. Neither can failure spur me to purchase a new shovel and expose the taproots of the subject. It is more salubrious to buy a grubbing hoe and, tossing the old sod aside, replace it with a fresh topic. Language, as I wrote earlier, can be as willful as bittersweet. All too frequently, it resists being trained to a trellis of well-wrought paragraphs and fails to capture thought. How much better to mutter ghormanhydras and abandon the subject. Certainly, Myrtle Reed's remarks are happier and, in fact, curative, purging grume from the bloodstream. "Young men," she wrote, "believe platonic friendship possible; old men know better—but when a man learns to profit by the experience of another, we may look for mosquitos at Christmas and holly in June."

June hasn't arrived yet. Days are dank, and "the spousal time of May," as Coventry Patmore hymned, hasn't hung "all the hedges with bridal wreaths." I am eager to spot bloodroot and narcissus in the dell outside my study. I want the lilacs behind the garage to bloom and their perfume to drift through the kitchen window. I want to stop wondering whether liberty and equality can co-exist without qualifying the meaning out of both. When I step off a sidewalk on campus, I want to smell pineapple weed. I am ready to say that I won't mow the front yard until dandelions have gone to seed. If someone questions my fondness for dandelions, I'll quote James Payn and respond, "What are a few wild oats in a world of wheat?" Nevertheless, I am impatient. By now the forsythia that separates our yard from that of our neighbor should be yellow as sunrise. But then I know that in New England, as Mable Osgood Wright wrote, "we have no calendar of Nature, no rigid law of season, or of growth. The climate, a caprice, a wholly eerie thing, sets tradition at defiance and forces our poets to contradict each other. The flower which one day declares the harbinger of spring may be a lazy vanguard in another year." That's true, but a book I transplanted into my study from a library discard sale (paying fifty cents) puts it better: "The golden days of autumn are full of their own beauty. The grey days of winter's mist and fog have theirs, but there is something in the tender blue days of the rainy springtime that sets the heart appraise, and brings out as nothing else can, the meanings of leaf and bud, of flower and tree."

"A life-long habit of story-telling has much to do with the production of these pages," George Washington Cable, stated at the beginning of *The Amateur Garden*. A flower garden "is itself a story, one which actually and naturally occurs, yet occurs under its master's guidance and control with artistic effect," he explained. "A well-designed garden is not only a true story happening artistically, but it is one that passes through a new revision each year." All the essays in *My Garden, Too* are designed. Despite the effort I put into them, though, I don't care what effects they produce. I simply hope people will enjoy them enough to refrain from bad language. My pages, like those of Cable, have been shaped by habits not only that of telling stories but also that of seeing the world as composed of stories. I like to think the flowers in my garden true although many plants are grafts, that is, a shoot of this inserted into the stem of that. I am still revising my bed and will probably be doing so until, as the saying puts it, I get measured for a new overcoat and become a resident of a different sort of plot. The revisions do not adhere to a schedule but are happenstance. Yesterday was sunny. I got up early and raked the back yard, filling a garden cart with the shells of hickory nuts. Afterward Vicki and I set out on an excursion unlike yet similar to one of David Fairchild's plant hunting expeditions. We drove to Blue Spruce Farm in North Franklin to watch draft horses in a plowing competition. The horses were Belgians and Percherons. Both are massive and look like boulders ripped from escarpments, the Belgians settling on a dry plain and bleached by sunlight, the Percherons falling into marshy damp and blanketed by black-on-black lichens.

I didn't intend to discover things for my garden, but I did. Near the horse barn a table sagged under pots of food. The food was for teamsters and their families, but when I strolled over to the table, a woman said, "Would you and your wife like lunch? We have more than enough. Please join us." I thanked the woman. Vicki is diffident, and I had to lead her to the table and hand her a plate. Then I served myself a bowl of jambalaya thick with shrimp and sausage. Afterward I ate a palm-sized slice of a two-layer vanilla cake. "You approached the table hoping one of the women would offer you lunch," Vicki said later. Vicki sounded reproachful. I thought her tone "a bit much" because she ate more than I did: macaroni and cheese, beans, a salad, and dessert. I ignored Vicki's criticism and responded to her implied question. "Sure," I said, "I ambled over on purpose. I was hungry, and I knew someone would invite us to lunch. I'm a professional horticulturalist, expert at manipulating days into narratives." "Anyway, enough culinary chatter, it makes me bilious. You know the old saying: a person should never open his mouth except at another's table." If it is possible for a man to snigger at himself behind his own back, then I did so. I have cadged countless meals, and every time I simultaneously want to pat my shoulder and kick my bottom. Still appetite should not be denied. "Some philosophers despise the stomach, but we cannot get along without it," James Friswell wrote. "Our limbs may fall off one by one, our taste decay, our senses leave us, our minds be wrecked, but King Stomach lives, and will live supreme. . . . Business may trouble us, politics worry us, and money-matters drive us mad; but we all eat and eat heartily."

As Vicki and I talked, we wandered behind the horse barn. At the edge of a pasture grazed a pair of Lineback cows, one an American, the other a Gloucester. While the heads, flanks, and shanks of the cows were black, their bellies were white, and a broad white line ran over their backs along their spines and dripped down their tails like a wash of paint. Sight of the Linebacks was bright and cheering. It made us feel good-natured, and Vicki smiled and called them "bovine pole-cattles." I had not seen a Lineback before, and for me the cows were exotic, not quite as exotic as many of the plants Fairchild sent home from around the world but nevertheless new to me. I told Vicki that I planned to take the pair back to Storrs and plant them in a book. "On the page with the sausage tree which Fairchild discovered in Egypt." "That will please your grandfather," Vicki said. "Didn't he have Jerseys and Guernseys at Cabin Hill?" "Yes," I said musing, remembering sitting on the floor of the screened porch watching cows trail across the lowlands toward the Pamunkey River headed for the milking barn.

Rummaging

Many experiences enriched my childhood, but nothing bettered rummaging attics and barns. When I grew up, I didn't stop rummaging. I simply shifted my explorations to libraries. School did not make me a teacher. Instead barns and attics taught me to notice the visible and the palpable. The fragrance of the musty and the manured awakened sense and thought. Rummagers like me often write prose that is corny and occasionally rank. Never, however, is it abstract. It is always concrete and understandable. Instead of sitting in classrooms waffling on about the creative process, instructors should encourage students to see for themselves. They should pack them off to barns or send them armed with pads and pencils to hunt old-clothes in their grandmothers' attics. Paradoxically, the more people hold and see the tangible, the more they appreciate the world but the less certain and judgmental they become. Meaning becomes muddy, and they eschew doctrine and age into flexibility and humanity.

Of course, people hanker for clarity despite knowing that it is artificial. The "deep slumber of decided opinion" and the assurances of commonplaces are alluring. The heroes of childhood, Arthur Rowe said in Graham Greene's *The Ministry of Fear*, are uncomplicated. "They are brave, they tell the truth, they are good swordsmen and they are never in the long run defeated. That is why no later books satisfy us like those which were read to us in childhood — for those promised a world of great simplicity of which we knew the rules, but the later books are complicated and contradictory with experience." In preaching that the end of learning was "to repair the ruins of our first parents by regaining to know God aright, and out of that knowledge to love him, to imitate him, to be like him," Milton appears naïve to present-day adults — even to people who having found the world too much with them long to change their lives, people whose hopes have been eroded by daily life and who know that satisfaction and happiness are both temporary. Such people recognize, often regretfully, that fervent Pentecostal leanings bend their holders out of thoughtful shape, indeed out of truth.

In *The Pleasures of Life*, Sir John Lubbock spoke more commonsensically, at least to the inhabitants of my fallen neighborhood. The important thing in education, he wrote, "is not so much that every child should be taught, as that every child should be given the wish to learn." Alas, as much as Lubbock's statement appeals to me, years have taught me that firm declarations are raised on sand. Only the old acknowledge the truth of and delight in James Beresford's sweetly-sour, damned-if-you-do-and-don't *The Miseries of Human Life, or, The Groans of Samuel Sensitive and Timothy Testy* (1806). "What, my poor Sir," Sensitive asked Testy, "are the senses, but five yawning inlets to hourly and momentary molestations? What is your House, while you are *in* it, but a prison filled with nests of little reptiles; of insect annoyances, which torment you the more because they cannot kill you? And what is the same house when you are *out* of it, but a shelter out of reach, from the hostilities of the skies?" The thinking septuagenarian leans on a walker not the everlasting arms and emends John 9:25 so that instead of "I was blind, but now I see," the verse reads "I once saw but now I am blind."

"O Life, long to the Fool, short to the Wise," Abraham Cowley wrote. Today's wisdom is tomorrow's foolishness. What is true, however, is that for the bookish rummager long ordinary days seem deliciously short and exciting. I have never eaten in a starred restaurant, but I have dined upon mince and slices of quince using a runcible spoon. Although Walter Scott neglected to mention me, I gave the fair Ellen a leg up when young Lochinvar swung her to the croup of his charger and thundered away from Netherby Hall. From Nokomis, not a meteorologist, I learned that the rainbow was the heaven of flowers. After the "wild-flowers of the forest" and the "lilies of the prairie" perished on earth, they blossomed "in that heaven above us." I heard rats gnawing Bishop Hatton into a skeleton. I begged Mary to avoid the sands of Dee, but she was headstrong and raced off alone to call the cattle home. During a snowy gale, I picked up "The Vision of Sir Launfal." Soon after, the season changed, and I watched the flush of life "thrilling back over hills and valleys." Such recollections exude the musty aroma of a lavender bag discovered in the drawer of a Victorian dressing table. While the busy herd may ignore such remembrances or think them over refined, for the aging rummager they shine like birthstones redolent with glimpses of the past.

Amid sweeps of attic dust my admiration for animals rooted and started into green, as did my fondness for sentimental narrative verse. Outside the lecture hall, high purpose drifts away and people read, as John Livingston Lowes put it, as they have always done, "for the delight of it, and for the consequent enrichment and enhancement of one's life." In the nineteenth century, the Australian poet Alfred Chandler told the story of an "old crippled mare" named Bess. For a moment, the poem made my eyes glisten, and this harsh world seemed a kinder place. On seeing Bess stumbling about in a paddock, a young man observed that she was useless and wondered why her owner didn't shoot her. Twelve months after he and his wife Mary settled in the wilderness, Bess's owner explained, Mary had trouble giving birth. It was "death or a doctor," the man said, and the nearest doctor was thirty miles away through swamps and mallee "with scarcely a track." I sprang "to the back of that bonny old mare," the man continued, and felt "a sort of prayer." The journey was an ordeal: along dry creek beds, over sharp ridges, across a broad plain, into a snow squall, and then through a bush fire thick with falling trees, sparks, and curtains of smoke. The prayer was answered. The doctor was home. Immediately he jumped on a pony and set out following Bess back to the man's farm. At the fire, though, the pony balked, and the doctor mounted Bess. With Bess leading, the pony eventually followed. Miraculously, the doctor arrived in time to save Mary and deliver "Jack." Once she reached the gate in front of the house, though, Bess collapsed. "We nursed her for months, and we watched her with care," the narrator recounted, "For gratitude gets to be purer than prayer: / Though paralyzed then into maimed helplessness, / We'll love her forever, our bonny mare Bess!"

Animal books are the forerunners of animal days. Mammals change as they shift from sentences to yard and field. However, for rummagers nurtured on paper menageries, animals never disappear. Instead they scamper across the pages of life. This fall a skunk moved into the back yard and hibernated in a den abandoned by a fox. Because the skunk was almost albino, I named her White Tail. Her hibernation was intermittent, and on warm winter nights, she roamed the yard and the woods behind the house. I followed her tracks in the snow. I worried that she'd stray and be run over by a car, so I put sundry dog foods by the mouth of her burrow. I hoped the food would supplement her diet, and she wouldn't wander the nearby roads to stock her larder. I succeeded. White Tail survived the winter. Recently she announced her presence by spraying Vicki's and my dog Suzy. Since then White Tail and I have talked twice. No dosage of emeritus years can purge the schoolmaster from my system. When I met White Tail, I broke into the hortative and lectured her on the dangers of automobiles. I suggested that she confine food shopping to back yards. In summer, yellow jackets nest in the ground. "Their grubs," I said, "will supply all the nutrition you need." White

4

Tail heeded my warning. She didn't thank me, but after I stopped talking, she turned away from the road and shuffled off into the wood behind our house.

I don't know whether the sentimental precedes having pets or having pets precedes the sentimental. Perhaps reading in which happenstance rather than purpose selects books is responsible for both. Whatever the case, pets and sentiment are intertwined. In January, our dog Binky died in her bed under the kitchen table. Binky lived with us for six years, but she was much older. She was a tiny Chihuahua and had spent most of her life on a puppy farm. When her productive breeding days ended, the "farmer" tossed her aside. I suspect Binky enjoyed her richest dog years in Storrs, roaming marsh and pasture with Vicki and me, seeing river and forest for the first time, sampling the smells of shore and woodland, and playing with Jack and Suzy, our two other rescue Chihuahuas. Binky and I understood each other, and whenever she wanted to go outside, she came into the study and pressed her nose against my leg.

The morning after Binky's death, I dug a grave in the side yard on a slope below a shagbark hickory. The day was dark, and an icy drizzle fell. The ground was frozen, and I battered through topsoil and till into clay using a crowbar. I sliced roots and pried up and broke rocks bigger than foot stools. Digging the grave took three hours. The crowbar was heavy. Time has leached strength from my arms, and when I finished the grave, my shoulders ached. The grave was a construct of Egyptian and Indian tombs shaped by childhood reading. I fluffed up the hard bottom of the tomb with a mattress of soft compost on which I laid a sheet of pink grocery-store rose petals. Binky's shroud was one of Vicki's old T-shirts. "The smell will be familiar," Vicki said as she wrapped the body, "and the dark won't frighten our girl." To provision Binky for the afterlife, we scattered dog biscuits and bacon bits near her muzzle. For companions, we put two of her toys in the grave, the first a stuffed red and yellow turtle, the second a small shaggy monkey who during six years of being tossed about the house lost half his tail. Atop Binky's shroud we then scattered daisies — for memory's sake eight yellow and white blossoms, one apiece for me, Vicki, our three children, Francis, Edward, and Eliza, then Jack and Suzy, and finally one for an unknown friend. "Who?" I asked Vicki. "I don't know," Vicki answered, "maybe a squirrel Binky chased every spring. Maybe a chipmunk or perhaps an imaginary companion, a friend from Binky's dreams."

Rummagers expect the unexpected. They realize that life is disorderly and that stability of mood is rare. A neighbor noticed me returning the crowbar to the garage and asked what I'd been doing. When I explained that I buried a dog, he frowned and said, "That's too bad." But then he smiled and said, "That reminds me of a good joke." A man, he recounted, felt poorly and visited his doctor. The doctor examined him after which he said, "I hate to tell you this, but you've only got a week to live." "Oh, Lord," the man exclaimed, "what should I do?" "Well," the doctor replied, "there is a spa downtown next door to the Sam Davis Hotel. When don't you go there and have a mud bath every day?" "Will the baths make me live longer?" the man asked. "No," the doctor said, "but they'll accustom you to dirt." I did not want to hurt my neighbor's feelings so at the end of the joke I chuckled and said, "That's good — one for the books." "I thought it would cheer you up," my neighbor said, "losing a dog is tough." Often medical matters make me laugh. Two days before Binky died, a cardiologist examined me. At the end of the appointment, he said, "There's only a three percent chance that you will have a stroke this year." I hope to dine out on that remark through December, but then I can't be certain. I don't sleep as well as I did a decade ago. This morning I woke up sweaty and exhausted — worn out from dreaming that I was loading cartons of honey into railway boxcars.

Rummagers are not great travelers. The local satisfies them, and they don't need to wander afield to enjoy quickening surprise. For me libraries are archipelagoes of exhilarating paragraphs. Last week I read John Burroughs' *Indoor Studies*. I stumbled across the book in the mausoleum section of the university library. It had not been checked out since Burroughs' death in 1921. If a man wanted to escape himself or a guilty conscience, Burroughs advised, he should not retreat to the country but should flee to the town. "If he is empty, the town will fill him, if he is idle, the town will amuse him; if he is vain, here is field for his vanity; if he is ambitious, here are dupes waiting to be played upon; but if he is an honest man, here he will have to struggle to preserve his integrity." Burroughs' remarks appeared in an essay entitled "Solitude." Solitude insulates a person from corrosive social fret and is especially appealing to rummagers freeing them to drift apart from others. Sometimes, of course, the insulation frays, and what a person finds in a loft brings the present disturbingly to mind. Edwin Whipple died one-hundred-and-thirty years ago. He was and, despite being forgotten, remains one of America's better critics. Shortly after the last presidential election, I read his "The Ethics of Popularity." The essay seemed composed for Now. "The relation between the people and the amusers, teachers, and leaders of the people," he wrote, "is in continual danger of being withdrawn from the operation of those moral laws which govern the other relations of life and perverted from being a means of mutual benefit into a course of corruption. The idea is mischievously prevalent, that the true method of reaching the heart and brain of the people is to ignore the best sentiments of the heart and the best sentiments of the brain; that to hit hard it is necessary to strike low; and that all successful appeals to the masses suppose in the orator a previous elision of the first letter of the word" [the word is *masses*]. Such politicians assume the people, he continued, are "rude, coarse, credulous, prejudiced, illiterate, and sensual; that they are strong in their appetites, weak in their minds, incompetent to feel grand sentiments or receive great ideas."

I am too much a rummager to be comfortable in the brassy political present. If I must confront balderdash, let it be that from the past, quackery that has lost its edge and aged into eccentricity. Most rummagers are Romantics. They turn through the forgotten in hopes of discovering bits of things that have sifted through time both from history itself and from their earlier selves. The Greeks made Mnemosyne or Memory the mother of the nine muses. Memory often kindles warming, creative associations—something attractive to the elderly eager to stem the race of recollections cascading from their lives. "Precious years of memories / Oh, what joy they bring to me," Hank Williams sang in his version of "The Old Country Church." The problem is, however, that frequently the facts unearthed by memory like the facts "of this case," as the young lawyer declared in court, "are not true." As well as giving birth to the muses, memory is the mother of error and inaccuracy. In October in Price Chopper, I saw an old man wearing a T-shirt across the chest of which was printed "I Talk Only To Myself." "Yes," I thought noticing that the man's grocery cart was almost empty. "You are probably so conceited and unpleasant that nobody will break words or bread with you." Later when I couldn't remember two of the five items Vicki ordered me to buy at the grocery, I revised my opinion. I decided that getting things wrong had so exhausted the man that he had sworn off conversation with anyone other than himself, the one person who would not point out his mistakes or think them symptomatic of galloping intellectual lassitude.

The day the library reopened after Christmas, I checked out three books: John Buchan's *Green Mantle*, Algernon Blackwood's *John Silence*, and *Adele & Co.* by Dornford Yates. That night on settling down to read, I discovered not only that I had read the novels before but that I owned hardbacked copies of all three. Disgruntled, I crammed the books on a shelf in the study. In doing so, I noticed *Uncle Wiggily's Ice Cream Party*. "Where did you get that?" Vicki asked on seeing me holding *Uncle Wiggily*. "Where or when—I don't know," I said. "I've never seen the book before." Uncle Wiggily Longears was a companion of my childhood, maybe my closest friend. I remembered him and his muskrat housekeeper Nurse Jane Fuzzy Wuzzy, but Jackie Bow Wow, Suzy Littletail, the rabbit girl, and Billie Wagtail, the goat boy, had slipped from mind. How could I have forgotten Bob Cat, Woozie Wolf, and "the bad Blue-Nosed Baboon," all of whom threatened to nibble Uncle Wiggily's ears? Gosh, I appreciated being invited to the party in the hollow stump bungalow. Uncle Wiggily served ice cream molded into different shapes. My dessert looked like an apple dumpling. "You will really like this. It's scrumptious," Nurse Jane said when she handed the ice cream to me. To Jackie, Uncle Wiggily presented an ice cream castle, and while twinkling his pink nose, he gave a doll's baby carriage scooped out of blue ice cream to Suzy Littletail. To Billie, he served an "ice cream image" of Skeezicks, a mischievous but skinny, harmless crow-like creature dressed in a red hat and a red and yellow striped suit resembling long underwear. "Did you enjoy the book?" Vicki asked that night at dinner. "Oh, yes," I said, "And if the nutcracker doesn't break through the ice when it's trying to roller skate with the cheese knife on the pantry shelf, I'll tell just how much."

"Only when vitality is low," George Santayana wrote, "do people find material things oppressive." In winter when I become mind-bound and my vitality sinks, I purchase an across-the-counter tonic, a Caribbean cruise, three weeks on a Holland America ship. In the past when Vicki and I first visited the Caribbean, sights were fresh, and we travelled. Now the islands have become so familiar we rummage. Although itineraries determine the course of our trips, we rarely impose purpose on individual days and once ashore we meander. If one lives spontaneously, if only for a few hours, life becomes shapeless and suddenly rich with possibilities and interest. Of course, habits eventually slice so sharp into the adult's character that no pumice stone can rub deep enough to eradicate them. The "book of living nature," Burroughs opined, was inexhaustible. "One can read it over and over, and always find new passages and new meanings. It is a book that goes to press new every night and comes forth fresh every morning." Since childhood, Nature has been my paddock. Hardly a day passes without my rummaging out of doors, even if the outside is my small yard in Connecticut. Weather does not deter me. After ice storms, I check on the welfare of the little creatures who live on our property. "That's what a conscientious neighbor does," I tell Vicki when she warns me that I will slip and break a leg. "And that will be sunset for you," she says, "at best a walker but more likely a week of pneumonia followed by a pall of lilies."

"To go abroad, or, not to go abroad, is hardly the question with English people nowadays," Nona Bellairs wrote in *Wayside Flora; or, Gleanings from Rock and Field Towards Rome* in 1866. Likewise, Vicki's and my going on a cruise in winter is hardly a question. Bellairs left England in February and like us travelled to escape snow and everyday routine. Bellairs loved the natural world, and she packed three trowels, one of which was "flat like a mason's." She did not bury the trowels in her luggage but carried them in a black tourist's bag which she hung around her neck. Also, in the bag were the tools of an amateur naturalist: a knife, paper, string, old gloves, a drinking cup and "a bottle for refreshment," sticking plasters, a journal, and "a book of poetry for moments when scenery and conversation dulled." "Oh, the horror of that black bag during an uphill scramble on a hot day!" she exclaimed. Behind the cover of her dressing case she stored a blotting book in which she dried plants. Part of her luggage, she said, "consisted of a large basket with leather handles, and lined at the bottom and about half an inch up the sides with tin." "In this basket was a little tin kettle, with some tea and sugar, for out of the way inns where English tea was not to be had." Before leaving England, she looked for but could not find a small guide to "continental flora." Eventually she discovered a helpful book in Italy.

Although 150 years separated Vicki's and my cruises from Bellairs' travel, much was similar. Holland America serves inferior tea, so Vicki packed three tins from the English Tea Store, one containing English Breakfast tea, the second Irish Breakfast, and the last Scottish Breakfast. I have long delighted in the natural world and my study is a library of guide books. I selected two for the cruise, one to the birds of the West Indies, the other to tropical trees. The guides also served as blotting books. Between their pages I stored seeds and pressed flowers and leaves. In years past, when Caribbean flora and fauna were unfamiliar and before my muscles slumped into cellulite, I carried a backpack that bulged like Bellairs' black bag. Now I leave it in Connecticut as I do knives, hand lenses, binoculars, notebooks, and guides to, among others, flowers and vines, weeds, corals, shelves, and fish. On all trips, however, I take a poetry anthology. On this cruise, I took *A Book of Famous Verse* selected by Agnes Repplier and published in 1892. The poems themselves were wayside flowers, well-loved and familiar, Repplier testified. "The love of poetry," she said, charmed and brightened "the gray routine of life" and lifted a person "for some brief, sweet moments from all the cares, and vexations, and drudgeries of earth." Natural objects, Bellairs wrote exhibiting comparable enthusiasm, are "invested with thrilling interest, speaking to the heart and mind with powerful effect for good."

Instead of strapping a pack on my back or noosing a bag around my throat, I wore a Safari Vest, something called a Weekend Traveler. The vest had at least thirteen pockets. Four times I counted them, and each time I got a different number. There were inside pockets and outside pockets, obvious and hidden pockets, unsealed pockets, pockets sealed by Velcro, and pockets shut by zippers, some of these last pockets snug within other pockets. When necessary I put my passport, wallet, and boat identification card in pockets. In another pocket I stuffed small bills for tips. I carried two pens and a pencil in separate pockets. I jotted down observations on scraps of paper which I kept in an upper pocket, and I crammed plant specimens into a big pocket stretching across the back of the vest. Sometimes I put a plastic bottle filled with water in a side pocket. To keep the vest balanced, I usually stuck a container of sunscreen into the side pocket on the opposite panel of the vest. Once the vest was loaded, I was ready for heat, scrambles, and, in Bellairs' words, "simple, open-eyed, open-mouthed wonder."

Burroughs slightly misread the book of nature. Nature is not fresh every morning. It seems that way because memories are evanescent. Not the gemstone sea and sky, but trees were the first things I noticed in the Caribbean. In mid-winter, the woods surrounding Storrs were gray and leafless. Deciduous trees appeared hobbled and in high winds limped like old men. On ankles and trunks ulcers gaped incurable, and on the ground, branches lay like crutches abandoned by the moldering. In contrast on the islands the many greens shined in rainbows, their freshness not having slipped out of memory so much as out of my every day. Sometimes ornaments brighter than Christmas decorations adorned the trees. On this trip butterflies swarmed over the fruits on an Indian mulberry: yellow and black zebra longwings, orange-barred sulphurs, and Gulf fritillaries, these last, gritty and rusty but nevertheless glowing like honey. A troupial landed in a workaday divi-divi. Almost as if a switch had been turned, yellow, white, and black glimmered, the colors fluty like the calls of the troupial itself.

Once I looked at trees, I noticed birds: a West Indian woodpecker foraging bromeliads in a botanic park in Grand Cayman, within a crepe myrtle in Tortola a pearly-eyed thrasher hiccupping chirps, and on St. Thomas little green herons still and nubby on the aerial roots of mangroves. Under Poincianas on the grounds of St. George's Cathedral in St. Vincent, cattle egrets perched atop stone sarcophaguses looking like they had been pulled from a frieze and painted white. Nearby a flock of anis searching for insects in the grass periodically raised their heads and stared down their ridged beaks at me. Nature may be fresh, but too often man appears old and soiled, and occasionally a sighting sank my spirits — on the Belmont Estate on Grenada a solitary red-crowned parrot in a coat hanger cage. The bird's name was Rainbow. "Hi," Rainbow said repeatedly, the word clicking dully like a stone wedged between the treads of a tire on an automobile creeping down a back road.

In observing trees, I rummaged, reading, not purposely as in class but randomly. Certainly no one my age fools himself into believing he can read a place closely. Sometimes paragraphs are illegible, but in struggling to decipher them I spot the unexpected. In identifying a tree of life above coastal rocks pocking a shallow cove in the Bahamas, I noticed jumbles of snails: helmets, turbans, cowries, and limpets. Black and white nerites clumped together like handfuls of different-sized marbles, black stuttering electric across their shells. Minute hermit crabs pulled themselves and their houses over the limestone under the water, moving erratically as if tracing cuneiform script. Tiny mussels clung together in shiny cornrows. In studying the feathery headdress of blossoms on a coral bean near San Gervasio on Cozumel, I noticed one then a mess of black spiny-tailed iguanas. Black bands circled the animals' bodies almost as if a cooper had wrapped metal hoops around them. As I walked a forest path, several bobbed their heads at me. They did not bob at Vicki, and most stopped when I dropped to my hands and knees, snorted, and bobbed back.

Looking at trees in the Caribbean was like opening a huge loaf-shaped trunk in the attic and discovering old but familiar clothes: high buttoned shoes, pantalets, a smoking cap, and a corset missing its laces among a laundry of other items. There stood a papaya. Its crown was sparse and windblown, and beneath the leaves, fruits bunched like lipomas. Here grew breadfruit, avocado, and an African tulip tree, its branches ablaze with candelabras of scarlet flowers. A few flowers bloomed on mouse trap trees. The blossoms were yellow with dark sunken throats and looked like those of black-eyed Susan thunbergia, a vine I hang every summer in a planter by the kitchen door. Because the prickly green fruits of soursop supposedly deterred cancer, I gave up coconut smoothies, my favorite, and drank only smoothies made from soursop. From a spur a calabash pursed out from a branch in a green balloon. On mangos, small flowers burst upward in buffering, scratchy panicles. While seed pods dangled long and slender from cassia looking pulled and rolled, those on sausage trees hung down resembling weights in a massive grandfather clock. On travelers-trees leaves flared shuffled like cards. On Bismarck palm, they fanned into circles of enormous gray shutters. Glory cedar was pink with blossoms. Teak was white, and the great brushy apricot flowers of cannonball tree smelled like allspice. Sometimes a tree evoked distant memories. Seeing jacaranda in full purple triggered recollection of Vicki's and my yard in Mosman Park in Western Australia. "Why did we leave?" I said to Vicki sinking into nostalgia. "We were so very happy."

Occasionally an individual tree seemed admirable and aristocratic, almost, perhaps more than human in appealing dignity. The mahogany at the side entrance of St. Mary's Anglican Church in Bridgetown, Barbados, rose big-browed and austere. Here and there gray streaked its bark giving the trunk a silvered wise appearance, and a philodendron with weighty green and yellow leaves wound through its branches, each of the leaves seeming the lining of an academic hood. Geometric walks don't wind through my arboretum, and my plantings are not clipped into topiary. Instead the arboretum is weedy like life itself—a thought that appeals to people worried that rummaging has made them so content that their lives are and will always be abnormally orderly. On this trip, I planted a stand of rainbow eucalyptus, their trunks quickening strips of green, orange, blue, and gray. and then with its bark claret but warty with gold, two red birch, erythrina velutina, a relative of the coral tree. I didn't consider sunlight, wind, or drainage when I planted the trees. I simply stuck them onto a page.

The phrase being one's brother's keeper smacks of prisons or at the least intrusive nosiness and repulses me. Still, perhaps I should have been careful to prevent my arboretum from growing so rank that visitors lost their spiritual ways. Along paths I should have planted sycamores shipped from the United States. The trees are so beautiful that in their presence people feel reverent. Pentecostals call the sycamore the Christian or Redeemer tree. Plates of bark peel from the upper parts of the sycamore's trunk leaving the surface to appear white and smooth especially to someone on the ground gazing skyward. On the lower trunk the bark is rough and gray and often dark. For the believer the lower trunk represents a mottled unsanctified earth-bound life. After a person accepts "Jesus Christ as Savior and Guide," sin falls from him like bark from the tree. The more spotless his days, the higher his spirit ascends and the closer he approaches heaven, his life now white as the sycamore's upper branches.

Let me assure all castigators that I did not see the tree described in *Malleus Maleficarum* or *The Hammer of Witches* (1486) in which lady necromancers hung a bird's nest containing twenty or thirty penises, maintaining the hatchlings' vigor by feeding them oats. Although many trees widespread in the Caribbean are native to distant regions of the world, the Norfolk Island Pine and the African tulip tree, for example, fertility trees endemic to Europe don't appear to have spread to the islands. Several varieties of such trees have long flourished on the continent, the most common resembling a bush gardenia and depicted in illuminations of a manuscript of the *Roman de la Rose*. In illustrations nuns harvested fruits from the trees and placed them in wicker baskets. The fruits were white and curved looking like sugar-coated crescent cookies popular during Christmas. The second common European variety is native to Tuscany and appeared in an ancient fresco. The tree was medium-sized and busy with branches. Its leaves were reddish and heart-shaped, and like those of balm of Gilead poplar dangled at the end of long slender stems. Growing high in the tree and thus insulated from ground-chilling mists, the fruits ripened in the sunlight free from sour rot and black mold.

Nobody, as the country song puts it, is going to get out of this world alive. But if he rummages, he may be so busy that he won't notice leaving. One should never allow death to spoil a sunny day. In my arboretum appeared a miscellany of sights and experiences. Dazzling, practically flashing, amid rows of plants were the candied stalks of shampoo ginger and heliconia with bracts sharper than the teeth on large crosscut saws. A zoo of animals roamed scrub and forest: agouti, coatimundi, Mona monkeys, and red-eared turtles. Carved on tombstones were names I'd not seen, Scatliffe and its progenitor Scatcliffe, this last three letters removed from Ratcliffe, Mother's maiden name. In Tortola Vicki and I ate jerk pork at Dareo's, a stand on Lower Estate Street in Road Town. Behind the stand chickens foraged a dry creek, the scratching sounding like water sputtering from a dry pipe. For lunch at her kitchen in St. Lucia, Silvia sold lamb neck, pig tail, and cowheel soup. "If God is for us, who will be against us," she wrote on the board listing her menu. Years ago, I'd have bolted pig tails with abdomen-may-care gusto. But I have aged into culinary caution. I have reached the limit of hanging my head in nausea, something I did so often in the past it resembled an addiction.

Late one Friday Vicki and I drank Hairoun beer in S & D's Hideout, "Shop 23" behind the markets and bus terminals on Lower Bay Street in Kingstown on St. Vincent.

Although crowds jostled boisterous and exuberant along the bay, buying, selling, smoking bales of marijuana, and drinking rum and beer, we were the only tourists. The shop was smaller than a pantry. Inside was a bar, S the female bartender, one stool, and four chairs. Vicki and I occupied two of the latter. In a third sat a man who said he wanted to go to America "after Trump." In Antigua, we rode in Nellie's taxi. Pasted to the back window was a Harvard sticker. Nellie's son was a junior at Harvard. "He won't return to St. John's. He's a chemist. He will go to graduate school in America. I miss him terribly, but," she said then stopped and smiling pointed out a colony of egrets.

In St. Lucia at the Central Market in Castries, I bought my only real souvenir, a mahogany lion. The lion was nine inches long and stood five and a half tall. He was both polished and rough. He was male, and while his mane was studiously luxuriant and resembled the nemes worn by ancient pharaohs, his mouth gaped, and his fangs looked like teeth cut into a Halloween pumpkin. The carver was Rastafarian. During a previous cruise, he and I chatted, and he recognized me even remembering that I lived in Connecticut. Familiarity costs money, and I felt obligated to purchase a carving. I liked the lion and paid forty dollars for it, fifteen dollars more than I would have paid had I haggled. However, dickering with a person the quality of whose life depends upon an insignificant amount of money makes me feel petty. In any case I was a good patron. While in the market I convinced a hesitant costumer to buy a wooden mask. At first the man balked at the price twenty-two dollars. "Peanuts to you," I told him outside the shop, "but not to him." Later that day I bumped into the Rastafarian on Jeremie Street, and he thanked me for helping sell the mask. "But," he said, "since I gave you such a good price on the lion, you should buy something else from me." "Maybe on my next visit," I said then we talked about money. Often, he recounted, he didn't sell anything for four or five days. "Many tourists don't want to pay anything for a carving; yet, they will stay in a hotel that costs a hundred dollars a night." "A hundred dollars!" he exclaimed. "If only you knew," I thought.

Every spring I dig through the discard sale at the university library. Always I discover books that enrich my living, among my finds last year, *One Thousand Poems for Children* given to "Dorothy Dear" by "Mother and Dad" on Christmas 1923. Almost every night for three months I read a handful of poems. Although I had not read them in a long time, most were familiar, poems like Landor's "Rose Aylmer," Peacock's "The Priest and the Mulberry-Tree," and "You Spotted Snakes" from *A Midsummer Night's Dream.* "You spotted snakes with double tongues, / Thorny hedge-hogs, be not seen; / Newts and blind worms, do no wrong; / Come not near our fairy queen," the First Fairy and I sang to Titania. For the rummager discards or things which seem insignificant are frequently sources of unexpected pleasure. Even when I dream I read. Last week, for example, I dreamed about a sign inside a medical-arts building directing sanctified patients to the office of a "Christian Dermatologist." Accordingly, verbal scraps marked my island meanderings. Stamped on license plates in Tortola was the tag "Nature's Little Secrets." A blue Honda parked outside St. Ann's Day Nursery at the Social Center in Roseau, Dominica, belonged, the license stated, "to Ms. Sweet." "How sweet do you think she is?" Vicki asked. "I wouldn't want to argue with her over a parking place," I said. "But certainly, she's sweeter than the woman we saw in St. Maarten wearing a T-shirt saying, 'You Can't Drink All Day . . . If You Don't Start in the Morning.'"

In the Caribbean, not just cars but their parts are canvasses. Painted in thick yellow strokes around the sidewall of an automobile tire standing in front of a house in St. George's in Grenada was "One Day You Happy The Next You Sad." "Cleopatra Upstairs," a sign on Tudor Street in Bridgetown, Barbados, read. "Cleo" was a preaching hairdresser. She fashioned Crunch and Palm Rolls, the Invisible Pineapple, even a "Messy Bun with China Bang." "God loves You," her sign announced to prospective patrons, "He's always in control." Cleo wished folks who could not stop for a hairdo well, telling them to "Have a Blessed Day." On the wall of a building across the street someone painted, "When A Mate's Life Turns Stormy, The True Friend Stands By Him." A wag devoted to the truth emended the sentence, changing the period following "Him" to a comma and adding "If The Mate Has An Umbrella."

Placid and organized — bailed in barn terms — life on the ship did not lend itself to rummaging. Most passengers were comfortably sedentary. The only people able to take a three-week cruise in February are the retired. "This," Vicki said one evening at dinner, "is a Hospice Cruise. The purple you see on passengers' arms and legs are not tattoos. They are senile bruises." I jogged alone on the Sports Deck. Never did another member of the Almost-Dead Runner's Society join me. For my part, even though cataracts photoshopped my appearance in the mirror, I couldn't shed awareness of my age. Guides and taxi drivers addressed me as poppa and grand-poppa. Only once in the ship did I hear anybody grumble. Inside the men's locker room attached to the gymnasium were two showers. One morning as I dressed to jog, a man wrapped in a towel entered the room. Because both showers were being used, the man sat on a bench and waited for one to become free. We began to talk but almost immediately were interrupted by the occupant of one of the showers blowing his nose. It sounded like the harrowing of Hell. "My God!" the man exclaimed. "What shower did that noise come from?" On my replying that I couldn't tell, the man stood and said, "Screw this. I'll bathe in my room. Here, my chances of choosing the shower in which the fellow blew his nose are fifty-fifty. If I go into that shower, either one of my feet will stick to the tile and lifting it will rip all the skin off the bottom or I will slip and fall and break my hip." "Some people," he ended, "some damn people."

Vicki's and my cabin was on Dolphin Deck, deck one, the lowest and cheapest of the passenger decks. When we boarded, I suggested that for the first week while riding the elevator down to our cabin we should get off on deck three, the Lower Promenade. "That will cause people to raise their estimate of our means and thus hold us in greater esteem," I said. "Once off the elevator we can creep downstairs unnoticed." "What?" Vicki said. "It is an old and respectable ploy," I explained. "Years ago, when air conditioning was expensive, inhabitants of Belle Meade in Nashville who owned cars without air conditioning drove with their windows rolled up until they reached the anonymity of Harding Road, creating the impression that they were as flush as their well-to-do neighbors." "Even during July and August?" Vicki asked. "Especially then," I replied. "Impressions are substance."

Passengers on the cruise were temperate. In the formal dining room, speech never rose or dropped an octave. People had led corporate lives and were adept at assimilating and in tamping down the disruptive both within and without themselves. Rarely, however, do the successful reach their end times without regretting the undone—the injustices they ignored, the truths they allowed to be buried beneath paragraphs of dead words, the occasions when they didn't shout "to hell with it" and decamp "having nothing," yet, as Henry Wotton put it, having all. To mitigate regret, sometimes they provoked small hullabaloos. Vicki met a retired school principal and frequent cruiser who roamed corridors at night and at least twice during every trip changed room-service breakfast orders hanging on doorknobs outside cabins. If the person in the cabin ordered orange juice, she switched it to prune, coffee to soy milk, corn flakes to Fruit Loops. She especially enjoyed changing an unhealthy ham and cheese omelet to a vegetable omelet, one thick with extra onions and peppers. "Just doing my duty as my brother's dietician," she told Vicki.

The woman was traveling with her first cousin and one afternoon late in the cruise we met them for tea. The cousin was a retired accountant and had worked for a medical group associated with Emory University. Idleness bored her, and to quicken days after retiring she worked as a clerk in small shops. "Four to be exact, all in Myrtle Beach, South Carolina," she said, "Tic, Tac, Tacky" which sold souvenirs, puzzles, and electronic games; "Brown Cow Ice Cream and Candy," "Bessie's At Your Convenience," and "The Blessed Cross," a store that sold religious, "mostly Protestant," memorabilia. As could be expected of someone kin to the principal, the woman wasn't an ordinary clerk. "When I was an accountant," she said, "I handled enough money to last several lifetimes." Consequently, in the stores shoplifting interested her more than buying and selling. At the convenience store men were the worst offenders addicted to stealing SAE 30 engine oil for their riding mowers. While teenage boys tried to filch games from Tic, Tac, Tacky, girls and small children stole candy and ice cream bars from the Brown Cow. The bar of choice was the old-fashioned ice cream sandwich, "reassuring," the woman said, "at a time when no one honors tradition." The store that suffered most from pilfering was The Blessed Cross. Its losses amounted to more than those of the other three shops combined. "Everybody stole everything — men, women, children, the old in wheelchairs or behind walkers, adolescents wearing sweatshirts proclaiming 'The Bible Changed My Life,' and pregnant women so large they couldn't bend to choose items to swipe so they just raked trays off counters. They took crucifixes, statues of the wise men and the holy family, paper napkins with the Star of Bethlehem printed on them, bibles, prayer books, backpacks decorated with a patch depicting angels carrying Jesus to heaven, the wound in his side a small zipper pocket, baseball caps, on the crown Jesus at bat swinging a cross, and then jewelry decorated with stones mentioned in Ezekiel's description of The Garden of God, rubies and topaz, onyx, sapphires, diamonds, and jasper." "Thievery comes easily to Christians," the woman explained. "They feel no remorse. Once outside the store, they pocket their loot and ask God to forgive them and to absolve them from their sins. God is the bank that always grants loans. Once they pray, true Christians are free to go and steal more."

In slipping under the rails of the social fold and rambling without purpose, rummagers become the prey of eccentrics—strangers whom others avoid or don't see because conventional responsibilities determine the focus of their lives. Nowadays when I repress concerns about governance to meander worry-free amid thoughts insubstantial as cirrus clouds, someone invariably attempts to plant a boutonniere of his notions in my buttonhole. Such people don't limit their grinding to axes. They possess a tool shed of honed bettering ideas. Two days after Vicki and I returned from the cruise, a man approached me in Dog Lane Café and gave me a photocopy of a four-page broadside. The man served as spokesman of a group dedicated to forming a nation, he explained, "one truly committed to the proposition that all men are created equal." "I've noticed you in the café," he said as he pulled up a chair and sat at Vicki's and my table. "You seem right sorts, and I hope you'll support this proposal." Because I taught for four decades, he also assumed I could introduce him to former students able to help popularize the broadside. I liked the boys and girls who took my courses, but I didn't keep up with any of them. None became friends or correspondents. At end of each semester, I wished them well, stuffed high grades into their backpacks, and put them up for adoption.

The broadside described a plan to build a wall sealing New England off from the "remainder" of the United States, the cost estimated by Ganache, Patricelli, and Wolfe of New Haven to be $6 billion dollars, considerably less than the $22 billion for erecting a wall between Mexico and Sunbelt States in the Southwest. In the plan as first proposed, Lake Champlain constituted both the border and a natural wall between the new nation and old America. Construction of an actual wall would begin, the broadside detailed, at Ticonderoga and extend south to Long Island Sound following the present boundaries of Vermont, Massachusetts, and Connecticut. However, at this initial stage plans were "to indulge in a pun" set in water. An hydrologist suggested reducing costs by shifting the border west, paralleling the course of the Champlain Canal as it joined the Hudson River then following the Hudson to Long Island Sound. Reducing the cost of the wall, supporters surmised, would appeal to Connecticut Yankees. Also attractive was the inclusion of Long Island in the new nation, particularly portions of Nassau and all of Suffolk counties. Yet, some advocates of "the United States of New England" disagreed and opposed any border that swept New York City into the new nation. "Its population would overwhelm the country," they argued, "and transform a predominantly rural land into one dominated by high-rise urban concerns."

Constructed out of Barre Granite blocks mined in Washington County, Vermont, the wall would embody the positive features of the Maginot Line. Atop the wall at appropriate intervals would be fire towers, "not, let it be emphasized, guard towers." "As Hunnish as some of their attitudes clearly are," the broadside declared, "we" do not consider the people excluded from the United States of New England to be actual Huns. Moreover, asserting that plans had been drawn to seize Nantucket by imminent domain and transform the island into the nation's Guantanamo was, the broadside said, a libel promulgated by diseased commercial interests in the Midwest. "If any islands must be turned into temporary picnic and confinement shelters, they will be the Isles of Shoals, probably only Star Island on which several hotel buildings already exist."

Also atop the wall would be platforms serving as the bases of gigantic wind turbines. These would reverse the flow of effluvia spewed from the coal burning industries west of the wall. "We want our nation to be beautiful for spacious, unpolluted skies," the broadside hymned. For the record, The United States of New England was a temporary name chosen to facilitate the country's appearance in atlases. "The long-range intention," the proposal explained, "is to pry the contiguous provinces of Atlantic Canada—New Brunswick, Nova Scotia, Prince Edward Island, and Newfoundland—free from the dominance of Ontario and the despoiling three provinces to the west, particularly Alberta with its tar sands." "Perhaps Labrador will join the group," but, the broadside assured nervous Quebecers, "we do not believe in manifest destiny and are not land-hungry." Until Atlantic Canada became part of the confederation, Boston was projected to serve as capital. Once the Canadian provinces were integrated, the broadside suggested that Halifax could replace Boston. If disagreement arose, Portland, "it has been mooted," might be a good compromise.

Emigration was to be encouraged, especially from the intellectual colonies of Vermont: Washington, Oregon, and Northern California. "The number of immigrants may be small, particularly since negotiations between British Columbia and those western outposts of sanity and integrity are supposedly underway, the intention being to form their own nation, The United States of the Pacific Northwest." We have not learned, a footnote attached to the broadside testified, whether a wall will insulate the U. S. of P. N. from contingent states and provinces. "In any case the U. S. of New England will not subject immigrants to ethnic or religious tests, though, to be honest, worshippers of the Great God Gun will be discouraged from applying for visas." Planners envisioned that the bright new New England would have a coast guard but not an army, navy, or air force. "The Guard will steer wandering captains away from reefs, but its main duty will be to clear coastal waters of the swirls of plastic waste pushed north by the Gulf Stream." With aggressive militaristic ideologues controlling the territories to the south and west, timid advocates of the U. S. of New England questioned the wisdom of not having an army or, alas, "a modest nuclear deterrent." Most proponents of the new country, however, believed that a tapestry of Alliances Cordiale with the enlightened nations of Europe and Central and South America based on trade and mutual respect would deter intrusive behavior.

The U. S. of New England, its advocates hoped, was destined to become a peace broker and the guardian of sister nations. "Of course, many people," the broadside noted reluctantly, "find peace of mind and country boring to the point of seeming immoral." Such people would be encouraged to emigrate, and to speed them on their way, the nation planned to offer financial good-bye incentives. Founders hoped life in the new nation would be pleasant, but they refused to promise a lobster in every pot or quinoa on every platter. To support education and cradle-to-cremation healthcare, taxes would be high. For its part, education had to remake itself. "Higher education ought to be a reality not simply a phrase." "Education must awaken curiosity and spread beyond STEM studies to ROOT and FLOWER studies. It must make people aware of their natures and histories, their capacities for the humane and the inhumane. It must not simply produce shrill, self-serving utilitarians, but instead community-minded stewards of thought and decency."

An addendum observed that the spectacle of massive athletic programs attached to undistinguished universities would vanish. Sports would continue but on a recreational not professional level. Indeed, Departments of Recreation were scheduled to expand. Instead of becoming fans and sitting through hours, "minds and bodies becoming clotted with plaque," students would be encouraged to become participants: hike, climb, swim, wander afield to learn about fields and the worlds about them. According to one story, when Marie Antoinette learned that French peasants had no bread to eat, she said, "let them eat cake." Sports have unfortunately become, as a descendant of Karl Marx recently stated, the "opiate of the people." "Let them watch the Super Bowl, the World Series, March Madness, and the World Cup" has become the contemporary equivalent of the queen's remark. By numbing and callousing the mass mind and transforming probing questions into orchestrated, manipulative cheers, the addendum declared, sports fomented the rise of moral pauperism. They dulled the individual conscience and diverted attention from pressing social problems such as "the corroding inequalities of wealth and opportunity."

The broadside was longer, proposing, for example, a unicameral legislature, the seats determined not by gerrymandering but by population, its members selected in a lottery. I could have continued reading, but after three pages I was tired. I knew that the proposal's criticism of athletics would alienate some potential supporters of the new nation. I suppose I should have revised the pages expanding their appeal, but beside being weary I resented the man's thrusting himself upon Vicki and me and then scrutinizing me, searching for approval as I read. Also, a footnote contained a dozen suggestions for statements to be printed on bunting, the colors green, white, and blue — white for clouds, blue for the ocean, and green for woods and fields. No statement was snappy and memorable. All were soporific, and despite agreeing with their declarations, I didn't want to force down two cups of black souring coffee in hopes of jump-starting myself into fashioning better alternatives. The single slogan I remember was, "Just say YES to compassionate socialism."

Anyway, Whipple had undermined my interest in government. He made me so cynical that I distrusted even the man who showed me the broadside. How would democrats behave, I wondered, in this the twilight of proportional representation? Whipple suggested an answer. A demagogue, he wrote, "was a democrat emancipated from democracy." In accounting for Robespierre's descent into brutality, Whipple wrote, "Like all incompetent men who are cursed with power, he tried to make violence do the work of insight and foresight. He slew because he could not think. He ended in being fiendish because he started in being foolish" — a statement "applicable to the occupant of the Fifth Avenue White House," Vicki lamented privately later that night. The next day in my study she read a paragraph I'd copied from St. John Adcock's "The Real Thing," Under the veneer of conventional decency, Adcock believed, lurked primitive human nature. All people, he declared, were familiar with accounts of responsible individuals suddenly spurning decorum and artificial restraints and "yielding to the natural heathen in the blood" running "amok through the proprieties with an unblushing abandon worthy of the rudest of our rude forefathers." "Yes," I thought, "and in doing so staging spectacles that appeal to masses of people. Man is an animal that pants after blood on television and in the newspaper, cheers the grab and smash of ice hockey and football, and in some smoldering part of his being longs to shed responsibility and decency and revel in naked barbarism."

The cruise exhausted me more than I realized, and I couldn't muster my thoughts and stand them at attention in an orderly line. "A fellow on a cruise I took recently told me a good joke," I started to tell the man. "It's an old chestnut. Is a hippopotamus a hippopotamus or is it a really cool opotamus?" I did not repeat the joke because although the broadside was occasionally playful, the man himself was intense and not in a jocular mood. Four tables away sat my friend Bert. Just before his twelfth birthday Bert's mother told him that the person he thought was his father wasn't his father. His real father, she said, was an alien, and he had impregnated her with a ray beam. The alien lived six light years away on another planet, and after siring Bert, the alien went home for a short visit. He was now, she revealed, returning to earth to fetch Bert. "He will arrive on your twelfth birthday and take you to a home on his planet." I suspected our tablemate wouldn't enjoy the anecdote. When Vicki and I heard it, however, we laughed and laughed. Somehow, Bert's story seemed more important, and more enduring, than any political fervor, no matter its serious, elevated intention. Oh, how I wish I'd had the imagination to fashion such a tale for Vicki's and my children. Then maybe the taproot of our family tree would have been salubriously other-worldly, and the children would have blossomed into wondrously odd people. If they'd had an alien for an ancestor where would they have gone to school, if they went to school? Certainly, they would have easily escaped becoming their jobs, the fate of so many good students.

Contributing to my lack of energy was the fact that on retrieving my car at the airport after the cruise, I discovered the battery was dead and the hand brake frozen. As a result, Vicki and I did not get back to Storrs until after midnight. "Thanks," I said to the man, "I really appreciate your showing these papers to me. You have given me much to think about. But I must go. I have an appointment for an electro-cardiogram." Rummagers become inured to contrary truths. Consequently, they become comfortable with uncertainty, not only keeping incompatible opinions in mind but accepting them. As a side effect, rummagers lie easily and frequently. On this occasion, however, I told the truth. I had an appointment with a cardiologist, albeit the next afternoon. As I spent the previous three weeks outside traipsing across islands, so doctors would spend the next three weeks rummaging inside Vicki and me, seeing what ticked and what needed rewinding. Ahead lay two cardiograms, not one, a pair of blood tests, a colonoscopy, an examination measuring pressure in my eyes, and an eight o'clock visit to a urologist sixty miles away. For her part, Vicki had a mammogram then a physical. A dentist cleaned and examined her teeth, and twice she saw an ophthalmologist. During the second appointment, he inserted capsules of steroids into her eyes.

"And if," as Howard Garis, Uncle Wiggily's biographer put it, "the automobile doesn't run over the milk bottle, and turn it into an ice cream cone for the trolley car," I'll tell you the results of the medical parsing. Then again, maybe I won't. Oh, shucks, at the end of a long essay almost anything goes unnoticed. "I could put you in the hospital and treat this with radiation," one of the doctors told me. "On the other hand, you are seventy-six and this ailment won't kill you for ten years. Actuarily speaking, something else will get you before then, so why don't you spare yourself the ordeal of the hospital?" What I should really describe are the West Indian whistling ducks I saw on Grand Cayman or in the shallows off Klein Bonaire the batfish I watched flattening itself into the sand. Or maybe I'll sit in the Ruins Rock Café near the harbor in Roseau and drink Kubuli beer. No, it would be better to go to the Jerk Centre in Ochos Rios and with a couple of Two Stripe beers wash down an order of fried plantains and half a chicken. That reminds me. When Vicki and I were in Ochos Rios, I spent an afternoon alone exploring the town. It was Ash Wednesday, and the streets were crowded. Five or six merchants asked me if I wanted weed. In a small souvenir shop when the owner learned I didn't have grandchildren, she pointed to the rear of the shop, said, "Come into the back. We'll make a child who'll give you grandchildren." The woman was good-natured and generous, but the invitation came fifty years too late, and I declined. In hopes of assuaging the woman's feelings, however, I bought a present for Vicki in the shop, a hand-carved wooden chameleon that cost seven dollars. "Ash Wednesday is the reason the woman was so warm-hearted," I told Vicki when I gave her the gift. "It's a holiday, and folks feel ecumenical." "The carving is an anole not a chameleon," Vicki said, "and, yes, holy days should be memorable. But how do you suppose people hereabouts celebrate Christmas? It's the big red-letter holiday." "I don't know," I replied. "But in December we could take another cruise and find out."

Re-Reading *Nicholas Nickleby*

Decades of sprinting through crime novels in which plot mattered more than any other consideration made me a poor reader. When I was young, I read Dickens' novels four or five times each. I ambled and mulled characters. I talked to them and advised them. Sometimes they advised me, and I listened recognizing the spirit of the Sermon on the Mount. I spent afternoons and evenings with Mr. Micawber and Sam Weller, the Cheeryble brothers, the Golden Dustman, Betsy Trotwood then patient loveable Agnes Wakefield. Although Uriah Heep and Daniel Quilp intrigued me, I steered clear of knowing them socially. I explored the worst-of-times slums and bleak houses where many of Dickens's characters lived. In those best-of-times elsewheres when life blossomed for Esther Summerson, Florence Dombey, and Lizzie Hexam, I smiled and was a bright dinner companion. Dickens's world was bigger than my imagination, and I hardly noticed the insignificances flickering on television or flashy on the covers of magazines at checkout counters. I never opened *Sports Illustrated* or *People*, and later when *US* appeared, I knew the pronoun did not include me.

However, until last month I hadn't looked at Dickens in four decades. I am not sure why. Perhaps teaching and the narrowing that accompanies breaking years into terms and dividing books into genres and courses into themes was responsible. Consequently, to appreciate Dickens anew, I had to brake my eye. I limited reading *Nicholas Nickleby* to fifty pages a day. In "Tradition and

Individual Talent," T. S. Eliot emphasized the importance of "natural receptivity and necessary laziness." Laziness makes receptivity possible. After I read fifty pages, I closed the book and sat quietly. Occasionally I muttered "Gee" or "Holy Cow," but I didn't try to wring analysis from the moment. Pondering Dickens's novels removes the reader from the fretful evanescent exterior world and opens doors into the interior life where people live and where they become vital characters in stories of the self. Instead of being bedtime narcotics, the novels invigorate curiosity and appreciation. They show that life is richer and more seductively diverse in its inconstancy, in joy and sadness, in simply itself, than a person can ever understand.

The characters that roamed the pages of *Nicholas Nickleby* made my small town seem hang-nailed: among others, Sir Mulberry Hawk, Madame Mantalini, Vincent Crummles, his daughter Ninetta "the Infant Phenomenon," Newman Noggs, and the mad gentleman in small clothes, worsted stockings, and black velvet cap who courted the Widow Nickleby by tossing vegetables over the garden wall—marrows, onions, turnips, and especially cucumbers. "That's what my books are," I thought, "marrows and turnips, maybe not digestible but nonetheless fun." As I smiled at the antics of the insane suitor, I recalled one of my onions. Thirty years ago, I wrote a description of my father. For the sake of the narrative, I implied that Father had gone over the garden wall. Shortly after the piece appeared, Father ambled into the golf shop of the Belle Meade Country Club in Nashville. "Good Lord, Sam," a man said springing out of a chair and addressing Father. "I read your son's piece and I thought you were dead. I missed the obituary in the newspaper, and I want you to know I regretted not going to your funeral." "You shouldn't feel bad," Father replied. "I suspect that fairly soon the opportunity to atone for the oversight will arise."

John Burroughs said that Thoreau spent his life

searching for the wild, "not only in nature, but in literature, in life, in morals." For my part I spend much time hunting the playful. Dickens' world was as dark as it was bright. Thousands of people, Nicholas Nickleby stated, were born into circumstances that wrapped "their very cradles' heads" and like curtains blocked light and smothered virtue and opportunity. How many people, he asked, had no chance of life. "How much injustice, misery and wrong there was," he lamented, "yet how the world rolled on from year to year" careless and indifferent. Yes, and as a person ages pessimism clouds his view of man and man's doings. He doesn't grow indifferent, but he accepts the fact that he cannot change the course of the world's hard spinning. At best, he can be cheerful, a state of mind that takes effort to achieve. To be cheerful one must be disciplined enough to misread both Dickens and life.

No longer do dreams make me laugh so raucously that I bounce from under the covers smiling. Now they provoke anxiety and seem cartoonish parallels to the moody worries that infect the day. Three weeks ago, a friend told me he was heading for the last roundup. We were drinking coffee in a café. "This is the last time I'll be able to meet you here," he said. "Maybe you didn't notice but I'm drinking regular rather than decaffeinated. If I'm going out, by god, I want to leave riding a good hearty buzz, not sinking under a waterish whimper." That night I dreamed that Vicki forced me to go to bed with a razor in my mouth. The next morning, I determined to find something light-hearted to dull the sharp edge of the brisket saw. I refused to allow Dotheboys Hall to provoke a diatribe against the failures of schooling. Instead I recalled an anecdote from John Cleese's *So, Anyway*. . . . When Cleese was a student at Clifton College, a secondary school, he and a couple of classmates occasionally folded a scrap of paper into a rectangle. On the outside of the fold, one of them wrote "For Foster" or the name of another student in the school. They then placed the paper on a table in the library after which they loitered nearby watching to see if anyone opened the paper. Someone usually noticed the paper and unfolded it. On doing so he discovered written on the inside of the paper statements like "Is your name Foster?" and "You are being watched." "Are you sure," Vicki said when I read her the anecdote, "that it wasn't you, rather than John Cleese, who studied at Clifton College?" In *Gleams of Memory*, James Payn, the 19th-century critic and novelist, recalled that when he was small he hid under "the dinner table when there was a party" and nipped "at the legs of the guests, both male and female, to give them the impression" that he was a dog. I read Payn's account to Vicki. "That also sounds like something you might have done," she said. True confession to a mate is unwise. I didn't feel obliged to inform Vicki that in prenuptial years I'd frisked about in a similar canine manner, the difference being that I was in the trouser, not short pants, stage of life. Moreover, an excess of fortified libations not youthful exuberance caused my scampering about beneath tablecloths. In truth the best-natured and most decent oldsters of my acquaintance were once blue-ribbon agronomists who in the spring times of their lives sowed lush crops of soul-sustaining wild oats. "Yes," I said to Vicki, "transforming a dining room into a kennel and toes into Eukanuba and ankles into chicken tenders must have been good toothsome fun."

Meringue quickly dries into splinters, but when it is fresh and feathery, it tickles. For those disposed to look the playful lurks practically everywhere. After listening to the anecdotes from *Gleams of Memory* and *So, Anyway . . .* , Vicki went upstairs, and I began reading Clyde Edgerton's *Lunch at the Piccadilly*. The book contained an album of songs. My favorite was "The Safety Patrol Song," the refrain of which declared, "I'd like to be in the safety patrol, / Wear a clean white strap. / Shine my shoes and stand up straight, / And wear a sailor's cap." In eighth grade, I belonged to the safety patrol. I wore a white strap, and although I didn't shine my shoes or have a sailor cap, I stood straight at the end of Westover Drive across from Parmer School. I held a bamboo pole with a yellow flag attached to the tip and guided younger students across Leake Avenue. "That was the high point of my school years," I told my friend David after singing the refrain in the university locker room, adding that wearing the strap was the closest I ever approached to military paraphernalia.

Childhood delights often disappear during a person's middle years only to reappear like Lazarus during old age. When I was a schoolboy, my favorite tickler was the shaggy-dog "I've got a banana in my ear" tale. Until recently I had not thought about the joke in decades, but now, unaccountably, it has risen, and I tell it to strangers always alarming them by erupting into raucous laughter. Two men, the story goes, meet on a street corner downtown in Nashville. The men are ordinary businessmen. Both wear gray suits, wingtip shoes, and blue and red striped regimental neckties. Sticking out from the right ear of one man, however, is a banana. "A mighty fine one, really yellow and not too green or ripe, just the ticket to top off your breakfast cereal," I tell listeners. At this point I usually digress into a paragraph describing the virtues of breakfast fruits, particularly if my auditors appear impatient. For the record I am especially fond of blueberries although I reassure people that "I don't mean to disparage the blushing gals — raspberries and strawberries." About now, eyes may begin to roll, reminding me of berries spilled across a drainboard at the edge of a sink. But that's enough narratology, on with the story: "You've got a banana in your ear," the first man says when he sees the second man. "What?" the other man responds, cupping a hand behind his right ear to aid his hearing. "You have a banana in your ear," the first man repeats raising his voice. "What's that?" the second man answers leaning forward. "You've got a banana in your ear!" the first man shouts, clearly irritated. "I'm sorry. I can't hear you," the second man replies. 'I've got a banana in my ear." Usually the story and I stop here, but if the person whom I have seized by the tympanic membrane doesn't smile, seems ill-at-ease or unnaturally sensitive, I forge on. I note that the second man is a gentleman and knows eating alone in the presence of others is rude. Consequently, he plucks the banana from his auditory canal and after peeling it and ascertaining that it is not marred by unsightly bruises offers the first man a fraternal bite.

After jocularity has been stripped away and the flesh chewed and digested into metaphor, the banana could be thought a natural hearing aid, one that blocks sound rather than amplifies it. Today loss of hearing soothes more than it perturbs. Jabber and blare swirl through the hours "smothering thought," as my friend Josh puts it, "and overwhelming personality." Radios caterwaul and televisions blather unceasingly: in the cardiologist's office and the orthodontist's chair, in the lavatory at the café and at the meat counter in the grocery store. Hikers and runners wear earbuds, turning lonely trails and wilderness paths into scratchy sound studios. Three of the four people whom I meet every day in the university gymnasium collect televisions, usually three, placing one in the kitchen, another in the family room, and the third in the bedroom. Vicki and I have a single television. Alas, radios clutter our house and day. There are at least two in the kitchen, one in the study, two in our bedroom, one in the garage, another in the attic, and two in the basement, one of these last at the bottom of the stairs on an all-purpose table, the other across the room on a shelf above the washing machine. I cannot be precise about the locations. The radios swarm and wander about. As soon as I switch one off, another squawks. I don't know how they procreate, but shortly after I murder one, a descendant soon appears in its place. Oh, well, a writer ought to be able to silence a bore, even if the bore is himself. In any case I hope the otologist's prescription is right: telling the banana joke once a day keeps tinnitus away.

Reading *Nickleby* animated my genial spirits. I run six miles a day with David. He is a long-time, long-distance runner, and since his 39th birthday, has tracked his mileage. Shortly after Smike slipped away from Wackford Squeers and Dotheboys Hall, David reached 90,000 miles. That afternoon Vicki and I gave him a bottle of Scotch that cost $90, well, to be accurate $89.99 before tax. Finding the appropriately-priced bottle wasn't easy. The clerk in the liquor store was too helpful and insisted upon showing us tasty Scotches that cost $68 or $75. After we paid for the Scotch, he said, "Let me remove the price tag for you." "No," Vicki insisted cradling the bottle. "If you take the price off, we'll return the bottle."

"David," I said later when I handed him the Scotch, "the 90,000 miles was manageable, but if you are decent enough to feel responsible for the financial well-being of your friends, you should decrease the daily allotment of mileage. 100,000 miles would break the bank and shred Vicki's purse." For the record, neither Vicki nor I drink hard liquor. Never do spirits in our house rise above beer or on special occasions $10 plonk. Only once have we drunk anything that cost $40, and that was a bottle of Champagne, given to us as a Christmas present. Moreover, David is eighty-one, and he's unlikely to reach a hundred thousand miles. He and I are now moving so slowly that workmen see us coming and have time to fashion witty remarks. "Fellows," a surveyor said recently as we drew alongside, "don't worry. The man with the torch will be along soon, and he'll lead you into the stadium." "Guys," a man trimming a hedge warned shaking his clippers at us like a school-principal's index finger, "don't you know there's a speed limit around here?"

In late winter, cold jabs through days like sciatica. Juncos dart rheumatic as if being cuffed in and out of the air, and until the appearance of Lent lilies, playfulness can become disruptive. During the first week of March, Allison telephoned three times to inform me that the warranty on my car had expired. "Hellfire," I told Vicki, "the warranty on me has expired. The treads on my feet have split, and my carburetor is hinky." During the third call, Allison offered to connect me to a warranty specialist. She didn't react well to my responding with a snort-and-honk speech impediment phrase, in the middle of which lay unseemly osculatory instructions. "I'm sorry. I didn't get that," Allison said. "Would you mind repeating what you said?" "With pleasure," I answered, and taking a deep breath, replicated my previous remarks. Immediately thereafter, Allison ended the call, and during the past two months neither Allison nor any of her friends—Tiffany or Laura—have telephoned. Their concern for my welfare on the highway was probably not deeply felt. Still, I miss their calls, and the gals should know that I have improved the snort and honk by adding a shriek, the sound, I must confess because I am a good academic, plagiarized from the cry of a red-tailed hawk.

The sentence that hops then comes to a crisp full stop appeals to me in Sparrow Winter, this last a Connecticut appellation describing late April when the temperature bounds up and down like sparrows flitting erratically across the ground. In contrast summer is the time of languid paragraphs and dreamy thought. Adultery, Thorne Smith wrote bracingly, "is the best-dressed of all the vices." A remark as eternally stylish, Josh said, "as a sleeveless sweater vest, an Argyle checkerboard of blue and white diamonds covering the chest, the white, as befits those to the country club raised, slightly off color." A conservative, Douglas Jerrold wrote, "is a man who will not look at the new moon out of respect for that 'ancient institution,' the old one." "No reader could wish that quip longer," I thought, buttoning my jacket prior to walking to the library not sure whether I should sling a raincoat over my arm. The third week in April, a publishing house offered me the "opportunity" to update a twelve-thousand-word encyclopedia article I wrote sixteen years ago. "On completing the revision," an editor stated, "you can choose a hundred dollars worth of books from our list." I declined the offer. "$100 of books," I wrote the editor, "wouldn't supply enough pages to keep the privy of a constipated bachelor in paper for two months." I might have accepted the chore if the editor had offered me something less probable than books, say, a pair of shoehorns that glowed in the dark, one hot and scarlet, the other white and icy, or maybe a teakettle that sang like Wilson Pickett when it steamed, my choice being "In the Midnight Hour," or if that was out of stock Melanie Safka's "Look What They've Done to My Song, Ma."

Four days later, the editor of a literary quarterly solicited an article from me. "I'd like a description of university life from the perspective of a retiree. I'd especially value any suggestions you might make on how to improve the reputation of the humanities." How many times, I wondered, had I spooned through Pablum dished out by apologists for the humanities? Inevitably the servings were sweet with good intentions, but withal lumpy and innervating. Because they appear to live apart from the main currents and many of the temptations of life, teachers are often treated as secular clergymen. Cultural deacons draft them to preach, expecting their sermons to be slightly priggish and safely formulaic — jam containing dollops of pectin and no seeds. Recently I read "On the Study of Literature," an address John Morley made in 1877 to the Students of the London Society for the Extension of University Teaching, "The thing that matters most, both for happiness and for duty, is that we should habitually live with wise thoughts and right feelings," Morley concluded stirring in a bromide compounded to elicit applause and agreement rather than thought. I thanked the editor for writing but resisted the temptation to wrap myself in truisms and wax Delphic. I explained that the subject was too easy for my talents. To the end of my reply, I attached a footnote obliquely justifying why I punted, as sports aficionados say. In the note I quoted the first number of *Salmagundi*. "Our intention," Washington Irving and James Paulding declared in 1807, "is simply to instruct the young, reform the old, correct the town, and castigate the age. This is an arduous task, and therefore we undertake it with confidence." Perhaps the actual reason I did not embrace the editor's invitation was that I've become a winding-down wind-up toy. Age has loosened my main spring and writing about matters for which not much thinking is required quickly exhausts me.

Dickens' novels are three-volume circuses. Small non-fictional carnivals abound in everyone's every day, however. If a person is alert to the light-hearted and the odd, he will see shows that outdo the performances of Vincent Crummles's troupe. Across Doddley Road, opposite Green Square in Providence is a popular French restaurant. On weekends, the line of patrons snakes along Hammond Avenue and coils around the corner of Doddley. Because the restaurant's menu is extensive and the wine list "a sommelier's fantasy," once customers are seated, they spend an inordinate time ordering. They take so long they inhibit the flow of people in and out of the restaurant, thereby, the owner claimed, reducing potential profits by a third. In hopes of shortening the period diners spent before ordering, the owner hired a culinary consultant. She suggested attaching metal sleeves to the backs of lavatory stalls and into them inserting menus and wine lists. "The idea," I explained to Vicki, "was that people would multitask and return to the dining room having chosen their dinners." Vicki has a graduate degree in common sense, not business, an M.C.S., not an M.B.A. "I assume that after their visits to the Necessary House," she said, "many customers will order Ca Ca Vin."

Television serials are the contemporary equivalent of the 19th century novel published in weekly or monthly parts. Raymond, Michael, and I, all of us former English teachers, meet for pizza and talk once a month. In bygone days, we would have discussed books and maybe the comical doings of colleagues, our tone affectionate and not censorious. Nowadays we talk about television programs and rarely chat about members of English departments. When we do mention university teachers, we are more critical than appreciative, thinking many to be careerists, people whose doings lack the spirit-elevating lift of helium. Recently Ray sent Michael an email reminding him that a new season of "Fargo" was about to begin on television. "Be and sure and see the first installment," Ray wrote. "No can do," Michael answered. "I'm in Tangiers." I suspect an unacknowledged desire to escape the present and sail the choppy seas of Victorian England provoked my reading *Nicholas Nickleby*, Dickens himself serving as both cruise director and tour guide. On the other hand, I have long imagined escaping to places vague and barely visible, if not to Tangiers like Michael then to Persepolis, Isfahan or maybe travelling to Magadan on the Kolyma Highway, the Road of Bones built by people imprisoned in Stalin's forced labor camps.

I realize that outside the pages of books. I will never visit any exotic places. I have come to believe that DNA so controls me that despite aching to get away I won't go anywhere unless a ticket is stuffed into my pocket. I am not simply my father's son. I am him, and he rarely spent a night away from Mother and me. Father's hands are my hands: the palms soft and fingers long and slender, their movements easy and expressive. Veins creek across the dorsals or backs never stopping and eddying, the skin silver and reddish, stepping stones of liver spots winding between the colors creating paths from the knuckles to the wrists. As I am now a domestic library, so, Father was in the past. He read on the bus going to and returning from the office. At work, he kept a book open in the top drawer of his desk. He read before and after dinner, often romantic verse. I remember his reciting lines from Thomas Moore's "Lalla Rookh." "Now, upon Syria's land of roses / Softly the light of eve reposes, / And, like a glory, the broad sun / Hangs over sainted Lebanon; / Whose head in wintry grandeur towers, / And whitens with eternal sleet, / While summer, in a vale of flowers, / Is sleeping rosy at his feet." When Father was a child, he read so incessantly that his parents worried that he'd become sick. To break the addiction, they sent him to military school for a year. The cure failed. "The only thing the military taught him," Coleman his brother said, "was the names of books librarians hid so children would not discover them."

In part I am also Father's brother Uncle Coleman. I managed the last decade of Coleman's life. Thrice a year I flew to Houston to visit him. When I arrived, he was usually listening to gospel songs on the radio. I am an atheist. Now, though, that eighty lies just below the next bend of my back, I, too, listen to religious songs. I even jot down lines: "When the fire comes down from heaven, this old world will melt away," "As he hung there on the tree, he prayed for you and me," "Precious Lord, take my hand; lead me home" or best of all "If there's a phone there in Heaven, Jesus, put me through." "Put my Mama on the line," the supplicant begs. Give me "one more chance to tell her that I love her." Dickens' novels are ragbags of families, in *Nickleby* not just the two branches of Nicklebys but also the Squeers', Kenwigs', Cheerbyles', and the Crummles'. Often while reading *Nickleby* I thought about the Pickerings, my musings evoked both by the novel and by lines from old, sentimental songs the book somehow suggested: "When you and I were young, Maggie," "Silver threads among the gold," and then from "Lorena," "The years creep slowly by, Lorena. The snow is on the grass again."

I thought much about Grandma Pickering. I was her only grandchild, and she doted on me. Regrettably, I never appreciated the extent of her love until long after she died, that is, until I reached sixty and my house and life were quiet. My children had scattered, and the things of the world that I'd gathered seemed trifling. Why, I wondered, had I spent so much of my life writing books and accumulating knick-knacks: paintings, china, citations, rugs, sideboards, and honorary degrees. After graduating from Sewanee, I spent two years at Cambridge getting a second B. A. When I first went to Cambridge, I wrote Grandma Pickering every week. I stopped writing after four months because she didn't answer my letters. After I had been gone a year, Grandma died. On my returning home, Father said, "She loved your letters, Sammy." Then he handed me a stack of letters she'd written me. "She was old and got confused," he said, "and sent them to the wrong address, Massachusetts, not England. I saved them for you. She was so proud of you."

Relatives consigned to oblivion purposely or by mistake often wander onto the boards in Dickens' narratives and play important roles: Smike the feeble-minded child of Ralph Nickleby and in *Barnaby Rudge* Sir John Chester's brutish illegitimate son, Hugh. Although they lay deep under the turf of years, I suddenly wanted to know more about my lost relatives. I knew much about my great grandfather William B. Pickering. In 1861 when he was seventeen, he left Ohio University and enlisted in the Union Army. After the battle of Stones River early in 1863, he left what had become the Army of the Cumberland and became adjutant of the Fifth Tennessee Cavalry. He spent the remainder of the war stationed in and around Carthage, Tennessee. After the war ended, he married and settled in Carthage. Among his children was my grandfather Samuel Pickering. Of Daniel F. Griffin, Grandma Pickering's father, I knew little. He was from Georgia and supposedly was notoriously quarrelsome. Upon getting into trouble with reconstruction authorities, he was forced to leave Georgia, not, however, before being shot. He settled in Franklin, Tennessee but once more he quarreled with neighbors, and consequently he moved to Texas. Texas not proving to be to his liking and his purse, he returned to Franklin where, when my grandmother was young, he was stabbed to death, either in a brawl or by an aggrieved husband.

Ralph Nickleby learned that Smike was his child only after Smike's death. As a person ages the future contracts and the past expands and becomes alluring. The abusive life at Dotheboys Hall made Smike feeble-minded. What, I asked, unsettled my great-grandfather and made him difficult to get along with?

The answer was war. I exhumed muster roles and discovered that in March 1861, Daniel Griffin enlisted as a private in the 36th regiment of Georgia Infantry. He was sixteen years old. A year later he was "discharged by expiration of term of service." Shortly thereafter he was appointed 2nd Corporal of the 2nd Company E, 1st Confederate Regiment. On July 22, 1864, he was wounded at Atlanta. On September 17, 1864, he was in a hospital in Columbus "wounded," after which he disappeared from official records, invalided out of service, I assume. What I couldn't find was where the war took him. Was it to Fredericksburg, Spotsylvania, Chickamauga, and Nashville? Many Georgia infantrymen fought at Stones River. If so, did he and William Pickering come within a Minni ball of each other? Such speculation is the stuff of a novel. What seems clear, though, is like that of Hugh in *Barnaby Rudge,* Daniel Griffin's classroom was brutal. Although not predictable, it is not surprising that he like Hugh became difficult and died violently. Of course, allowing a novel to unravel into family story, if only for a moment, must be a recognized critical error. Call it the Personal Fallacy. But then isn't the best reason for reading personal, be it diversion, entertainment, or to be led into realms beyond the page?

Last month I read an essay entitled "How to Make Biscuits." As I read memories rose fluffier on the baking sheet than the biscuits themselves. Years before I left Tennessee for England, a friend advised Mother to buy stock in Martha White Flour. "Martha White Self-Rising Flour has got hot rise," a contemporary advertising jingle declared. Almost as if it were rich with Crisco and buttermilk, baking powder, salt, and flour itself, the stock heated up and swelled, making my attending Cambridge financially possible. Perhaps, I thought as I read the essay, biscuits were the reason I didn't become a banker or lawyer or settle and marry in Nashville. Maybe the popularity of biscuits was responsible for my becoming a teacher. "Diet in the service of psychology," Vicki said. "What will you discover when you read about fried chicken, corn on the cob, snaps, turnip greens, country ham, tomato aspic, and fudge cake?" "Me," I said. "If I read closely and thoughtfully I'll discover me."

In *Nickleby*, Mr. Curdle, notable for writing a sixty-four-page study of the deceased husband of the nurse in *Romeo and Juliet*, quizzed Nicholas on the dramatic unities. They are, Curdle said, "a kind of universal dovetailedness with regard to place and time — a sort of general oneness." In life oneness is an umbrella under which anything and everything shelters: cucumbers, jiggers of Scotch, the Georgia Militia eating Goober Peas, and, as improbable it may seem to people shackled to the literal, Fanny Squeers walking arm in arm with Annie Laurie, both with brows like snowdrifts and necks like swans. Early in April, Vicki and I attended a memorial service for Joe Cary, a man with whom I shared an office for a dozen years when I first taught in Storrs. "When my father died," Joe's daughter recounted, "he was reading *Nicholas Nickleby*." "Did you hear what she said?" Vicki said jabbing me. "How much more of the book do you have left to read?" On my guessing a hundred-and-ten pages, Vicki said, "as soon as this service ends, we are racing home. You are going into the study and start reading. I'm locking the door and not letting you out until you finish the novel. What a bad sign!" I obeyed Vicki and finished the book. The next morning, I started re-reading *Barnaby Rudge*. Oh, how I have enjoyed spending evenings in the Maypole Inn warming at the fire and observing characters from the novel: Gabriel Varden, the locksmith, and his daughter Dolly rubbing the only hand of Joe Willet, her one-armed soldier, Simon Tapperwit glowering at Joe and displaying his legs, Miggs jealous and scowling, fueling her resentment with pages from the *Protestant Manual*, and then Barnaby himself, on his shoulder Grip the raven rocking back and forth proclaiming, "I'm a devil."

In summer, Barnaby, Dickens wrote, walked and ran and leaped until he became tired. Then he lay "down in the long grass or by the growing corn" and gazed upward at the "light clouds as they floated over the blue surface of the sky." Sometimes he picked wildflowers: "the bright red poppy, the gentle harebell, the cowslip and the rose." He watched birds, fish, ants, and hares. He smelled the air rich with the fragrance of beans and clover and fell asleep amid the murmuring of the wind. Summer is two months away, but spring has arrived in Storrs. Daffodils and tulips are red and yellow in Vicki's planters. The curtain of periwinkle at the edge of the wood is blue with blossoms. In the high grass dandelions spread buxom, and Quaker ladies spackle barren patches in the lawn. Redbuds are magenta, and the color glows like a glaze on Mexican pottery cooked for the tourist trade. On Norway spruce cones are rose-purple and look like stoppers plucked from small bottles of expensive French perfume. In the afternoon garter snakes wrinkle across paths, their tails lagging cedillas. At dusk the rabbit that lives in the brush pile behind our house leaves his home, and the fragrance of the saucer magnolia becomes moist. During the heat of the day the aroma of skunk cabbage rises from nearby marshes. Not many people like the smell, but I do, and so would Barnaby.

A robin is nesting in the yew by our side door, and across the street a groundhog has moved into a burrow under our neighbor's front stoop. Soon blossoms will break from forsythia and tumble crinkled to the ground looking like fallen stars. Almost every day Vicki and I walk until we are tired. "The true art of walking consists in being rather than in going," Stanton Kirkham wrote in *As Nature Whispers*. Unlike Barnaby, we are not able to gambol spontaneously, freeing ourselves from personality and letting the spirit of nature "take possession of us." We are too worldly, too conscious, and too old. We have enjoyed too many books never suffering, as Kirkham put it, from "literary indigestion." Still, we delight in moments. We marvel at the maples' red blossoms. We shake catkins dangling from birches, and the lemon-colored pollen powders our fingers. We lean into golden larches and sweep the brooms of new needles across our cheeks. Sometimes we run, at least mentally, but never do we lie down. This is high tick season. Two days ago, I flicked two off my trousers and plucked a half dozen off Jack and Suzy our resident Grips.

Uncommercial Traveller

The Uncommercial Traveller is a collection of articles and journalism from Dickens' middle years. In the preface, Dickens wrote, "No landlord is my friend and brother, no chambermaid loves me, no waiter worships me, no boots admires and envies me. No round of beef or tongue or ham is expressly cooked for me. . . . No house of public entertainment in the United Kingdom greatly cares for my opinion of its brandy or sherry." I travel, he explained, for "the great house of Human Interest Brothers." "When I come home from my journeys, I never get any commission. I know nothing about prices, and should have no idea, if I were put to it, how to wheedle a man into ordering something he doesn't want." In the *Traveller* Dickens described roaming mind and place. He dissected memories and explored morgues, poorhouses, and the aftermath of shipwrecks. He wandered churches and graveyards. He talked to Mormon emigrants headed to the Great Salt Lake and to the inhabitants of Rats' Castle, a slum in London, home to thieves and the disease-ridden poor. He ate a meal at the Whitechapel Self-Supporting Cooking Depot. He visited the Preparatory Day School he once attended now cut up "root and branch" by a railway. The school, he recalled, was "remarkable for white mice," judging that "the boys trained the mice better than the masters trained the boys." At a Flemish fair, he was fortunate to see a ventriloquist and a face-maker just before they supposedly departed for Algeria. While the ventriloquist followed the buzzing of a bee across a window pane eventually capturing and imprisoning the insect in a bottle, the face-maker transformed his face and thus himself into a jamboree of characters.

Would that I could add the face-maker and the ventriloquist to the carnival of memorable people I have come across in my wanderings. For Dickens scholars, the *Traveller* is a sampler of revealing treats. In "City of London Churches," Dickens described a shower which drove him and the original of David Copperfield's Dora Spenlow into a church. While walking to Wapping Workhouse, he patted the leg of *Dombey and Son*'s wooden midshipman. For my part, however, the years I devoted to literary study have ended, and much of the pleasure of the *Traveller* and of reading itself arise from associations with my life. When Dickens was a boy, a nursemaid told him ghoulish stories. According to the nurse, a month after each of Captain Murderer's marriages, he handed his bride a golden rolling pin and a silver pie board and asked her to make a pie crust. While the bride made a crust, the Captain produced an immense silver dish which he filled with flour, butter, eggs, and "all things needful, except the inside of the pie." When the bride asked what kind of pie "this is to be," the Captain said, "A meat pie." Then the bride said, "Dear Captain Murderer, I see no meat." "Look in the glass," the Captain answered laughing robustly. He then told the confused bride to roll out the crust. When she finished, he shouted, "I see the meat in the glass."

On the bride's staring into the mirror, the Captain sliced off her head and chopped her into bite-sized pieces. After salting and peppering her, he crammed her into the pie and sent it to the baker to be cooked. Later he devoured the pie finding the bones especially savory. The Captain got his just, not desserts, but main course, when he married the vengeful sister of one of his earlier dinner companions. As the girl rolled out the pie crust, she swallowed a poison distilled from toads' eyes and spiders' knees. The Captain "had hardly picked her last bone, when he began to swell, and to turn blue, and to be all over spots and to scream." He continued to swell, turn blue, scream, and become increasingly dappled "until he reached from floor to ceiling and from wall to wall; and then, at one o'clock in the morning, he blew up with a loud explosion." When our children were little, Vicki and I kept a haberdashery of spooky costumes in the attic. We filled it with, among other regalia, madmen's wigs, masks with nightmarish angel-maker expressions, dead hands with long green and yellow decaying fingers, and fiendish pets, one of which was a three-foot long rubber scorpion that could be worn around the neck like a scarf. I entertained the children by lurking in closets and behind furniture from which I unexpectedly rose like Old Mister Grim, pawing and snorting. Alas, nothing I did matched the nurse's scrumptious account of Captain Murderer. Indeed, from the perspective of a father with three all-too-well-adjusted adult children, I realize that none of my tricks was as funny, memorable, and as emotionally educational, as the biography of Captain Murderer. "How limited my imagination was," I thought as I read about the Captain.

After retirement transformed me into a superannuated man, I became an uncommercial traveler. Like Dickens' narrator, I sell nothing, and there is nothing I wish to buy. No shopkeeper calls me by name, and in cafés and streets I am anonymous. I am free from necessity and follow whim not schedule. I do not mind doing favors for other people, but I refuse to let them do favors for me. I avoid intellectual and emotional encumbrances, and when others attempt to snuggle close in order, as they blather, "to know the real you," I drift away. Frequently I rely upon hypocrisy and caulking dishonesty to insulate myself from familiarity. Unfortunately, hypocrisy demands exhausting and ultimately impossible vigilance, and I occasionally lapse into intimacy which in turn leads to careless intemperate honesty and disrupts calm of life. Perhaps the most efficacious way to keep familiarity at a distance is to perfect talking about nothing, mouthing insipid soporifics that lead nowhere and which dull the mind, anesthetize memory, and spread balmy boredom over heartburn, that is, chat about tight shoes, lawnmowers, the colon, or having one's teeth or house power-washed. "My word, isn't the weather nice?" a woman said to my friend Josh recently. "The sun makes a body feel so warm." "Yes, I have always thought the sun makes a difference," Josh answered then continued when the woman hovered nearby looking at him expectantly. "And snow makes a difference, too. It makes a body feel cold, but when the sun melts the snow, a person does feel warm." "Yes," the woman answered. "You are so right. I couldn't agree more."

When many people age, they gather crowds around them like comforters. Friends and relatives, they say, keep winter away from the heart. In my case the comforter would smother not warm. My favorite visitors are those who never leave their houses. Having been an only child may be responsible for my asocial behavior. When I was young, my mind to me was not a kingdom, as Edward Dyer put it, stored with regal surfeit and peopled by princes and courtiers. It was an ordinary suburban place, but it sufficed, and although I cannot describe what I did, if I did anything during my hours alone, I was content. Today's rigorous chumminess requiring hugs and first names repulses me. I refuse when a new acquaintance suggests a glass of wine. The invitation falls on ears deafened by the honky-tonk warning of Ernest Tubbs playing the guitar and singing, "I'm just drivin' nails in my coffin every time I drink a bottle of booze." In "I'm Sorry. You Have the Wrong Number," Wendell Berry comes close to capturing what I think about the robocall present. "It's true, I may as well confess, / That most dead people I do not miss, / And I am further remiss in this, / That many living I will not kiss. / I don't love everybody, damn it. / A man must love within his limit. / Against love's collectivization, / I propose love's specification. / When you're out of intimacy's range, / It is most cordial to be strange."

No man knows himself well enough to explain his past. Maybe being an only child had no formative influence upon my character. What is clear, however, is that as I slump into my Cialis years, I am reclusive. My shadow autobiography occupies thought more than my actual biography. Vigor quickens paragraphs of the former, and its pages are crazed with oddity instead of decay. "What If" serves as subtitle to a signature of chapters. Although I repeatedly start chapters, I never finish reading them. Unlike accounts in my actual autobiography which grind steadily through declarative sentences to periods and dead ends, tales in my shadow autobiography are seductively unfinished, enabling, encouraging, me to peruse their beginnings repeatedly, something Dickens understood. "There are not many places that I find it more agreeable to revisit when I am in an idle mood, than some places to which I have never been," Dickens wrote, adding, "I never was in Robinson Crusoe's Island, yet I frequently return there."

The imagination of the wintry adult is darker and more active than that of youth. In contrast to optimism and hope which blind and make youth drowsy, pessimism is caffeinated and keeps a person awake—fitting for an uncommercial traveler. On my wanderings, I meet detail donors, that is, people, manifestations of whose DNA surface in my fictional characters. At the Sunday morning flea market held at the Mansfield Drive-In, a battered man standing at a trough urinal said to the person next to him, "I'm like you. No Social Security. We'll die on the street." Both men shuffled and wore baseball caps. Printed on the crown of one was "Celtics," the name of the professional basketball team in Boston; on the other, "Huskies," the byname of athletic teams at the University of Connecticut. At the cash register of a bookstore in Hartford, I met a psychiatrist buying the most recent novel by Danielle Steele. "Rubbish to read on an airplane," he told me. The man flew from coast to coast once a month. "I've never used a bathroom on a plane, and I never will," he said. The man refused to take non-stop flights. He also avoided flights in which he changed planes only once. "My travel agent knows to book me on two-stop flights," he elaborated, "flying, for example, from here to Atlanta where I change planes for Dallas or Denver where I change again. She schedules my trips so that I have time between legs of the trip to go to the bathroom. Never, ever, will I micturate on a plane." While I waited for Gengras Volvo in East Hartford to tune the engine of my car, a woman selling insurance introduced herself to me. "I've had four husbands and six proposals," she testified. "I wouldn't mind another husband or two, but I'm over fifty and too fat for younger men. Insofar as older men are concerned, aside from an occasional date, I don't have much use for them. They are all looking for a nurse with a purse."

"You're mad!" Lyndon Parker, the companion and amanuensis of the detective Solar Pons, exclaimed in August Derleth's *The Casebook of Solar Pons*. "It becomes me," Pons responded. Pons' madness was genius inherited from Sherlock Holmes. Never have I met a mad genius or, for that matter, a detective. Practically every day, however, I chance upon the odd, that is, people whose conversation cloaks their gray lives with checkered eccentricity. "How different the world would be if societies were ladder-less and all people earth-bound," a stranger confided in Price Chopper. Before I could mount the first step toward a reply, he changed the subject asking, "Have you ever noticed the number of 'EXIT' signs in a building? You teach at the university. There are thousands on the campus. Why don't you count them?" The troubled are particularly susceptible to the numbering virus. Last winter a man with midnight-black eyebrows and fingers thinner than screwdrivers approached me while I hunted for a crime novel in the Mansfield Library. "Can you guess," he asked, "the number of murders depicted in books on a six-foot shelf in the fiction section?" On my saying I had no idea, he told me he'd counted the murders on one-hundred-and-twelve shelves. Four-hundred-and-eighty-one murders occurred on the average shelf. In the first four chapters of a celebrated best-selling novel, he said, fourteen people and two dogs were killed. "Not gun control," he said staring at me. "We need book control."

Libraries resemble hornets' nests, their aisles papery cells. Amid the stacks drones forage for audiences. They lack stingers, but they have, as the tired expression puts it, bees in their bonnets, and if encouraged by a nod or a smile, they alight buzzing with words. "Indignation about statues that represent persons now out of favor would end," a man told me last month, "if we removed all existing monuments and replaced them with statues celebrating imaginary people — teachers, musicians, writers, preachers, generals, statesmen who never existed." Engraved on the plaques of imaginary novelists, he said, would be the titles of books they didn't write; on the plaques of generals the names of famous battles not fought, and on those of politicians, elections neither won, lost, "nor tied." "What an idea," Josh said later. "Who could be offended by a monument honoring Asenath Templeton's discovery of a cure for a disease that never existed or a memorial for Florita Dortch who satisfied the dreamy hankerings of untold numbers of hopeless people by fashioning an easy-to-follow recipe for pie in the sky?" "Not even a rabid sectarian could spade up theological grounds to object to a non-existent divine's non-existent description of a non-existent place," Josh continued warming to the topic, "a netherworld in which the naughty endured a carnival of punishments, say, sizzling in deep dish frying pans awash with brimstone and chili peppers, or having their innards gnawed into frass by cancerous worms with teeth sharper than carbide meat hooks."

Like Dickens' preparatory school, the two elementary schools I attended have vanished, one torn down, not to accommodate trains, but for a housing development, the other for a small park. When I last visited the second site, a boy called Whitey, not pet mice, came to mind. Before ethnic nicknames became culturally unpalatable, boys often addressed each other using the names of Indian chiefs. Geronimo was the most popular followed by Crazy Horse, this emended to Crazy Scott or Crazy John or, as I remember, in one instance to Crazy Wahoo Bill. Emendation was simple and popular, and Whitey changed Cochise to Cocheese. "It's too bad you were too young to be witty," Josh said when I told him about the "monikers." "'Hey, Cocheese,' someone should have said. 'How's the old Gouda? Has Monterey Jack found a girlfriend? His trouble is that he thinks dependable English Cheddar boring and can't stop fantasizing about nibbling the exotic, preferably from over the waters, say, Sap Sago or Torta del Casar. Anyway, what's Stilton up to? Is he still melancholy and blue-veined? Any Crackers sashaying around with Brie? I reckon she has been on the shelf too long and isn't as fresh as she used to be.'"

Josh has been a fictional companion so long that I am unable to jettison him. Like a periodic fever, he reappears and spots my sentences. The most effective treatment I know is to shut my pencils in the desk, pack my traveler's bag, and decamp for half a page at least. Slipping away from Josh does not guarantee peace or quiet, however. When Dickens' traveler became weary, he sought "instant rest," interposing, as he put it, "a fly-leaf in the book of my life" in which he prorogued writing for "a brief session of a few weeks." The session was shorter than he hoped, for "begging-letter writers came out on the fly-leaf" and bedeviled him. Times simultaneously change and remain constant. Today's importuning writers are not individuals but organizations. Their causes are almost always good and deserve the support of the decent. Nevertheless, the stacks of mail exhaust me. Hardly a day passes without my receiving solicitations from, among three score others, World Wildlife, PETA, the Campaign to Defend Democracy, Planned Parenthood, Cystic Fibrosis Foundation, Princeton University, NPR, the Physicians Committee for Responsible Medicine, International Animal Rescue, Earth Justice, Sewanee, Audubon, the Connecticut Humane Society, and the Sierra Club.

My carpetbag resembles a doctor's bag hemorrhaging medical anecdotes. "I now have double vision," an old friend told me recently. "Gosh," I said, "you live alone. Do you get somebody to drive you to the grocery and run errands? Life must be difficult." "Not really," my friend answered. "I bought an eye patch. Whenever I drive, I put it on over one eye, and the double vision goes away." At my age, vision is physical not intellectual. The vision of Clay, a distant cousin, had so deteriorated that last fall he had operations on both eyes. After the surgery, the doctor assured Clay that his sight would improve. "Improvement will be gradual, but it will occur," the doctor said. Several days later, the physician's assistant examined Clay's eyes and prescribed new glasses. Weeks passed, and Clay's vision did not improve. In fact, his sight worsened when he put on his glasses. Eventually, he returned to the doctor's office, and the assistant re-examined his eyes first without then with his glasses. "Good Lord," she exclaimed after he put on his glasses, "These aren't your glasses. Somebody made a mistake and gave you the wrong prescription. No wonder you are having trouble seeing." Their salad days having wilted and becoming splotched by mildew and leaf spot, many uncommercial travelers resemble J. B. Priestley's Aunt Hilda, a character in *Bright Day*. "Her favorite talk, when she was out to enjoy herself," Priestley wrote, was "of minor ailments leading to major ones, of operations and tragic breakdowns, of dissolution and death."

Although I don't purchase anything during my travels, I run across shelves of strange items. For sale in Mackey's in Willimantic was a cemetery of plastic crosses made from translucent boxes. The crosses were two feet high. On each cross was a switch and a small solar panel. When the switch was turned on, a bulb inside the cross glowed. "Perfect," a customer said, "for standing atop the grave of a beloved cat or dog." On sale at the flea market was a cast iron garden hose holder suitable for mounting on the side of a house or garage. The holder resembled an andiron. The back of the holder corresponded to the part of an andiron nearest the fire and could be screwed to a wall. The middle section of the holder resembled the leggy middle of an andiron and was long enough for a hose to be wrapped around it. The front was decorative, not with an andiron's conventional cannonballs or urns, fanciful owls, or cowboys drawing pistols as I once saw but with a lighthouse. The light house was ten inches tall and stood in a grove of bushes, two on one side, four on the other. The foundation of the lighthouse was orange. On it sat a blue platform. From the platform, the lighthouse rose looking like a black and white barber's pole. At the top of the pole was another platform. Atop it was the revolving light, its windows also black and white. The roof above the light rose to a point and looked like a small cap topped with a button. The holder by my back door at home was plastic and gritty with dirt, and for a moment I was tempted to buy the holder thus becoming an apostate to uncommercial traveling. I resisted the urge, however, and returning home wandered the internet, discovering I could buy the holder online for $28.99 postage included.

Rarely are uncommercial travelers young. Time blinkers and focuses, and instead of being attracted by the glittering, uncommercial travelers notice the crape-draped things of end moments. On the town square this past spring middle school students selling Girl Scout cookies shared a table with elderly women hawking Senior Citizens cookies. The four women to whom I spoke were widows and had baked for decades. "Punching dough," a woman in a wheelchair said, "for patisseries of husbands, children, grandchildren, and now great-grandchildren." A box of Senior cookies cost six dollars, a dollar more than a comparable box sold by the Girl

Scouts. "Inviting us to share their table was sweet and we did not want to undersell the girls," a woman explained. The cookies themselves were soft butter cookies "easy on dentures." The cookies were not iced and had simply been dusted with powdered sugar. Next spring, the women planned to enlist more bakers and to drizzle melted chocolate over some cookies and add peanut butter to the ingredients of others. "We want to attract widowers not afraid of ovens. Men are addicted to peanuts and baking with peanut butter ought to make one or two boys pitch their canes and spend a couple of mornings in the kitchen." Profits from selling the cookies were more intangible than tangible—happy afternoons visiting with people on the town square rather than dollars and cents. All cash revenue from the sales was donated to the Wellness Program at the Senior Citizens Center, the bakers themselves having already donated the ingredients and their time.

Replacement heels for work boots were the most singular item I came across. For sale in a cobbler's stall at the farmer's market in Coventry, the heels were an inch and a half taller than the heels on commonplace work boots. Inserted into each heel at different heights were a dozen capsules resembling the soft gels containing fish or cod liver oil that health enthusiasts swallow by the handful. Instead of dietary supplements, the gels held liquid air freshener, the fragrances including lemon-lime, apple orchard, lilac, piña colada, and baby's breath. As the heels wore down, individual capsules split and released the freshener, banishing, a handwritten card pasted to a box of heels stated, the aroma of cow pie from pasture, boot rack, and screened porch. The heels were long-lasting and would, the card assured skeptical purchasers, "dispense perfume throughout the active farmer's day for eight months."

Along with squash and corn, stalks of Brussel sprouts, carrots and cauliflower, oddities fill barrows at farmer's markets. Three years ago in Coventry, a woman sold

"Undertakers Masks." Carved from wood, they covered wearers' faces and resembled ritual masks worn during African tribal ceremonies. Mouths on the masks curved upward into smiles looking like the waxing crescent of a Cheshire moon. "Because obsequies require under-takers to remain solemn hour after hour, their facial expressions cramp and harden into dour grimness," the woman explained. "Restoring mobility to the epicranius muscles is laborious and often involves massages and hot compresses," she continued. "To prevent frighten-ing their blessed little ones after leaving the meat locker and returning home or on route unnerving cashiers at the grocery store if their wives ordered them to pick up a comestible or two, morticians don masks wreathed in smiles." The masks were popular, and the woman quickly sold the fifteen she brought to the market. I saw two of the purchasers. Both appeared to be so good-na-tured they seemed incapable of frowning. "What did you expect?" Vicki said. "Coals to Newcastle, owls to Athens, tulips to Holland — that's the way of commerce."

The uncommercial world I wander is familiar and pedestrian — unremarkable in comparison to the space opera landscape of actual buying and selling. Two years ago, a former student sent me an advertisement osten-sibly clipped from a Bengali newspaper. Unlike most of the paper the advertisement was in English. Written for Memsaabs new to the subcontinent and whose digestive systems had not adjusted to Indian cuisine, the ad cel-ebrated the virtues of "Cool Below," a flame-retardant tablet that purported to extinguish "Fire in the Hole." The ad described the catastrophic effects of wind colic on Europeans who ate hot Indian food before their "organs" developed internal sprinklers. On one fatal occasion when a young missionary let fly a rouser after eating an especially peppery vindaloo, she expelled flames not wind. The flames ignited a cotton sari recently given to her by a kindly Hindu monk. Within seconds she was immolated. The only part of her not reduced to ash was her right hand. It held a bible, "a fire extinguisher of another sort," my student commented. The advertisement was half a column long and contained several memorable testimonials praising Cool Below. However, the ad strained credulity. It asserted that to prevent forest fires during droughts the government of Arunachal Pradesh forbade inhabitants from serving combustible food— "unless accompanied by condiment dishes overflowing with Cool Below."

Reading advertisements is more addictive than nicotine and is a prelude to insanity. Buying is pestilential and so weakens the immune system that hordes of people succumb to bankruptcy. However, indiscriminately perusing ads has a worse effect. It so skews a person's view of the world that before he realizes it his compass has broken and losing his way he sails into the windward side of reason, never to return to the safe harbor of good sense. The gullible reader is so buffeted by the dizzying claims of advertisements that maintaining levelheadedness becomes impossible. In December a correspondent in Arkadelphia, Arkansas, sent me a notice cut, he said, from the For Sale section of the *Daily Siftings Herald*. "Guard Possums," black type at the top of the clipping stated. "A burglar may have been pursued by a lion or elephant or a fast boa constrictor, but until he's had a possum snapping his heels, he ain't never been chased," the ad began. "Pure bred, registered possums, free from any taint of raccoon or armadillo—raised naturally in dens under stumps. Vaccinated, weaned, and fed earthworms, corn, berries, and squirrels killed on the highway. Practically tame, learn names quickly, and are easily trained to come, fetch, and defend property better than a pit bull. Once a thief hears your possum growl and screech, sees it flatten its ears, weave from side to side, and opening its mouth show its teeth and start drooling displaying hydrophobic symptoms, he will surely skedaddle."

"Praise the Lord and Pass the Possums. Home security is cheap at any price," the advertisement concluded.

"I am asking only fifty dollars for short-tailed possums and seventy-five for long-tailed." In Connecticut, ADT dominates the market on home security systems, and sales of Guard Possums would be small. Connecticut is, however, plagued by ticks, and Lyme disease is epidemic. Possums are omnivores and are particularly fond of the ticks that bedevil inhabitants of the Nutmeg State. "Like a mower chewing grass, opossums mulch ticks by the thousands," the associate director of the Tick-Borne Diseases Research Center at Windham University said. "Lyme disease would almost disappear from Connecticut if homeowners rid themselves of dogs and replaced them with opossums." The associate director opined that the commercial possibilities were vast. Along with mowers and weed trimmers, lawn care companies could keep a passel of possums in stock and every spring subject yards to the "thorough cleansing of marsupial grazing." Like a Wellness Examination, the grazing would be preventive, and secondary health insurance companies, if not Medicare and Medicaid, would likely reimburse homeowners for "the cost of such a salubrious contraceptive."

Also for sale in Arkadelphia was a rescue possum. Its previous owner was a recently deceased member of the Holiness Church on Sylvia Street and a past Grand Matron of the Eastern Star. In an accompanying letter, my correspondent said that prices were negotiable and that the long-tailed cost more than the short-tailed because the extra length of caudal appendage made them more elegant. Insofar as the rescue possum was concerned, it had a blot upon its escutcheon and could be obtained for free. Its owner was a spinster who died in her kitchen shelling peas. Neighbors did not find the body until after she had been dead for eleven days. She was very fond of her possum, named it Fred, and allowed it to room in the parlor. Unfortunately, the woman did not store much food in her cupboard, and after devouring the peas, little remained in the house for Fred to eat except, and here my correspondent ended his explanation with an ellipsis. He added, however, that all possums ate carrion, and that he did not believe Fred had acquired an abnormal taste for omophagia.

Only glaucoma enables the uncommercial traveler to avoid advertising as masses of people turn themselves into sandwich boards and wear clothes decorated with fillers. A few are light-hearted. Often, however, these reflect a grayer reality: "I'm Nobody. Nobody is Perfect" on the shirt of a nondescript man eating alone in a Subway restaurant or scrawled across the shoulders of a T-shirt worn by a man sitting at a desk in a library writing with his left hand, "Everybody is Born Right-Handed. Only the Gifted Overcome It." Animal bores stalk the aisles of big box stores. "My Shelter Dog Rescued Me" is more a Pentecostal invitation to share good canine tidings than the happy reflection of a contented pet owner. Occasionally animal signage strays from fabric to flesh. Tattooed on the upper arm of a large woman I saw in Stop & Shop was a Valentine's Day heart. In the left ventricle a contented cat stared out a window; in the right a Chihuahua sniffed the breeze, a grin pushing its whiskers up. For many people dog days occur not only in summer but through all the seasons. In a recent number of *Venice* "Fort Lauderdale's Magazine" appeared a full-page advertisement for "Bark Appétit." In the ad a terrier mix stood on its hind legs behind a kitchen table. The dog's front legs were spread wide and rested atop the table. Between its paws gleamed a stainless-steel bowl. "Everyone in the family deserves real food," the copy declared. "Food for Dogs delivers the best home-cooked meal possible for your beloved pooch. We use USDA Human Grade ingredients and recipes developed by board-certified veterinarians and executive chefs." Our pooches, Vicki said when she read the magazine, "would turn up their muzzles at such a diet. They prefer rodent and deer droppings, vomit on the campus after a party weekend, and hors d'oeuvres more interesting than Human Grade Food." "Are you referring to Mia's love of earthworms?" I asked. "Yes, among other creeping and crawling dishes," Vicki answered.

Some walking advertisements are crass, "Drink Naked," being an imperative printed on a shirt of a man unable to distinguish wit from vulgarity. Other advertising I saw recently was so narrowly evangelical that it repulsed passersby and isolated, this last probably increasing the smug contentment of the wearer: "My Savior Is Tougher Than Nails," in black capital letters on the chest of a shirt worn by a man elbowing through a crowd. Under the statement appeared a cross and a nail, this last a roofing rather than a box or common nail. Travelers who are commercial rather than uncommercial wear shirts that announce the places they have visited, Aruba, Panama, Honduras, Cartagena, the Galapagos, and Penguin Islands. The conversation of such travelers is bland and dining near them, eating a hamburger and French fries or a three-selection Chinese meal in a fast food emporium, is an easy experience. In contrast, just the sight of shirts trumpeting athletic teams located in places like Oklahoma, Texas, Ohio, and South Carolina makes me bilious. I would enter those states only if I were enclosed in an armored half-track. On the other hand, no matter how seasick I became on the trip from Galway, I'd like to visit the Aran Islands and meet Saint Gregory. Thoughts of his youthful indiscretions made Gregory feel so guilty that he gnawed off his lower lip. God, as the theological platitude puts it, moves in mysterious ways. After the frenzy of autosarcophagy passed, Gregory sprouted a golden lip, a prosthesis that glowed brighter than a lighthouse and guided flotillas of sin-tossed sailors into moral harbors.

Fiction imposes the delusion that causes lead to effects and that effects must have causes. The better read a person, the more he expects unity and consistency both on the page and in life itself. He assumes that his actual non-fictional days will resemble fiction and that an understandable and analyzable glue will bind the miscellaneous doings of his weeks together. The truth is that one thing follows another. Sometimes the two are related. Sometimes they are not. At least they are not related until mind revises the simple and the complex, the ungrammatical and the grammatical and forces them together into fiction. While I searched for the garden hose holder on the Internet, I ate three squares of Dove Dark Chocolate. Each square was wrapped in shiny red foil. Printed on the inside of the wrappers were Dove's equivalent of the advice proffered by Chinese fortune cookies. "Forget the rules and play by your heart," the first wrapper advised. "You have a nice laugh," the second judged. The third affirmed my uncommercial wanderings, "You are exactly where you are supposed to be." "Well," I muttered recalling Barry Cornwall's brackish lines, "I'm on the sea! I'm on the sea! / I am where I would ever be."

I suddenly felt dyspeptic, so I turned on the television. On the screen was an advertisement for a medical alert device. Across the nation elderly people were falling at an alarming rate. While a man tumbled down the stairs in his house, a woman collapsed on the floor in her bathroom. Later her cousin slipped on the kitchen floor, and a viewer could only shudder imagining the hordes prone in basements in front of washing machines or curled like balls in walk-in closets, their cries muffled by clothes cinched around them by cables of Velcro. I was interested in the devices, not because I considered buying one, but because uses of them had metastasized. Because nuisance suits are more common than starlings, two state colleges in the deep South hung alert devices on hooks outside showers in their gymnasiums. The schools required emeriti and faculty seventy or over to wear them in the shower. If, a sign read at one college, "you are caught not wearing a device, you will lose your shower privileges. Your health is important to us." As could be expected, the rule upset aging libertarians, and they accused the schools of unconstitutionally curtailing their personal freedom. The schools did not relent although they changed the requirement into a "strong request." To avoid accusations of ageism, the schools, and they must have been in cahoots, tied the regulation to filing for Social Security. Once a person began receiving retirement benefits, he was urged to wear a device.

Commerce is all-pervasive. No matter where a person is, he is exactly where he should be to notice the mercantile. Early in the spring, I attended a memorial service celebrating the life of a retired faculty member. The celebration was held in an auditorium in the Dodd Center at the university and home to rare books and special collections. Sitting on a table at the entrance to the auditorium was a wicker basket overflowing with "Facial Tissue Pocket" packs. Made in China and "Latex Free," the packs were one inch tall, three long, and two wide. A box containing a hundred packs cost $39.99 at Staples. Although the tissues were for people whose memories made them tearful, the paper wrapping each pack was joyous and colorful. Rows of small spheres the shape of lemons decorated the wrapping, forty-two lemons to a side, six rows, each row containing seven gay lemons, green, red, yellow, and blue. I filched three packs. I took them home and put them on the kitchen table. Until the tissues ran out, I used them to mop up the milk that invariably sloshed out of my cereal bowl during breakfast.

Life is fragile, and from the perspective of the aged, evanescent. Occupying much of the mature uncommercial traveler's time are the funereal and the near-funereal. In February, my son Edward and his wife Erica spent a fortnight in Costa Rica. One morning as they were hiking through the rain forest, Erica screamed. Edward was standing on an eyelash or hooded palm viper — not a snake whose acquaintance one should make six miles from the nearest town. "What did you do?" I asked Edward. "I lifted up my foot and shooed the snake into underbrush beside the trail." Edward was more fortunate than Lee the wife of Stanley an old friend living in Fremantle in Western Australia. One morning Lee left home to stroll on South Beach. Unlike the rain forest in Central America, South Beach is a fang-less landscape. While walking to the sand on a path cut through beach grass, however, Lee stepped on a dugite. The snake bit her just below her calf. Later that morning she died. One Saturday last fall, when Teddy, a friend from elementary-school days, went to fetch the newspaper at the end of his driveway, he stepped on a hickory nut and rolling his ankle fell and hit his head on the asphalt. On getting up he was a little woozy, but the feeling soon passed. After lunch he raked leaves and that evening watched an episode of the Russian crime series *Silver Spoon* on television. Sunday morning, however, Ann, his wife, could not wake him. The Rescue Squad raced him to the local hospital where doctors discovered he was brain dead. "By Monday," a mutual acquaintance recounted, "he was body dead, too."

No matter the care he takes, no matter how assiduously he avoids Aunt Hilda's banana-peel conversation, the traveler cannot avoid death. The deaths of family and friends startle, but little deaths pervade the hours and slip by almost unnoticed. Although Keats wrote, "the poetry of earth is never dead," many lines are catalectic. The mock orange and cranberry bush in the back yard didn't survive winter, and the salts the town sprays on the roads to melt ice poisoned the snowbell and the panicled golden rain tree by the driveway. Last week a red-tailed hawk plucked a gray squirrel out of the side yard. To replace Binky who died earlier in the spring, Vicki adopted Mia a rescue dog, part terrier and part Chihuahua. The day after arriving Mia killed my favorite squirrel, Stumpy, a gray squirrel with a rabbit's pom-pom tail. In early May Vicki and I watched a robin constructing a nest in a yew in front of the house. At the end of the month a cardinal built in a lilac behind the garage. Both birds laid eggs. The eggs never hatched. Crows destroyed the clutches. In June, an eastern cottontail cropped grass by the walk in the front yard. She nibbled every morning and evening until the end of the month. The day before public school let out for summer vacation, the term's last yellow bus flattened her in the road.

Not only is taste epicurean, but it is bound to time. No longer can I stomach love poetry. Age has changed my digestion, and sugary thoughts often give me mental dyspepsia. Most verse I read now swings to the embalming rhythm of the dance macabre. Often stanzas are gay. Nevertheless the dance is the last dance and concludes with someone being put to bed with a shovel. Recently I read Frank Stanton's funeral elegy, "The Cremation of Jinks." On his deathbed Jinks instructed that his body be cremated. His wife obeyed the request. Afterward she stored his ashes in a container in a corner dim. Eventually, "as most widows do," she took another comforter. For the wedding feast she didn't spare the expense and hired six cooks to prepare barbeque. While cooking they ran short of the spice "that makes a dinner nice." On searching the house for ingredients, they discovered Jinks' ashes and thinking "him" black pepper shook him over the meat. "The widow," Stanton wrote, "found it out too late; but nothing could she do: / The guests declared they'd never eat a finer barbeque! / And the widow kept the secret, and long her sorrow nursed / For that second husband's wedding feast, they seasoned with the first!"

As aging travelers scroll through their lives, many conclude they were born at the wrong time in the wrong place. People whose existences were laboriously conventional often feel nostalgic for homes they never knew. My years in Tennessee and Connecticut have been happy. I have always been popular. Smoothing away collars, shoulders, biting cuts, and profile contours from one's character shapes the key to unlocking popularity, but it can also turn a person into a round personality-less shaft. Dissatisfaction with themselves and with their presents may be the reason many uncommercial travelers delve into family history. As Dickens' uncommercial traveler traced Dickens' own footsteps through the lanes of Rochester, so I wandered scrapbooks. I spent much time with the Pickerings of Athens, Ohio, especially with my great-grandfather William B. Pickering, in part because I look like him.

Will's path through the Civil War was clear, and I followed him from the Army of Ohio to the Army of the Cumberland at Stones River. After Stones River, he joined the Fifth Tennessee Cavalry. Before the battle he was General O. M. Mitchell's Private Secretary when Mitchell "took possession" of Huntsville in April 1862. "We captured," Will wrote, "21 first-class locomotives and a few cars belonging to the Memphis & Charleston R. R." He also sent an anecdote printed in the *Huntsville Democrat* to the *Athens Messenger*. "A man in Federal uniform rode into Fayetteville, Tenn., on Sunday last," and "conversing freely with the citizens, said he belonged to an Ohio Regiment." After first removing the cap, the man let "a citizen, who asked permission" examine his gun. Later he dined at a tavern all the while keeping the gun on his lap. Then after having his horse fed, he left town. "The citizens thought him one of Morgan's men, notwithstanding his representation. A short time after, however, they were undeceived. Coming 4 or 5 miles on the road to Huntsville, he overtook an old white man with four negroes and three wagons of bacon, he forced them to drive their wagons close together, put fodder under them, take out the mules and retire a few steps. Then, lighting a match he set fire to the wagons." The soldier then rode on to a church a few miles away "where preaching was going on." He stopped and "asked the minister if any soldiers" were present, explaining that "if there were, he wanted them. Receiving a negative answer, he rode away, and crossed the road, 10 miles this side of Fayetteville, with two other Federals" and disappeared. "The owner of the bacon and wagons returned to Fayetteville with his negroes and mules and reported his misfortune. Several men went in pursuit of the bold marauders but failed to find them."

Despite the man's saying he was from Ohio, Will's sending the anecdote to his hometown newspaper struck me as odd, unless Will himself were the Federal soldier. If he identified himself, Will knew the story would upset his parents, and they had worry enough. Two of Will's brothers had also enlisted. Later in the year his older brother Levi would be killed at Perryville, and his younger brother Joe captured by Stonewall Jackson's troops at Harper's Ferry. A benefit of being an uncommercial traveler is that one is free to speculate. No customer hovers nearby debating whether to make a purchase. My speculations neither cost nor gain me anything. If a reader thinks my mulling erroneous, so be it. I prefer to think Will was the soldier. Printed inside the wrapping of the last piece of Dove candy I ate were the words "Why Not?"

Yes, indeed, why not? Monday while jogging, my friend David asked me to name the Irish song written for the plumbers' guild. As music aficionados know, the song is "Danny Boy" famous for pipes calling from glen to glen and down the mountain side. Did I answer David's query correctly? You bet I did, but then maybe you shouldn't take my word for it as uncommercial travelers are rarely inconvenienced by truth. The first requisite of a good reader, listener, or traveler is ignorance, feigned or actual, the second, an inclination to tell or accept a lie. Truth is a mist; too much knowledge confuses; and the lightning-bug flash of the anecdotal vanishes. Or as Sherlock Holmes put it in "The Boscombe Valley Mystery," "There is nothing more deceptive than an obvious fact." When Cavaliers captured George Wither, the 17th-century Puritan poet, so an old story states, they wanted to hang him immediately. Sir John Denham saved his life by intervening and saying to Charles I, "I hope your majesty will not hang poor George Wither, for as long as he lives, it cannot be said I am the worst poet in England." Now that is an anecdote to brighten the matutinal rite no matter the season regardless if the account is apocryphal or historically accurate.

Jogging

Five days a week I jog. Rarely do I vary my path. Most days I run ovals around the university track behind the gymnasium. Occasionally I run a noose following Discovery Drive west away from the campus until the pavement ends at Route 44. Then I turn left and shaping the top of the loop follow 44 until I come to Hunting Lodge Road. I turn left again east on Hunting Lodge and head back toward the university. After a mile I break from the road and entering woods circle toward my beginning on Discovery Drive cinching the knot of the run. Almost never do I vary my route. I have reached the tottering years in which ritual soothes. Neither do I hanker to break pattern and discover new places or a new self. Instead I greet the familiar fondly. My paths do not lead to a fictional enlightenment. Only when I was young did I titillate myself by thinking that the farther I wandered from the usual the closer I'd come to the exotic and the marvelous. Moreover, I have aged beyond seeking truths and am comfortable with uncertainty. Uncertainly is easier to live with than certainty. It fosters toleration and prevents ideology from clogging the heart with bile. No longer do I cannonade grasshoppers, as the old expression puts it. In the presence of intrusive, presumptuous busybodies, I remain silent. Only intolerance jars my speech out of the rhythm of quiet plodding.

Rarely are the decalogues of one generation those of the next, and I suspect that only people cataracted by ignorance or self-interest envision the numinous. I paste mind and feet to the earth, and when I climb above level ground, I attached one arm to a railing. To me cries for change sound like the early morning gangland cacophony of crows. I avoid the fevered who shriek and to better the lots of strangers cloud days with disorder and ugliness. Give me the restful ticking of a Victorian mantle clock. Once upon a time so long ago that it now seems fairy land, I would have enthusiastically agreed with Arthur Helps's remark that "to take an interest in many things, is one of the greatest of felicities." Now beautiful absence attracts me, and the restful simplicity of a Congregational Church appeals to me more than the bustling gadgetry of a gothic cathedral. While youth dreams about colorful impossibilities, age wonders how it can continue the ordinary: getting out of the driver's seat of a low car or reaching the top shelf of a kitchen cabinet. The conversation of aged joggers revolves around seven spokes: health, family, weather, athletics, government, travel, and money. Nothing startles. Unexpected things do not happen. Turns are gentle, and people don't cut corners. There are no startling ups and downs. No one trips over resentment or stumbles into inspiration, and the last half of a run is always silent.

Instead of poems that celebrate the open road, the siren calls of the west wind, and that place somewhere east of the Suez "where the best is like the worst," I fluff the cushions on my daybed, stack books beside me in my study, and read Barry Cornwall's "My Old Arm-Chair." "Let poets coin their golden dreams," Cornwall wrote. "Let lovers weave their vernal themes; / And paint the earth all fair. / To me no such bright fancies throng: / I sing a humble hearthstone song, / Of thee, — my old Arm-chair!" As I read, the grinding sounds of the opinion industry that mass-produce thought, and people, vanish. Sometimes a sentence in a book almost causes a hitch in my stride, for example, Siegfried Sassoon's description of Mrs. Edmund Gosse in *The Weald of Youth*, "Like all the best women, she had an element of masculinity in her." Or William LeQueux's quip that he found "wholesome roast duck" more to his taste than "Leda's whoreson swan." Or more substantially, William Hazlitt's hard-boiled judgment that "the great are life's fools — dupes of the splendid shadows that surround them, and wedded to the very mockeries of opinion." Better than all perhaps is Myrtle Reed's observation that "It pleases a man very much to be told that he 'knows the world,' even though his acquaintance be limited to the flesh and the devil — a gentleman, by the way, who is much misunderstood and whose faults are persistently exaggerated." But then after running across such statements I read on rarely pausing to agree or disagree. Almost never does the hitch last long enough to become a limp. In *On Trails*, Robert Moor described paths, writing "a path is a way of making sense of the world. There are infinite ways to cross a landscape; the options are overwhelming, and pitfalls abound. The function of a path is to reduce this teeming chaos into an intelligible line."

Neither the jogging paths nor the words I follow across a page make sense of the world. Pages may delight, irritate, or intrigue, but the thoughtful know that making sense out of any landscape without distorting is impossible. As a result, people fashion intelligible lines too narrow for pitfalls. Recently a priest said to me, "A man stays young as long as he is learning." A statement in Robertson Davies's *Fifth Business* immediately came to mind, "Whom the gods hate they keep forever young." I didn't quote Davies. The priest was ninety-two years old. Although his eyes twinkled like those of a cartoon Santa Claus, he lacked the strength to be other than serious. He had long been virtue's good servant, so I nodded and said, "how very true." Over a nearby pasture a fog hung whiter than a cassock, and high in the sky thin clouds were turning gold like the lip of a chalice. "You lied. You don't believe what the priest said," Vicki observed later. "Yes," I answered then quoted Bobby Macfarlane, "Don't worry. Be happy."

Of course, the sensible man worries constantly or at

least is observant. Two years ago, as I drove in Yarmouth, Nova Scotia, singing "Don't worry" so absorbed my attention that I didn't see the stop sign at the intersection of Beacon and Brunswick streets. If Vicki had not screamed prompting me to slam on the brakes and jerk the steering wheel to the left, I would have smashed into another car. People forever try to reduce chaos to a simple path. After thanking the priest for his advice, Vicki and I walked uptown and paid the insurance on our house. In the agent's lobby stood a whiteboard. Written on it were "words of wisdom" lifted from the "Dear Abby" column of a newspaper, "If you want your children to turn out well, spend twice as much time with them and half as much money." People slather words across days like cows splatter fields with bluegrass marmalade. Occasionally, the marmalade sweetens a moment. Sitting in a field behind the agent's office was an old green tractor attached to a hay rake. The name plate had fallen off the tractor's engine compartment. Painted in its place in rough yellow letters was "Barn Rat."

In the study my readings are miscellaneous. None increase my blood pressure. Some make me stretch and smile, Thorne Smith's *Turnabout*, for example, which begins, "Clad in a fragile but frolicsome nightgown which disclosed some rather interesting female topography, Sally Willows sat on the edge of her bed and bent a pair of large brown eyes on her husband." Or better perhaps, Clarence Day's observation in *The Crow's Nest*: "The most ordinary steamship agent, talking to peasants in Europe, can describe America in such a way that those peasants will start there at once. But the most gifted preacher can't get men to hurry to heaven." "A man sits in his pew," Day continued, "hearing about harps and halos and hymns, and when it's all over he goes home and puts on his old wrapper. 'I suppose I can stand it,' he thinks. 'I've stood corns and neuritis. But I just hate the idea of floating around any such region.'"

The heroine of Jean Rhys' *Good Morning, Midnight* describes my days when she says, "I walk along, remembering this, remembering that." Recently I read C. M. Doughty' s *Arabia Deserta* and followed footsteps I made four decades ago through Jerash and Wadi Musa. Afterward I climbed to El Deir at Petra. I recalled dreaming of a ghrol big as a camel with arms like chicken wings and a long beak with teeth as sharp as scimitars at the tip. I didn't see a ghrol, however, but I imagined hearing it lure travelers to their deaths by calling their names and sounding like their mothers and sisters.

I don't read to blaze trails through the brambles of knowledge. I read for entertainment and to pass peacefully through the daylight. Recollection is just recollection, and I don't imagine turning about and reversing my steps. The farms where the corn and cotton grew in old Tennessee and Virginia have become strip malls. Yet, in indulgent recollection I can pluck and shuck an ear, one sweet on the tongue and unlike grocery-store corn alive to the eye with worms. As one stride follows another, so one book leads to another. Sometimes the books are related, but generally they are not. No longer do I have gastric juices acidic enough to digest meaty literature. A milk diet suits me better. From the desert I traveled to Aix-en-Provence and helped M. L. Longworth's Antoine Verlaque and Marine Bonnet solve a murder. Verlaque is a judge and a bon vivant; Bonnet is his lover and a professor, and Longworth's novels are savory with learned appreciations of art and architecture, Cuban cigars, palate-teasing wines, transcendent meals, bespoke clothes, and country houses lustrous with high, crown-molded living—bonbon which armchair joggers experience only in epicurean dreams. Little that I read disquiets. Sometimes at the end of a paragraph I wonder about small things, for example, what cigar the Pope smokes— probably a Figurado, a sensible rounded Perfecto, very different from the Cigarillos smoked by the Vatican's most closeted, Machiavellian cardinals. Verlaque would probably know the brand, and although I don't smoke, I wish I could talk to him off page.

73

What causes the middle-aged to gasp in anticipatory dread only makes someone my age shrug in recognition. It doesn't cause him to pause and breathe deeply. After leaving Aix-en-Provence, I read George MacBeth's sonnet "The Worst Fear." MacBeth wrote the poem while dying from a motor-neuron disease. "Some days I do feel better," the poem begins. But soon the lines and MacBeth's health darken. He drops food. Drink chokes him, and people cannot understand him. The sadness which has become mundane and is a part of the everyday coffee conversation of people my age ends the poem. "The time has come when I put on my coat / With fumbling fingers, grappling with my fears / Of God knows what. Well, I know one that's worse / Than all the rest. My wife's become my nurse."

Because they are not intent upon going someplace or reaching a goal, aged joggers are good-humored. Hills tire them, but climbing doesn't provoke exasperation. Much life occurs off their paths, and they are more spectators than participants, the former even when they participate. In August, my friend David described a bus trip he made from Manhattan to Hartford. After a half hour's driving, the bus broke down and pulled into a service area. "During the four-hour wait for a replacement to arrive," David recounted, "The driver did her best to keep tabs on all the passengers. 'Where is the woman in the wheelchair?' she asked. 'In the Dunkin' Donuts,' someone replied. 'What about the old guy?' a fellow near me asked. Old guy? Old guy? I hadn't seen any old guy. I looked around for one. Then the truth thumped me between the eyes."

The lives of teachers are repetitious. For decades one semester follows another, and teachers jog through rounds of the same classes, saying the same things. When teachers retire, they shun the unknown and confine themselves to paths. Of course, repetition determines the course of everyone's life. About the only achievement that cannot be refined by repetition is suicide. While teaching, Josh collected classroom oddities. After retiring, he expanded his collection, and for ten years he has traveled the South in a circular fashion gathering the peculiar, all of which he describes to me in letters. "People's doings," he said, "are far more educational than ideas." He spent June in Alabama scrutinizing state government. "The foreheads of two state legislators are billboards, making them the most popular and best-known fellows in Montgomery," he wrote me. "The wrinkles on one spell 'God,' those on the other 'Tide,' this last the sobriquet of a football team at a state university."

Another prominent legislator trained possums to think they were dogs. "That's easy," the man told Josh. "All you have to do is name it Lion or Bryce, and then tickle its ribs so it grins and shows its teeth." Teaching a possum to bark and to bury bones were harder but could be managed by an experienced marsupial trainer. "It is much more difficult to make a dog think he is a possum," the solon informed Josh. "It takes more than a six-week yoga course to get a dog's tail limber enough for him to throw it above his back and wrap it around a branch, so he can dangle back and forth and swing in the breeze." Josh has a penchant for shaggy dog stories, and although governance in Alabama has long smacked more of the extraterrestrial than the reasonable, I suspect that his account of canines-to-be marsupials was chimerical — especially since in his latest letter he stated that "in Alabama six times more opossums than turkeys are sold during the Thanksgiving holiday." "Opossums are such a popular dish that the Departments of Human Development and Family Studies at the two biggest state universities offer courses in 'Carving the Feast Day Possum.'" Extraordinary numbers of student-athletes take the courses, and "I have been told," he said, "that in the athletic departments at both schools, plans are a-tail (ho, ho) for franchising fast-food opossum restaurants. Accountants predict that the revenue from the licensing fees will be enormous, topping the gilt raked in by monopolistic clothing and shoe contracts."

Best-laid anodynes go astray. Life is Mephistophelean and disrupts beatific absence, assuming the demonic forms of doctors' appointments, insurance flaps, car repairs, and fixes for chimneys, roofs, and the small machines supposed to ease living, but which instead break and complicate making sensible, passive people contemplate self-murder. What lies beyond the door is not difference but similarity and another door. In "The Road to Anywhere," Bert Leston Taylor wrote, "Across the places deep and dim, / And places brown and bare, / It reaches to the planet's rim— / The Road to Anywhere." The Anywhere is the Somewhere left behind. Believing that one has strayed from the familiar may vivify a passing moment, but it is delusional. Moods are seasonal and predictable. Every June Vicki and I leave Connecticut and spend summer in Nova Scotia. When added together, the months I have vacationed in Canada amount to five years. Vicki and I imagine that we are jettisoning the chores that clutter our calendar and make us feel trapped. We think that we'll escape the everyday and feel more alive. The truth is that going to Nova Scotia is quotidian. It's a routine loop in our path through the year. Our strides do not speed or slow. Our Anywhere may lie across the Gulf of Maine, but days on the rim of the Bay of Fundy differ only slightly from those in Storrs. I do not mow grass, but I split wood for the kitchen stove. The car battery dies, and a nail punctures a tire. Three days a week I jog eight miles. I follow a gravel road around Cedar Lake. Strangers wave when they see me. Drivers slow down and say, "Good to see you back." I always wave and say, "Thanks. I'm glad to be back." In July I run the Sheila Poole ten-kilometer road race in Yarmouth. This year I finished second in the Seventy and Over age division. As anyone who has seen me jog could guess, there were only two runners in my division. Early in the summer a man in a blue pickup paused beside me as I ran along Beaver River Road and asked a question echoing one I hear often in Storrs, "How far do you walk every day?"

Every summer Vicki and I eat lunch at the Rib Fest held on the Yarmouth Waterfront. People devour platters of barbequed ribs and chicken cooked by vendors named Crabby's or Alabama's Finest. In July Vicki and I each drank a Keith's India Pale Ale and split an order of pulled pork and ribs cooked by Billy Bones, paying $19.99 for the barbeque. In front of the vendors stood tables bending under pinnacles of trophies. Atop the trophies were gargoyles of pigs and chickens. "Look at those pigs and chickens," I said to Vicki, staring at the trophies. "I have," Vicki replied, "last year and the year before when you pointed them out." In August we listen to country and gospel music at the Coal Shed Music Festival. Momentarily I live on "Tulsa Time," and feel benevolent imagining traveling to the end of the railway and giving the dying man's love to "Rose." I'm glad that I was never the kind of guy who'd "walk on by" and "wait on the corner." Not even in my budding spring did I have "day dreams about night things in the middle of the afternoon." I wish that when the road turns rocky I could "bring it all to Jesus." But the "Dust" is thick on my bible, and I know there isn't "a better home a' waiting in the sky." Still, I try to keep on the "sunny side of life."

Familiar and sentimental, the music makes me pensive. I am a displaced person, and I miss the easy vanilla days of childhood when I didn't fret about belonging. I left Tennessee fifty years ago. I've lived in Connecticut forty years, meandering off occasionally and spending months here or there. Yet, not a day passes, in Canada, Connecticut, or elsewhere, without someone hearing my southern accent and asking where I am from. Identity and the concomitant sense of belonging do not arise from within; they are imposed from without. No matter what I do, say, or believe, no matter the paths I beat into a landscape, no matter how well I know a place or how long I lived there, strangers forever force me to be an outsider. "Not this again," Vicki said, when I mentioned feeling dislocated. "A little music is a dangerous thing. It makes you melancholy. Face it. You aren't clubbable. If you can't be chummy with people who resemble and think like you, how can you expect to be chummy with people unlike you?" Vicki said, grabbing my hand. "Clearly the time has come to lean on the bar at Rudder's, guzzle a pitcher of Blonde Rock, scoop sour cream up with bar chips, and forget where you came from, where you are now, and where you are headed" — which is what we did and what we've done for summer after summer. So far, as the gospel song puts it, the circle is unbroken.

Every July at a tag sale I buy an historical knick-knack always paying less than five dollars. This year in a battered scrapbook I discovered a crinkled eight-by-nine-inch certificate issued by the Marine Temperance Society of the Port of New York. The first two numbers of the date, one and eight, were visible but last two digits and the name of the man who subscribed to the "PLEDGE" had been worn away. An eagle spread its wings across the top of certificate; printed on a banner unfurled beneath the eagle was "We Abstain from All Intoxicating Drinks." Sketched on the right side of the paper were warehouses. In front of the warehouses, a sailor stood beside a seaman's chest and held an American flag. On the left side of the paper a dozen men wearing white bell-bottom trousers, short dark seamen's vests, and straw sailor's hats waited to unload two sailing ships, the first, three-masted and twelve to fourteen hundred tons, the second approaching from a distance, also three-masted but smaller, not over a thousand tons. "Such a find calls for a celebratory banquet at Pizza Delight," Vicki said holding the certificate. "Let's have the usual," I said, "the small Caesar salad and a six-inch pizza covered with mushrooms, pepperoni, and spinach." "Yes," Vicki answered, 'but don't forget the mead, Keith's Pale Ales." "Certainly not," I replied. "We are charter members of the Bay of Fundy Glass and Sandwich Club." "Did you make that name up?" Vicki asked. "Not quite," I replied. "An obituary I read recently said a woman belonged to the Land of Evangeline Antique Bottle Club."

Of course, every summer I remember items that I should have hooked but let get away, nondescript minnows transformed by time into angelfish. Years ago, at a yard sale amid a jumble of knick-knacks on a folding table I discovered two cigar boxes containing small commemorative toys probably collected by a summer resident. Contents of the boxes intrigued me, and although each of the boxes cost only two dollars, I did not buy them. I cannot explain why except to say that some days people are in acquisitive moods and other days they are not. Among the items was a tin hatchet celebrating George Washington's birthday. The hatchet was three-and-a-half inches long. Attached to its handle by a diminutive chain were three metal cherries. While the hatchet was in good shape, the cherries were spoiled. They had oxidized into bruises with only flecks of red paint remaining on the skins. On Lincoln's birthday Five and Dimes sold four-inch-tall metal stovepipe hats. Although brim of the hat in the box was bent, if turned upside down the hat would have made a good paperclip holder and conversation starter. Despite protestations to the contrary history is short-lived. Events and people slip quickly from recognition into the dementia of time. A metal lapel ornament was shaped like the American flag waving in a breeze. In the upper left corner of the flag was the usual blue canton of stars. However, the stripes on the field were not red and white but were black and orange, the colors of Princeton University. Before being president of the country, Woodrow Wilson was president of Princeton. "Maybe the flag was campaign paraphernalia from Wilson's campaign in 1912," Vicki said, "appealing to the school's well-heeled alumni." Most items in the boxes were mysterious. Attached, for example, to a two-and-a-half-inch squiggle of a snake were eight tiny feet. The snake's keeper was a careful podiatrist. None of the feet was broken, and when placed on a table, the snake looked like it was running. "To the sea on March 17, with St. Patrick close behind waving his walking stick," Vicki guessed.

My summertime reading differs in one respect from that in Connecticut. I do not read a newspaper in Storrs. Every morning in Nova Scotia, Vicki drives to Port Maitland and buys the Halifax paper at the Corner Store. I glance at headlines, but I only read obituaries. Most of the people described lived on trails. Like me they were not fast-paced. Throughout the day Jane spoke her special canine language to her dog friends. Retirement enabled Harold "to enjoy his favorite pastime sitting at Tim Hortons drinking coffee and watching movies on his iPad." "Heaven has gained another angel with the passing of," flocks of obituaries began. "Doesn't anybody die nowadays?" I mumble practically every day before crumpling the paper for fire starter. Undertakers fitted coveys of corpses with wings. Never did they wrap a carcass in an asbestos shroud. No garden emporium sold owners of crematoriums pitchforks soaked in potassium silicate. Only once or twice was a person's path to the "heavenly watering hole" preternaturally individual. The first image Mary Ann remembered "was a framed large black and white rendering of Jesus Christ hanging at the foot of her bed, eyes looking rapturously skyward, one hand over his sacred heart, his other hand showing the wound left by his crucifixion." Mary Ann said that "as a child the picture gave her comfort and influenced the idea of who she wanted to be — a warm, empathetic person who people naturally gravitated to for guidance and comfort." "Open that bible and redeem your poor soul," Vicki said after I read her Mary Ann's obituary. "I'm tired of hearing you say you are a WASA, a white, Anglo-Saxon atheist."

"One great difference between the persons of real life and the persons of fiction," Somerset Maugham wrote, "is that the persons of real life are creatures of impulse." Conversation is comparable. Storrs is a university community, and conversation rarely startles resembling that of Maugham's person of fiction. In Nova Scotia even though my rounds are similar each summer much that I hear surprises me. Outside the laundromat in Yarmouth, I heard a woman talking on a cell phone. "I got the soap and the blueberries," she said, "then my teeth fell out." Talk swirled around the laundromat as if there were more agitators outside than inside the building. "Do you want to go back to your room? Do you want to walk on the beach? What in God's name do you want to do," an exasperated father said to his son. The father was fifty years old and worn into stooping. His right hand was clamped on his son's left forearm. The boy was twenty-five and retarded. He was expressionless and swollen and shapeless like a link sausage. He didn't react even when his father smacked him on the cheek and implored, "Please, please say something." Eventually the father grabbed the boy's arm with both hands and walked him slowly along Water Street on the Rail Trail. I pitied the man. How bruising twenty-five years of no reaction must have been. I would have cried had I been able, but as my skin has shrunk into parched ripples, so my eyes have dried.

Talk often plods, but I share Josh's conviction that people's stories or even fragments of their narratives matter more than ideas. After we pre-paid our bill, ancient Joellen who owns the motel in which we stay before we return to Maine on the ferry refused to let us leave her office. Her conversation jogged nonstop from topic to topic, and for an hour, she described the death of her dog from diabetes and her hip replacement and recovery, complete with a tumble, a minute description of her physiotherapy, and her teaching other oldsters recovering from hip operations how to tie their shoes. One morning Austin stopped me while I was jogging and showed me a bird house he built for swallows. We chatted, and he told me a one-size-fits-all story. Eighty years ago, when Austin was a boy, a relative's child died shortly after birth. The father of the baby asked the local undertaker and carpenter to make a coffin. The man did so, and the child was buried. Two weeks later, the father met the undertaker on the street, paid and thanked him, then said, "I realize I should have given you the measurements of the child." "No, that wasn't necessary," the man replied, "bones of babies are easy to break."

The loop I jog in Nova Scotia always includes a couple of entertainments. One evening Vicki and I went to Ultimate Championship Wrestling, the Summer Explosion Tour in Yarmouth. We sat in the third row at ringside and ate onion rings fermenting in ketchup. Only two-hundred-and-fifty fans attended. In the first match Short Sleeve Sampson, a dwarf, wrestled Prince Akeem, a small black man wearing a crown and wrapped in a blue robe. The Prince made himself unpopular by insisting that everybody in the arena bow to him. In another match, The American Patriot leaped into the ring waving a flag and wearing a red, white, and blue body suit. His exuberant parochialism irritated the crowd, and when a man held up a sign reading, "You Suck," everybody agreed and like a chorus started shouting. The cry then morphed into "America Sucks." Quickly that became "Trump Sucks," and people stood and yelled, many shaking their fists and several at ringside picking up their folding chairs and banging them on the floor. "What did you think?" I said to Vicki later as we left the arena. "Astonishing," she said. "Let's go to Tim Hortons for coffee. I'll get a banana pecan muffin. I haven't eaten one this summer."

Every summer we drive to Annapolis Royal and spend a Saturday at the farmer's market. The excursion is always fun and memorable. This year our daughter Eliza accompanied us. While the gals roamed the market harvesting loaves of olive bread, almond and chocolate croissants, jars of jam, and a dish of spanakopita, I climbed the ramparts at Fort Anne. The yearly Encampment Days were underway, and members of the "84th Regiment of Foot 2nd Battalion (Royal Highland Emigrants)" marched across the grounds in kilts and red swallow-tailed coats that swept over and down their backs like the elytra of beetles. After re-enacting a battle with American irregulars who had sailed across Annapolis Basin, the soldiers retired to their camp on the grounds of the fort. Many soldiers and people in civilian clothes who I assumed were spectators lined up and entered a biggish tent. I joined the line. Inside was a table laden with food. I filled a pewter mug with soda and stacked an assortment of edibles on a plate: two slices of ham, a chicken drumstick, a helping of rappie pie, watermelon, and a man-sized hunk of fruitcake. After eating, I told a woman in costume that I appreciated the enactors putting on a lunch for themselves and interested spectators. "For spectators?" she said. "No, this is an anniversary celebration."

Two enactors had been married twenty-five years, and they decided to mark the day by renewing their vows and treating friends to lunch. I was the only guest who did not know the couple. The people not wearing period dress were friends who had driven to Annapolis Royal for the occasion. "Now that you are here," the woman said, "you might as well enjoy yourself." I did. A man described his breast cancer operation. "I met some Americans in Bridgewater recently. They were monsters, not like you," a woman cleaning a long rifle said. "I'll bet you have crashed a lot of weddings," a woman serving chocolate cake speculated. "No, this is the first," I replied; "but when I was young I invited myself to a graveyard of funerals." "Yes," the woman answered, "they can be fun, especially if a person discovers she's in the will." "I wouldn't mind renewing my vows." a woman wearing a big straw hat with daisies blossoming in the band said, joining the conversation. "But I have been married three times, and I don't know which husband to renew with." "My second husband is dead," she continued after a pause; "he didn't clean up well when he was alive, and I suspect years in the ground won't have improved his appearance. As for the other two, they were both mistakes and duller than ditchwater. I must have been out of my mind when I married them." "Lordy," Vicki exclaimed later when I informed her that I'd accompany her and Eliza to lunch but because I had already eaten I wouldn't order a meal. "Did you say anything to the bride?" Vicki asked. "I said 'thank you,'" I replied. "What did she say?" Vicki said. "She said 'you're welcome,'" I answered.

The day after Vicki and I settled in Nova Scotia, I cleared paths I first cut forty years ago. I clipped swamp candles, rushes, cinnamon ferns, and raspberry brambles. I chopped winterberry, alders, and wild raisin. Around my head swarmed punkies, black flies, and gray deer flies. Ticks scrambled up my legs. Because I have atrial fibrillations, I take blood thinner and by evening creeks of blood trickled down my calves. Each year brings slight changes to both place and me. This August, for example, mountain ash had few berries. As a result, cedar waxwing fledglings swarmed the hawthorns in the kitchen meadow. Fields were lush with low bush blueberries while along stone walls blackberry canes were barren. The branches of wild raisin bent into falls heavy with fruit, but the berries ripened slower than in the past, and at summer's end the bushes glowed with pecks of pink berries incandescent in the sunlight and flickering with yellow.

I cleared scrub from old trails to keep my balance. Summer in Nova Scotia and its familiar paths confine and support, and as I age into wobbling, restriction becomes less distasteful while maintaining equilibrium requires conscious effort. During the seventy-three days Vicki and I spent in Canada, we drove to Yarmouth fourteen miles to the south and had coffee at Tim Hortons thirty-one times. We drank medium-sized coffees in ceramic cups. I never ate anything, but Vicki frequently had a muffin, her favorite being blueberry. Sixteen other days we drove four miles north to D. J.'s Store in Salmon River. We usually went in mid-afternoon and drank coffee and shared a piece of bread pudding soaking in caramel sauce. Occasionally we ate breakfast always ordering two eggs, crisp bacon, and homemade white bread. Every Sunday morning in Connecticut we walk the dogs then eat breakfast out. We eat practically the same things we ate at D.

J.'s, adding cheese grits to our order at Toast in Storrs and hash browns to the meal at That Breakfast Place in Willimantic.

In *The Tent Dwellers* (1908) Albert Bigelow Paine described three weeks he spent trout fishing with his friend Eddie and two guides in Nova Scotia. The friends camped in and near what Paine called Lake Kedgeemakoogee or the Lake of the Fairies. Not far from our house in Beaver River, the lake is now part of Kejimkujik National Park. Paine described each day's fishing in detail. The stream in which I fished all summer was the natural spillway of life. I seined field and woodlot, air and shore line. Our wild place in Beaver River is tame, but, nevertheless, every winter I dream of harvesting a *Walden* of natural observations. Unlike Paine the sights I hook are always small. They are minnows and water striders — little things that beetle across pages shaking prepositions and conjunctions but which never disturb the heavy equanimity of nouns. According to Vicki I am not a Literary Lion or Donkey, but a Literary Periwinkle. When the tide is out, periwinkles creep across the damp sand, sometimes one behind another forming a train until they reach a granite boulder where they join other snails hobnailed together. "You inch along verb by verb unnoticed in your shell until you pull yourself onto a rock. Then slowly colonies of words and small polished details appear," Vicki elaborated. I liked the natural analogy. Snails make paths, but like sentences the paths are short-lived, tides washing away the trails of periwinkles and the glistening mucus tracks of land snails vanishing in the sunlight.

"The details are not polished but smoothed with an adze, a Cooper's adze. That's a smaller handier version of the Gutter adze," I almost said. Happily, I resisted turning the moment irritatingly academic. Years in a college town educate the spouses of teachers. The incessant evangelical celebration of the redemptive effects of schooling causes a jaundiced reaction, producing recusants immune to the elevated, secularists who see the earth clearly and steadily.

Every fall I spend days blowing, raking, and carting leaves. After the third or so stint, I dream about blowing leaves, and the next morning, I look forward to strapping on the blower. At breakfast one cold day last November I waxed into poetry, paraphrasing Wordsworth and saying, "One leaf from a vernal wood may teach a person more about life than any book." "No," Vicki said glancing up from her granola, "you were just meant to be a small engine on the back kind of guy."

Harvesting the out-of-doors can be blood work. Along with vigor age saps good sense. At summer's end I discovered blackberries growing through the branches of a grove of toppled spruce. Too tired to change clothes and don trousers and wrap my arms in a sweatshirt, I wore short pants and a short sleeve shirt when I picked the berries. The canes shaved me. Afterward I neglected the gravel pit of holes dug by thorns, but I measured the cuts slicing down the outside of my right leg. "Sixty-one inches," I told Vicki. "Age has made you shiftless," she said. "Not shiftless but fashionable," I replied. "The cuts are country tattoos." People as well educated as Vicki generally avoid telling friends and mates the truth. Rarely do truths rain on my parade as I am not a grand marshal, but occasionally Vicki's remarks dampen mood. However, there is consolation as an ancient story attests. One stormy morning a man met an old acquaintance sheltering in a doorway. Not able to recall the woman's name, he greeted her saying, "Isn't this weather dreadful?" "Well," the woman replied, "any weather is better than no weather."

Paine and Eddie fly-fished. Throughout the summer, I netted insects. All were familiar: hairy spotted tussock moth caterpillars, their mid-sections orange, both ends black, flaring from them teased white lashes, and mottled tortoise beetles, pronotum and elytra metallic and black splotched with greenish gold resembling the carapaces of box turtles. From the wavy grass of unmown fields came the songs of crickets, their shrill jangling more musical to me than the deep-throated moan of a fine organ. Nearby, sphagnum sprite damselflies clutched the tips of rushes, the ends of the insects' abdomens so blue and warm they looked like coloring-book candles lit in a nineteenth-century children's book to celebrate a fairy's woodland birthday.

Early one morning I jogged past a farm whose owner having aged into a walker drove his tractor into his barn and parked it in a stall. The farmer had not cut his fields in five or six years, and they were rough and guttural with high grass and wild raspberry. As I ran past, sunlight broke through a low mist, and suddenly the field nearest the road sang like poetry. Dew clung to orbs spun by hundreds of small weavers, the droplets first silver then yellow and blue in the refracted light turning the webs into jeweled Cleopatra broad collars. In September black and yellow argiopes hung their webs along the lane leading from our house to the Gulf of Maine. The webs looked like silver plates beaten to filigree thinness. In the hubs of the webs shined the runic markings of their makers, often n's or m's turned sideways. At times the loops I jog curled into themselves and back into the past. When I was young, I hunted treasure in the trash piles lining the alley behind the apartment in which I lived in Nashville. A garden spider was a sight more valuable than a doubloon, and whenever I discovered a web, life dazzled. Recollection is more fiction than nonfiction. But I think seeing spiders made the future brighten, and although I lacked the words to tack feeling into thought, made it glimmer with possibilities beyond school and becoming a cog in a social machine.

Across the lane from the webs of the argiopes, near a stand of highbush blueberries hung the web of another orb weaver, the garden cross spider. A white line resembling the drying ray on a daisy ran intermittently down the spider's back. When I peered into the web, the spider scooted along a trapline and hunkered down atop a clump of flat-topped asters. The flowers were shriveling, and their centers were browning and shredding, turning the color of the spider's abdomen, camouflaging and making the spider seem another lumpy disk. One night about the house air hung heavy with the oily fragrance of rotting animal. Clinging to the screen door under the light on the kitchen porch were eight burying beetles. The beetles wore Halloween gaiety. Fluttering across the midnight black of their backs were orange patches shaped like bats raising their wings in flight. Another evening shortly thereafter eight Virginia Ctenucha hovered around the door. When a person is alone at night, association runs deep and individualistic. Because of their orange heads, the moths seemed companions of the beetles. The wings of the moths were dark as funeral cassocks. Around the edge of each wing ran a soiled white fringe, turning the moths into cartoon priests — defrocked to be sure, their collars slipped, but still officiating at burials conducted by undertaker beetles.

As the conversation of joggers glides rapidly across topics protecting runners from wasting energy on exhausting mental effort, so seeing the natural in terms of the human comes easier than dissecting study. It is, however, a path that increases appreciation of the non-human and makes people aware of the cousinhood of all life. Moreover, a closer walk with the not-me can invigorate and be therapeutic. In Frost's "Dust of Snow," a crow knocked snow off a tree limb. The snow fell atop the poem's narrator, giving, he said, his heart "A change of Mood / And saved some part / Of a day I had rued." One night I slept fitfully and the next morning felt weary until I stepped outside. Blue joint grass was blooming, and a purple haze hung loose and velvety over the field behind the barn, cloaking the ground like a royal robe. My path through the summer was rich with eye-wash: magenta coral fungus growing under black spruce, spikes of hedge nettle pushing aside goldenrod and announcing the end of summer, their flowers hooded in regret, at night ghost crabs on the beach their carapaces pale but dabbed with yellow, elegant lichens their golden rosettes perennial funeral flowers blooming on tombstones, and

in September the leaves of alders drying, turning upward, and folding inward into pockets, at day's end their
undersides ochre as the sun smoldered and sank out of
sight across the Gulf of Maine.

When the pump for the artesian well committed suicide ninety feet underground four days before we were
booked to return to Maine, I didn't whack the kitchen table
and season breakfast with profane evocations of the deity.
Instead I sat down and wrote a check for thirteen-hun-
dred-and-four resuscitating dollars. Afterward I ate a bowl
of granola topped with blackberries and probably a couple
of small worms as I am not a careful washer of fruit. Then
I went jogging. I saw a masked shrew and a woodland
jumping mouse. The mouse was young and had recently
left the nest. Its coat was reddish gold, and the middle toes
on its hind feet stuck out forked and spiked. I shooed a
porcupine off the middle of a highway. Earlier in the summer I encouraged a young skunk to leave the Cedar Lake
Road. The skunk was recalcitrant, and only when I reached
down and threatened to grab it did it trundle down a ditch
and disappear into the woods. Throughout the summer I
plucked creatures off roads: green frogs, toads, garter and
red-bellied snakes, woolly bears and white hickory tussock moth caterpillars, red efts, a cedar waxwing fledgling,
and a handful of slugs — yes, slugs. Joggers are often con-
trarians. As public discourse has become cruder and more
violent, I've become gentler and increasingly private. To
me saving a slug is more important than . . . , and I cannot finish the sentence because almost everything in the
public realm that I once knew to be significant no longer
matters to me. My path often wandered past murmuring
pines "bearded with moss." At their feet spread "garments
green," the colors of the peat various and "indistinct in the
twilight." However, the woods I roamed were not forests
primeval, and the trees did not stand like Druids "with
voices sad and prophetic." Instead I heard birds, in early
July, the back-and-forth ball-bearing roll of chattering rob-
ins and early in the morning and at dusk the ululating

howls of loons as they flew to and from inland lakes. Loons fly fast and spotting them by following their cries was difficult. Flying black chevrons against a gray sky, Canada geese were easily seen. Hermit thrush whistled in the woods, but the only one I saw lay at the side of a road, its voice silenced. Cars undid a flock of birds, among others, goldfinches, yellow and magnolia warblers, blue jays, and a snipe bound in bars of brown and yellow. Roads were killing fields: chipmunks, red squirrels, dragonflies crinkled into foil, meadow mice, shrews, and scores of frogs with their legs bracketed behind them. From the asphalt I pried two score snakes crushed into graffiti, their scales flaking and silver in the baking sun. Machines were not responsible for all the dead animals I saw. One morning I disturbed a marsh hawk ripping a hare apart, roundworms spilling like pasta from the animal's innards. That afternoon on the rocks at Salmon River, however, I found a newly-killed harbor seal, its head almost sliced off by the propeller of a fishing boat. As I jogged through woods, I heard but did not see animals bustling away deeper into the trees. Usually, the animals were deer, snorting then sweeping and swishing through scrub like brushes across snare drums. During August, I surprised a doe and her fawn several times on Beaver River Road. But then after the doe raided Austin's garden "one time too many," he shot her. I saw the fawn once again, but it was gawky and adolescent and wouldn't survive the hunting seasons of man and coyote.

According to the *Book of Liang*, Malachy Tallack wrote, a Buddhist monk appeared in the Chinese city of Jingzhou in 499 A.D. The monk said he came from Fusang. "Fusang was a word that people knew," Tallack said, explaining that "the Fusang was a kind of mystical tree—a red mulberry and tree of life—that grew somewhere far to the east." Ten three-footed ravens perched in its branches. Each morning a bird carried the sun to Fusang where the new day was born. Vanity runs deep in shallow people. Occasionally I wished that the small things I saw would swell into myth or wax out of observation into unforeseen story. Why couldn't the scarlet fly agaric that thrust round through the grass in September be the beating heart of harvest? Alas, whenever observation slips the knot of the actual and sails beyond reason, I do something foolish — some small, not big, thing. At lunch while I imagined the ventricles of fly agaric packed with apples and squash, corn, parsnips, cauliflower and cranberries, I dumped blueberries into what I thought was a salad bowl half-full of almonds. The nuts turned out to be kibble and the bowl the dog bowl. I plucked the blueberries out and dropped them into the right bowl. However, jogging had so tired me that I didn't think to wash them before I ate.

The absence of tension during the day is often balanced by excitement at night. My dog Suzy is silent when she is awake, but when she's asleep she yips, barks, and shuffles her legs back and forth. The sight of pitcher plants burning in a bog and the rattling of semipalmated sandpipers made my spirits bound in appreciation, but they did not cause my heart to race. The paths I jogged in my dreams differed from the ones I followed during the day. Indeed, peaceful days seemed the prelude to stormy dreams. Perhaps the dreams were compensatory. Maybe straying from beaten rational footpaths at night reflected an unconscious hankering to live a less predictable life, to be a spanner in the works not a dependable cog, a desire to break out of the shell of the Literary Periwinkle and . . . well, who knows, maybe sprout feathers, grow a horn, or write long confusing complex sentences. One night I checked into Ninth Cloud Ophthalmology Clinic for a double eye transplant. Dr. Eugene Nrog was the surgeon. After the surgery Dr. Nrog's staff presented patients with sweets resembling wedding cakes. Standing on top were not a bride and groom but a stickman wearing red trousers and a blue blazer. Dr. Nrog stored his allotment of eyes on a board in a refrigerator. They were gelatinous and resembled eggs cooked sunny side up. He tilted the board and used the first two eyes that melted loose and seeped off the edge. What intrigued me about the dream were not the details which seemed relatively commonplace but my being able to see Nrog's horde of eyes when my eye sockets were empty.

Another night I dreamed I had a pet lady snake, a fer-de-lance named Nancy. The snake slept with my parents in the guest bedroom in Storrs, she in a snake box, they in chairs on each side of the bed like end tables. Nancy was good-natured and so warm-hearted she wouldn't nip a mouse even when hungry. But if she lost her temper and struck a harasser who pinched her on the cloaca, the result would have been catastrophic. To forestall such an event, I knew I had to decapitate my pet, so I bought a machete. The dream ended with my parents covering their eyes and my leaning over the bed weeping while swinging the machete down like the blade of a guillotine. When I woke, my cheeks were wet with tears. But as I had wondered about being able to see without eyes, so I revisited the dream and revised it. "Nancy was too long," I told Vicki at breakfast. "She must have been an indigo snake." "What? Not in Connecticut!" Vicki said. "Although one occasionally slips into Georgia, indigo snakes rarely leave Florida. Moreover, they are endangered, and killing such a beautiful creature should make you feel guilty and give you nightmares. You need to visit an eye doctor. He'll prescribe drops that will drive the glaucoma out of your dreams. In your next dream how about a candy-colored corn snake?" "Corn snakes don't wander farther north than southern New Jersey," I said. "In dreams," Vicki said, "corn snakes are affable and don't object to traveling in tourist-class minds. Also, they adjust well to captivity, and one would not disturb your sleep by shucking its skin and trying to escape from your dream."

Several dreams featured swashbuckling derring-do. Internecine warfare in American embassies is brutal, and in one dream two diplomats had long been rivals and enemies, each convinced that the other's machinations verged on the treasonable. The first man pondered encouraging the CIA to assassinate the second but then decided to let sleeping suspicions lie. The other man James Wilkerson suffered no compunctions, and he arranged to award the first man a Freedom Medal for Meritorious Service. Before presenting the medal, Wilkerson exposed it to uranium, making it toxic. When the first diplomat discovered that the medal was packed in a lead-lined box, he became wary and asked an acquaintance at MIT to subject the medal to radiochemical analysis. On receiving the results of the test, the man realized he'd barely escaped being murdered, and when both men were transferred to the American embassy in Kosovo, he immediately set about preventing a second attempt on his life. He contacted a gang of Serbian thugs frequently employed by American agents to affect what "the soft-minded judge to be crimes against humanity." The man paid the thugs to kill his enemy. They accomplished this easily bundling Wilkerson into a car in Pristina and driving him to an abandoned factory in the Industrial Zone where they shot him and disposed of his body by feeding it piecemeal into a sausage grinder.

Afterward they manufactured suxhuk seasoning the meat with traditional spices, among others, fenugreek, cumin, garlic, and sumac. Once the sausage dried slightly, they packaged it and delivered it to the American embassy where it was served at a banquet for the diplomatic community celebrating traditional Kosovan culture. Along with a platter of sausages each guest received an embossed card reading "James Wilkerson appreciates your attendance at this reception." The card was poignant because at the time Wilkerson was missing, and if truth will out, will remain so unless a second dream resuscitates him. In any case, no one knew who printed the cards and distributed them to the partygoers. Wilkinson's unacknowledged enemy praised the lavish appearance of the card and during the evening repeatedly said as he munched the sausage, "James has long been known for his good taste." "Heavens," Vicki exclaimed when I described the dream. "Can't you assassinate someone without firing a pun?"

The answer is "no." Tides wash away the footprints a person makes in the sands of time. But when he returns to the beach, he'll walk the same path and use the same language. It's better to be old than to be young. For the old life is predictable, and in the garden of forking paths, the old may pause to smell rugosa roses and momentarily lose their ways but eventually they'll set off on a familiar trail. In mid-September, Vicki and I took the ferry to Portland. As usual I waved at children riding the tourist train, Maine's Narrow-Gauge Railway. On the right of way, a handful of shafts of viper's bugloss had survived summer and were blooming. Along Commercial Street cars remained bunched together like balls of newly-hatched spiders. As we do at the end of every summer, we ate dinner at Becky's before driving to Connecticut. Vicki had a crab melt, and I a haddock Reuben. We drank coffee and for dessert shared a piece of pumpkin cream pie. We agreed that the following summer we'd eat somewhere different, the statement repeated for so many years that it had worn word-bare. Awaiting us in Storrs was a familiar round of doctors' appointments: matters of the heart, colon, eyes, teeth, and private parts. "The same fall jog," Vicki said. "Are you going to run the Manchester Road Race Thanksgiving morning?" she asked as I drove. "You bet. I've run the race at least two dozen times," I said. "Why stop unless . . . ?" "Unless what?" Vicki said. "Just unless," I answered.

My Study Window

I get up between six and six-thirty every morning.
I put on my writing clothes: broken-seamed, sagging
jeans, a long-sleeved shirt, usually a decade-old souvenir
celebrating the Manchester Road Race, white socks, and
slippers with ridged rubber bottoms. Then I go downstairs and turn the dogs out of the kitchen into the back
yard. While the dogs sniff and roam, I bolt a handful of
pills and brew a pot of tea, the favorite of the moment
being Buckingham Garden Party. While the tea steeps, I
let the dogs back inside. They scoot into their beds under
the kitchen table. After I wrap them in ancient Afghans,
I make breakfast—an essayist's breakfast, cleansing and
not clogging: all-natural granola, a banana, fruit, generally blueberries or raspberries, and sometimes a scattering
of raisins, the whole awash in soy milk. I imagine that
the breakfasts of novelists, particularly those who write
massive three-volume, month-killing books, are very different, consisting of at least two eggs, sausage or bacon,
four strips of the latter, two patties of the former, coffee,
hackneyed with creamer, and a stack of toast, most often
white bread dripping margarine, but if the writer fore-
sees a randy scene in the future, maybe anointed with
Smucker's jam, probably strawberry. Many poets, particularly lyricists, skip breakfast or simply inhale a pot
of black coffee. As a result, their hearts throb into irregular beats, and the lines of their verse bounce in and out
of rhythm. Images flash but quickly disappear bucked
hither and thither as the poets' blood pressures suddenly
rise then fall, initially mystifying and intriguing readers
but finally irritating them, making them long for the nar-

rative verse popular in the nineteenth century, poems that told stories and sauntered smoothly through beginnings and middles to understandable ends.

After breakfast, I go to my study. The room is not big and measures twelve by fourteen feet and was once a screened porch. When Vicki and I bought our house in 1983, the porch was in bad shape. Floorboards were rotten, and the screens had broken loose and frayed upward into rusting scrolls. For fifteen years, we kept the door to the porch locked, and because it was an eyesore, we avoided mentioning it. When my parents died, Vicki and I used my inheritance to update the bathroom in the house and convert the porch into a study. The room is comfortable with two Victorian chairs, coffee and end tables, a daybed, an oriental rug, and shelves akimbo with books and knick-knacks from a life calmly spent: postcards, rusty tobacco tins, paperweights, a prancing Staffordshire zebra, and wooden carvings, from the Caribbean fanciful creatures with no name, and from Australia striped goannas. Here and there are ends of china, among these last nothing valuable, typically a Royal Albert tea cup and saucer from the 1950s decorated with one of my favorite plants, Jack in the pulpits with their hoods spreading red and green. On the window sill a mouse perches atop the lid of a glazed jar bought at the Lucky Rabbit pottery in Annapolis Royal, Nova Scotia. The mouse is cute, and if he wandered into a nineteenth-century poem, he'd make friends with a lonely little girl and Sniffy her pet kitten. I don't plan to increase the menagerie of knick-knacks in the room although every Christmas my daughter Eliza urges me to winkle an hermetically sealed crystal box out of the possession of Aldine, an ancient apocryphal friend who lives in Beaverdam, Virginia. The box contains the thumb and trigger finger of a Confederate sharpshooter killed at Spotsylvania. Although preserved, the fingers haven't weathered the years since Appomattox well and are not things of beauty. Their skin is wrinkled and brown, and the cuticles have shrunk so that the nails hang loose looking like spoiled doll-sized aprons, on which slops of caramel have melted and hardened.

An assortment of paintings decorates the study walls, among them two small latter-day Connecticut Impressionist paintings, one wintry depicting a frozen stream and snow-covered fields, the other autumnal with maples orange behind a red barn and a gray house. The other five paintings are Australian. In one a red kangaroo lounges on its side; in front of it zebra finches pick through eucalyptus leaves; in another Arnhem Land's Rainbow Serpent wraps itself into a protective coil around five ochre-colored eggs. At the east end of the room a Venetian widow replaces the upper half of the wall. Below the window is a board table made from cherry. The board is two and a half feet wide and extends from one side of the room to the other. Under the top are cabinets of drawers; in the middle is a knothole for my legs. On the top itself are, among other things, a computer and printer, a telephone, address and note pads, an uncontrollable population of pens and pencils, migratory books, an eclectic assortment of containers, one the business end of an old chamber pot, and then a movable feast of plants, now an amaryllis and four pots of petunias. After breakfast I sit at the table in an office chair I bought at Staples for seventy dollars. I begin almost every day by gazing out the window. A neighbor's house lies just across a small dell, but still I can see a Norway maple, three red oaks, a Chinese witch hazel, two shagbark hickories, a winged euonymus, and a hedge of forsythia. Once upon a time the dell was a sunburst of daffodils, but now it is barren. Runoff from the chemicals sprayed on the road in front of the house to prevent ice forming in the winter killed the flowers. Early in the morning squirrels and chipmunks scurry about, and I watch birds: crows caterwauling in their black workaday overalls, red-tail hawks looking down and studying the menu, juncos in the winter, sparrows in the summer, and occasionally bluebirds greening my spirits, their azure backs peeled from the sky, their breasts clay shoveled from the earth.

I don't gaze long. Every morning Suzy follows me into the study and sitting at my feet chats with me, her words high-pitched growls. After she has had her say, she crawls into a round bed beside my chair, and burrowing into a mound of throws falls asleep. Later Jack will wander in and curl up in a bed next to Suzy's. He stares at me imploringly, and I cover him with a throw. Next, I open my first-class email, not that I receive much. Then I delete advertising broadsides and importuning clutter from people whom I once may have known but who now are strangers and who unaccountably wish to renew our acquaintance. Immediately afterward I loaf a bit, dozing and not quite thinking. In 1880 Thomas Hughes worried that loafing was becoming a lost art. For his generation, he stated, loafing was "the one luxury," adding that "a country without good loafing-places is no longer a country for a self-respecting man in his second half-century." I am in the second half of my second half-century. After disposing of emails, I treat ideas like lozenges. I roll them about in my mind, but soon I forget them, and they dissolve unnoticed.

Vernon Lee once said that boredom was leisure's worst enemy. Boredom turns agreeably mild people into busybodies and "chaos merchants," or if not that then into imbeciles who traipse after herds of the know-nothings who frequent auditoriums and stadiums. When boredom creeps up on me and I begin to fidget, I mutter "here we goes" and sitting up straight write two or three hundred words of therapeutic prose. While I am writing, Vicki usually appears and summons the dogs to their breakfasts, on the way announcing how she feels. Winter causes her to sink into "glumitude." Today she said, "I feel like a tiny tick on its back slowly wiggling its little legs." Shortly after Vicki leaves, I suffer from writing fatigue, and laying my pen aside, I start reading. My reading resembles walking as Louis Jennings described it in *Field Paths and Green Leaves in Surrey and Sussex*. Jennings advised people to walk by themselves, "then you can cry halt wherever you please, and have no one's whims or oddities to perplex and harass you." If you stroll unfettered by a companion—or in my case saunter through books—shy country folk may talk to you, Jennings wrote, and from them you may "pick up many a quaint saying or odd scrap of information."

In Aldous Huxley's *Crome Yellow*, Henry Wimbush said that "the proper study of mankind is books." In *Joyous Gard*, A. C. Benson stated that "no art, no literature are worth anything at all unless they send one back to life with a renewed desire to taste it and to live it." The morning he penned that remark Benson must have eaten something moldy. Certainly, something inedible caused him to swell distastefully pompous. The best books do not impact. They aren't literature. They simply entertain. Good morning books delight and lift one's spirits into smiles. Some volumes are as sweet and sharp as a breakfast clementine, say, for example, Joseph Epstein's collection of short stories, *Fabulous Small Jews*. In Epstein's "Felix Emeritus," Felix Arnstein moved into Northwood Apartments, a retirement home. Soon afterward, he joined a foursome of old men who ate together, one of whom was Morry Manzelman, resident funnyman. "You boys heard about the widow Schwartz?" Manzelman asked one morning. "She called the *Tribune* to place a death announcement for her late husband," Manzelman recounted. "The fella on the *Tribune* tells her that they charge by the word. 'O.K.,' she says, 'make it Schwartz dead.'" "'No, Madame,' the fella from the *Tribune* says, 'there's a fifty-dollar minimum, and for that you get five words.' The widow thinks a minute, then she says, 'O.K., make it 'Schwartz dead. Cadillac for sale.'"

A good morning book never causes indigestion. When worry threatens to spoil the day, a tablespoon of light verse is a good panacea, the more snake oil in the poetry the better. In 1830 in the *New England Weekly Review*, John Greenleaf Whittier quoted a stanza of what he labeled "Love-Sick Poetry." In fact, the verse is a tonic which simultaneously expands the lungs and reduces amatory fever to laughter. "I sings her praise in poetry / for her at morn and eve. / I cries whole pints of bitter tears / and wipes them with my sleeve." Shortly thereafter Whittier offered readers of the *New England Weekly* a second miraculous pharmaceutical. "Say, hath the lip no other bliss / Than words to give? O yes, O yes, / For one more near than friend or brother! / There! There! Another! O, another!" Much of the epithalamic doesn't scan well and rises to the poetic only in the telling. In an old Scots story, a childhood friend attended the wedding of a former schoolmate's daughter. "Might I congratulate you on a marriage to be proud of," the friend said as she hugged the mother. "Please do so," the mother replied, "on the whole the marriage is quite satisfactory. It is true, of course, that Kate hates her new husband, but then there's always something, isn't there?"

In *Old Acquaintance*, James Fields described Barry Cornwall's friend John Kenyon, known as "the apostle of cheerfulness." In the shank of the afternoon after the chores of the day are done, the preaching of such apostles is welcome relief. Because they have no high intentions, apostolic afternoon books exhilarate and make readers feel born again, perhaps not so newly fledged that they can watch the evening news with equanimity, but still refreshed. How uplifting it is to thrust aside concerns about furnaces and sumps, bills from plumbers, and all the aches caused by exercises that promise to invigorate but which always exhaust. How much better to follow P. G. Wodehouse's Clarence the 9th Earl of Emsworth as he putters across the grounds of Blandings Castle, first admiring his prize sow, the Empress of Blandings, next perusing a paragraph of *The Care of the Pig*, and then before becoming frazzled sniffing "at a rose or two" and possibly doing "a bit of snailing."

How reviving to take French leave from the keening of Social Testament prophets and read Washington Irving, say, the letter Mustapha Rub-A-Dub Keli Khan sent in 1807 from New York to Asem Hacchem, Principal Slave Driver to the Bashaw of Tripoli. "Thou wilt learn from this letter, most illustrious disciple of Mahomet, that I have for some time resided in New York: the most polished, vast, and magnificent city of the United States of America.—But what to me are its delights! I wander a captive through its splendid streets; I turn a heavy eye on every rising day that beholds me banished from my country," Asem began. "The Christian husbands here lament most bitterly any short absence from home, though they leave but one wife behind to lament their departure;— what then must be the feelings of thy unhappy kinsman, while thus lingering at an immeasurable distance from three-and-twenty of the most lovely and obedient wives in Tripoli! Oh, Allah! shall thy servant never again return to his native land, not behold his beloved wives, who beam on his memory beautiful as the rosy morning of the east, and as graceful as Mahomet's camel!" Although "the habit of reading" had frequently been denounced as a vice then praised as a virtue, it was neither, Andrew Lang wrote. Reading was simply reading. Although more innocent, reading "like opium-eating" unlocked "artificial paradises." It offered consolations to the sad and disappointed and distracted people from the darkness of the world. Insofar as teaching was concerned, Lang testified that books had taught him "not much."

Although crime can be fusty, mysteries are fine digestifs and knockout drops especially those flavored with detectives, among a station house of sleuths, Ernest Bramah's blind investigator Max Carados, Henry Bailey's Mr. Fortune, and Bennet Copplestone's William Dawson. While A. E. W. Mason's fleshy Inspector Hanaud started his mornings with chocolate, Fergus Hume's Mr. Gorby talked to his reflection in the mirror as he shaved. Melville Post's Uncle Abner's "God was a war lord," and

Austin Freeman's polymath Dr. John Thorndyke was expert in both medicine and the law. Occasionally I am indulgent and snack between meals. Generally, I season this reading. However, I monitor my use of spices, and the condiments do not provoke bilious discontent. The elegance of J. P. Marquand has long seduced me, and recently I read his *Repent in Haste*. The word *repent* brings other reading to mind. I am ashamed to confess that I have a peccant interest in theology. For years I have wanted to know what cosmetological text led St. Cyril of Padua to assert that Judas was bald and that Mary's hair was red. Someday I will find out, but I am not in a hurry. True enjoyment and hurry are poor companions. In any case, last week I finished Micah Ratliff's definitive *Famous Preachers and Their Mistresses Complete with Appendices Describing the Fortunes of their Bastards*. Grim but not quite so dark as Ratliff's appendices was Arthur Morrison's *Tales of Mean Streets*, stories describing life in the East End of London in the 1890s. In response to a note penned on a Christmas card by a Kremlinologist I knew at Cambridge, in January I read Varlam Shalamov's *Kolyma Tales*, a collection of short stories depicting life in the forced-labor gulag in Eastern Siberia during the 1930s and 40s. Perhaps to brighten a moment in days devoted to gray Stalinist Russia, the Kremlinologist collects colorful neologisms. On every Christmas card, he jots down a shiny coinage. This year his favorite expression was Barking Spider or to move from genus to species Arkansas Barking Spider. "I have overheard indigested unfortunates suffering from flatulence," he explained, "attribute the sounds produced by wind as it escapes their alimentary canals to barking spiders."

That dialectical nugget aside, in winter I usually avoid frozen landscapes and accounts of hypothermic lives. Shalamov's book was so good, however, that I made an exception for it. When I wander afield on a reading spree, I usually read a toasty book like J. B. Priestley's *English Journey*, a volume into which I started dipping at the end of January and finished a month later. Soon I'll begin F. Van Wyck Mason's *Three Harbours*, an ambling old-fashioned Revolutionary War tale, but then, on the other hand, maybe I'll peruse Andrei Gulyashki's *The Zakhov Mission*, an account of the doings of Avakum Zakhov, a Balkan counter-espionage agent, published in the United States in 1969 for the Crime Club of Doubleday. Sometime before summer's climacteric, I will glance at Valerie Wollaston's *Husbands*, anecdotes from the lives of poor men who married wealthy wives. After being purchased and kitted out with new wardrobes, some of the men supposedly either changed their middle names to Husband, or, if they had no previous second forename, adopted Husband. I also intend to read *One-Minute Prayers for Graduates* if, of course, I can block out enough time. The book is divided into sections typically entitled "Finding Healing," "Keeping It Real," "How's Your Perspective," and "Think about It." Thinking about it will be an exhausting but, I am sure, uplifting minute. In the book I hope to discover a section called "Freedom from Religion," which is the primary salutary benefit of sixty-second prayers. Provided that praying doesn't exhaust me, I plan to read what Carl Jung has to say about dreams before daylight savings time starts again. The night before last found me in a double-deep coffin. My lips were blue; my nose was red, and a carpenter was nailing the coffin shut. The nails were long and sliced through my chest into the corpse fermenting beneath me. Things looked bad until the carpenter began shellacking the outside of the coffin. Shellac nauseates me, causing a headache and knotting my stomach. In order to breathe fresh air, I woke myself. I ripped the nails out of my flesh, kicked the lid off the coffin, and hoisting myself out of the ground sat up in bed. "I really smelled shellac," I told Vicki. "I'd be dead now if I hadn't smelled it."

Aside from happenstance and my predilection for neglected books, no taxonomy links these last volumes. I suppose most fit Ruskin's definition of good books of the hour, that is, "letters or newspapers in good print" bright and pleasant, lively, sometimes factual, other times witty, but always evanescent. And, for the record, I discovered most of them while loitering in the stacks of the university library. Nowadays I rarely enter a bookstore. Book jackets blare and are too colorful, evoking pictures of graveyards blooming with bouquets of artificial flowers. Above the displays themselves posters making extravagant claims loom like highway signs. Instead of encouraging readers to mull and wander by-ways of thought, they steer them onto crowded interstates and discourage meandering pensiveness. Rather than allowing me to plod and appreciate, they jostle me into boorish combativeness. Last month just inside the entrance of a Barnes & Noble was a table piled high with leaden books. Above the books stood a green flagship sign. Printed on the sign in puritanically-bold white letters was "Books Celebrating Powerful Women." "I know Barnes & Noble is a feverish signatory to a lending library of ethical directives and stands spine and head cap against all bias, so next week I assume," I said to the clerk at the cash register, "the store will promote 'Books Celebrating Weak Men.'"

On another table lay an array of self-help treatises, among them a dozen copies of *The 7 Habits of Highly Effective People.* "Let's get out of here," I said to Vicki seizing her hand. "Effective people disturb, break, smash, and destroy. They cause turmoil and heartache. Aspiration is a manifestation of discontent. Effective people aren't happy and are egomaniacs always on the go. Almost never do they achieve laziness, purr, and grow wise. Because of them horrid books like *Self-Reliance, My Ass! Give Me $100,000!* become best-sellers. In contrast ineffective people don't wreck other people's lives. They are antiseptic and don't tamper or disparage. They amble and don't let ambition blight observation. They never get swept off their daybeds by fusses caused by passing isms. They stay out of the fast lane, and instead they fall by the wayside. They don't climb ladders. Instead they lounge in the shade of whatever old tree is nearby and savor the sumptuary pleasures of inelegant idleness. They can dance the double-shuffle and cut the pigeon wing without perspiring. They are fanciful and never turn the world topsy-turvy. They banish superlatives from their speech and exclamation points from their writing. Most are nameless and don't belong to groups and clubs. Unfortunately, because they are temperate, they suffer from fewer ailments than other people. As a result, they attract the unwanted attention of social scientists and nerve mechanics prowling for role models. The resulting intrusions scuttle calm, and, alas, some become martyrs to their health.

For the ineffective, much of what the effective ignore as nothings are somethings. "A book weaning people from effectiveness would be worth reading." "Yes," Vicki said, "when I come into the study and ask what you are thinking about, you say 'nothing.' At dinner when I ask what your books are about, you say 'nothing.'" Vicki sometimes goes too far—only a peccadillo but perhaps the reason I spend so many hours in my study. "Why don't you print a copy of the book you are writing now and afterward erase the file from the computer," she continued. "Then take the pages into the backyard, slosh gasoline on them, and burn them, turning your nothing into something: smoke and probably a social visit from the town fire marshal." Next November I am going to find an eighth-hand copy of Myrtle Reed's *The Spinster Book* and stuff it into Vicki's Christmas stocking along with the usual oranges and chocolates. All women can put Reed's observations to harmonious use particularly the spinster emerita who has been married to me for forty years. "There is nothing in the world as harmless and utterly joyous as a man's conceit," Reed wrote, advising that "the woman who will not pander to it is ungracious indeed." "Let the woman dearest to a man say tenderly," she suggested perspicaciously, "'You were so handsome tonight, dear—I was proud of you.' See his face light up with noble, unselfish joy, because he has given such pleasure to others!"

Books almost compel a person to ponder domesticities though in my house such matters rarely rise above sotto voce. In *The Humor of Homer*, Samuel Butler observed that in the *Iliad* woman was "a being to be loved, teased, laughed at, and if necessary carried off." In one book, Butler notes, the reader learns about "a fine bronze cauldron for heating water which was worth twenty oxen, whereas a few lines lower down a good serviceable maid-of-all-work" was valued at four oxen. Butler speculates that behind the evaluations lay malicious humor. I "am confirmed in this opinion," he continues, by noticing that although woman was on one occasion "depicted as a wife so faithful and affectionate that nothing more perfect can be found in either real life or fiction" woman was generally drawn "as teasing, scolding, thwarting, contradicting, and hoodwinking the sex that has the effrontery to deem itself her lord and master." "I find it impossible to determine," he writes, "whether or not this view may have arisen from any domestic difficulties between Homer and his wife." But, he concludes arching a verbal eyebrow, "we cannot refrain from contemplating such possibilities."

The arbitrary nature of my between-meal reading is conventional for a person at the end of his seventies. I lack both the discipline and energy to allow system to disrupt my leisure. Even though the disruption would be temporary, I'd resent it. In contrast to the oldster, youth thirsts to embrace a program that will steer him toward his goals, no matter that the goals smack more of seventh heavens than they do of achievable possibilities. Youth mouths the word *freedom* and imagines escaping the creeds which served him well during his school years but which he now thinks inhibiting. He lacks a past and doesn't yet realize that almost never do people attain satisfying freedom. Ultimately, of course, all freedom is evanescent. Responsibility and duty hobble. Love binds.

Time cripples, and age imposes convention focusing attention on health and for men specifically on the bedeviling trinity composed of heart, colon, and prostate. Every man over seventy is a physician, and his favorite conversation becomes coffee-hour consultations with his peers. Old boys are also mathematicians, experts in loss and subtraction and to whom ambition or addition has no allure. "The life of a reputation is like the life of a plant, and seems," Edmund Gosse wrote perceptively, "to be like the life of an annual."

Not by material splendor or prosperity could a people conquer the future, James Russell Lowell declared. "but only by moral greatness, ideas, works of imagination." "No voice comes to us from the once mighty Assyria but the hoot of the owl that nests amid the crumbling palaces." Lowell's words themselves are verbal hooting, melodious but nevertheless short-lived and forgettable. The only owl visible from my study window is a barred owl. He perches in a shagbark hickory and swivels his head. Sometimes he hoots, but then soon after he flies out of sight and mind. Sir Alfred Lyall said, A. C. Benson recounted, "that if a man had once taken a hand in big public affairs, he thought of literature much as a man who had crossed the Atlantic in sailing-yacht might think of sculling a boat upon the Thames." Squalls endlessly agitate public affairs, and people who sail turbulent political and corporate seas suffer unremitting bouts of life-sickness. Better to loiter on the daybed in my study casually feathering the pages of an entertaining book and from time to time jotting down an appealing remark, say, Macaulay's owlish description of Dante's angels as "good men with wings."

According to a shaman in Robertson Davies's *Quiet Time* "not being serious is a civilized luxury." Indeed, it is more than a luxury; it is the goal of civilization. In his *Characteristicks*, Shaftesbury said that gravity was "of the very Essence of Imposture." Although gravity is always suspect, I don't distrust it completely. But in the morning when the sun shines through the Venetian window, my study is light and airy, more hospitable to low humor than high seriousness, friendlier to simpletons than to preceptors. Recently a friend described the plight of two dimwits who rented a holiday cabin in Florida near the Everglades. Because the cabin's windows lacked screens, the rent was modest, "a steal" one of the dimwits said congratulating himself on his business acumen. The first night the dimwits were in residence clouds of mosquitos swarmed into the cabin. Someone living in an insect-less place had told the dimwits that light repulsed mosquitoes, so they switched on all the lamps in the cabin. When that remedy failed, they concluded they'd gotten things backwards. "In the dark," the second dimwit said, "mosquitoes will get lost and not be able to find us." Immediately the dimwits switched off the electricity. For a moment they thought they'd succeeded in confusing the mosquitoes, but then one of the dimwits spotted a pair of fireflies. "Oh, Lord," he moaned. "There's no hope. They've begun searching for us with lanterns."

Readers and writers are forever tempted to bound from observation to analysis. In part this occurs because accepting that most lives, particularly their lives, lack decisive moments doesn't come easily, especially to the bookish nurtured on the moonbeams of infantile critical books. They resist admitting they'll never enter a wood where a path divides. Plain sense strikes them as arid and smothering, and they resist acknowledging that they won't metamorphize into explorers and experience the excitement of choosing the wrong fork. Almost without conscious thought and as compensation they imitate immature Jack Horners, and sticking thumbs into books extract startling meanings. What they find, rather create, flatters them and raises them in their own estimation, making them crow "What a good critic am I." For a hundred and fifty years the most popular and enduring book of nature writing was Gilbert White's *The Natural History and Antiquities of Selborne*. The book was published in

1789 and consisted of letters describing the natural and human inhabitants in and surrounding Selborne village. For the most part White resisted analysis or, as Wordsworth put it, murdering to dissect. "What an equitable, harmonious, and gracious spirit and temper pervade the book," John Burroughs hymned, "and withal what an air of summer-day leisure and sequestration!" The bluebirds that scuttle past my window are simply bluebirds. My seeing them does not awaken self-knowledge. They were not created for the benefit of man. They are some of the "Works of this visible world," as John Ray wrote in 1691, but they are not, as he asserted of such works, "a demonstrative Proof of the unlimited extent of the Creators Skill, and fecundity of his Wisdom and Power." To endow them with meaning, to see them as anything other than birds not only obscures the sight itself but also spoils the summer-day leisure of my study. It sacrifices comfortable and sensible sequestration for the vexatious hurly-burly of the outside world and its gaseous insistence upon significance. The epitaph on the tombstone of W. H. Hudson in West Sussex is so simple that it's magisterial, "He loved birds and green places and the wind on the heath and saw the brightness of the skirts of God." When I look out my study window, I see birds and green and brown places. I watch the wind shake trees, and at sunrise brightness breaks through the panes, mantling the day, not bringing a god to mind but awakening appreciation and love, that is, awakening the godly.

To loiter well isn't easy. Eschewing profundity necessitates discipline and thought. My friend Josh resents strangers asking his opinion on controversial matters. When such a situation arises, rarely does he spoon out satisfactory truisms. "I do not have an opinion," he stated at a meeting of the town council years ago. When those words didn't quench the inquisitor's curiosity and she urged Josh to elaborate, he wrapped a garniture of "do not's" around his initial statement. He rolled his eyes toward the ceiling, seized the sides of his desk as he would were he standing at a pulpit, deepened his voice, and testified, "I do not smoke. I do not drink. I don't spit or swear. I don't lie or steal, but, I cannot take credit for such good behavior. It is easily explained. You see I'm not a Christian." The message was unambiguous and slammed The End down on the intrusive interrogation.

Literary matters, of course, have the potential to disturb sleepy dawdling by animating small disturbances. In 1848 Thomas De Quincey distinguished what he called "the literature of power" from that of knowledge. While power moved, knowledge taught. He compared power to a sail and knowledge to a rudder. Knowledge spoke to mere discursive understanding; in contrast power appealed to the affections and sympathy and through them addressed "higher understanding or reason." In comparison to a cookbook, a reader learned nothing from *Paradise Lost*. Milton, however, expanded a reader's capacity for sympathy "with the infinite, where every pulse and each separate influx is a step upwards, a step ascending as upon a Jacob's ladder from earth to mysterious altitudes above the earth." De Quincey's ruminations are seductively clear and have provided sundry literary critics with a handy tool. My study, though, is not a shed packed with parsing instruments. Moreover, the books on my shelves are not Rosetta stones, mysterious pages waiting to be deciphered. They are written in lucid English not Aramaic. Discovering obscure meaning in them requires misguided effort and siphons attention away from pleasing, sequestered effervescence. In one of the thirty-one verses of his "*Litania Nigelli*," John Stuart Blackie asked the Lord to deliver him "From a scholar who smells of books, from a sportsman who smells of horses, and a mother who smells of babies." Regretfully, Vicki's and my baby-years have ended, and bookish musk doesn't season my clothes or mood after I leave the study. Equine dander is a different matter. Despite my not having ridden a horse in twenty-four years, Vicki noses out whinnies in my conversation, adding in rude vernacular that often I behave like, if not the follicles growing on the southern end of a horse, then the end itself.

I wonder what De Quincey would make of a strolling player's jape I read recently. The tale is flea-ridden and lop-eared, but on the warped boards of a country stage it goes down well and is a shining example of the literature of power, at least as I classify literary vaudeville. A man visited a doctor because his legs looked like switches. "Doctor," the man moaned, "my legs are so thin and weak that I don't walk. I wobble." "My God," the doctor exclaimed pinching his thumb and index finger together into a circle and wrapping it around the man's shins with a distal joint to spare. "What happened to your legs?" "I come from a poor family," the man replied clamping his hands down on his thighs to prevent the breeze drifting in through the window of the doctor's office from lifting his legs into the air and knocking him into the wall like the rigging torn from a dismasted sail boat. "Poverty forced my father to economize, and whenever he bought me clothes, he purchased items four sizes too large to allow for growth. To keep the shoes he bought on my feet, I stuffed them with hay. For a time all went well, but then one cold day my calves got so hungry they went down to feed on the hay. They found the hay was so tasty they stayed down, and for years and several shoe sizes, I have not been able to entice them out of my shoes and lead them back up my legs."

In this grinding, competitive age, bystanders mistake intense loitering for fecklessness. Decades ago I gave up New Year's resolutions and the pretense of embracing life-enhancing changes. Why turn over a new leaf when the old is broken in and comfortable? Soiled and worm-holed by habit and use, the old is never stiff and blistering. However, no man can escape occasionally curtsying to truisms, if only to deflect vulgar curiosity. As a sop to mental hygienists educated into believing the humbug that others should have goals and should value and acknowledge conventional accomplishment, every June I make a public Vacation Resolution. I crook a knee before the clichéd but am careful not to tear a ligament. Before leaving Storrs for Nova Scotia, I pack a box of papers in the car. I tell the inquisitive that I have high literary intentions. I mention research and assure auditors that during the summer I plan to write something significant. When I'm bored, appearing to agree with Puritanical busybodies appeals to me, and last May I declared that I was going to work hard to ferret out institutional racism at the university. My failure disappointed all interested parties, except, of course, myself. "You cannot imagine," I lamented in September, "how insidious and the extent to which abuses are deeply and inextricably embedded in education."

The hero of William Black's novel *Mr. Pisistratus Brown, M. P., in the Highlands* is an iconic exemplar of the scholar-loiterer—a splendid role model. In the book Brown slips away from Parliament "for a week or two before the recess." In Edinburgh he meets the tale's narrator and explains that he left London "in order to do some work which will really be of benefit." I brought with me, he states, "a bundle of papers, documents, and letters bearing on the gross grievances of Her Majesty's Clerks of Custom, as regards salary and term of service, and I humbly think I cannot be better employed than in studying this important question." Almost immediately, Brown's working holiday becomes that better thing: a real holiday. Overnight Brown turns into a sight-seer and traveler. He rides in waggonettes and coaches. He sails in yachts and schooners. He hikes rocky trails and climbs mountains. He stalks deer and shoots hares and an aviary of birds, among others, gannets, wild ducks, grouse, and partridge. He carries the parliamentary papers on his journey, but he doesn't study them. He is too busy living. One night before almost settling down with the papers, he samples whiskey at an inn. When asked his opinion of the whiskey, he replies that the cautious man never pronounces upon whiskey until he has "tasted it twice." Although books rarely teach, sometimes lessons lurk amid sheaves of intoxicating words.

As reading spreads wider and becomes more habitual, large numbers of people, Henry Wimbush said, "will discover that books will give them all the pleasures of social life and none of its intolerable tedium." Books, Arthur Waugh wrote, "make the best friends, and the friendships that grow out of books remain the most enduring. For even a harsh word, or an unkind thought can be smiled away in the light of a cherished quotation." Satisfaction and contentment are the bricks and mortar of good manners. In my study I often disagree with writers, but never do I engage in tedious wrangling. "The boy is charming in Art, and sometimes quite virtuous in Fiction; but in real life he is intolerable. His wit is buffoonery, his humor is practical joking," James Payn wrote in *Gleams of Memory*. "He loves idleness, cruelty, dirt, and athletic exercises like the savage. There is a delusion abroad that he does not share the weakness of the adult for wealth and station; but he has in reality a very accurate notion on which side his bread is buttered and would sell his soul for five bob." "James, old lad," I'd say if I were talking to him before reviewing his book. "You have sacrificed sense for style and wit." Our chat would not wax contentious. We would not sling dingy words about. Still, few writers like to be criticized to their faces, and further immediate conversation might be strained. If I read Payn's statement in the solitude of my study, I'd mutter "well and brightly written, good fun, but unfair." Peace of mind in privacy, however, leads to peace of mind in company, and the truth is that if I met Payn on the street I'd praise *Gleams*. Conversation is meant for amusement and becomes dangerous when taken seriously. Like a good literary friend, I'd laud Payn's writing, complimenting him for not veiling reality. I'd gush and say, "to love truth is rare, but to write it is rarer still, so much so that it often seems unbelievable." "Have you no shame?" I'd ask myself later in my study. "Of course not," I'd answer after which I would cluck, kick my drumsticks about, then cackle joyously.

Eventually sounds would yield to sense, and I'd pluck a book off a shelf, probably a volume I purchased last spring shortly after Vicki and I returned home from a cruise, *My Memories and Miscellanies* written by Wilhelmina FitzClarence Countess of Munster and published in 1904. Last week I reread "True Refinement" my favorite chapter in the book. In the chapter FitzClarence used language to distinguish Shibbolethites from Sibbolethites, the former being the old-fashioned upper crust or crème de la crème who spoke proper English while the latter were the socially and linguistically not-quite quite. Although these last could be worthy and charitable, when it came to the test of language, they proved second-rate. What could be more grating to one's feelings, FitzClarence wrote, than to hear of people "riding in their carriages" rather than "driving" in them? "Going to get married" was a hateful expression found in novels "by authors who ought to know better" and who should have written "going to be married." She pointed out that in describing God, the Holy Writ declared, "Awful is His name." Of the misuse of *awful* by Sibbolethites in expressions such as "awfully jolly" and "an awfully nice little chap," she exclaimed, "Oh! what can we say to the prostitution of such a word." She said she wanted to protect young people nearest and dearest to her from being infected by the plague of slang. "What is more hateful to the English language, and to every sense of reverence and refinement?" she asked rhetorically. Particularly distasteful was the popular use of *ripping* to mean splendid, "opening up as it does, such unpleasant, disgusting thoughts."

FitzClarence did not limited her criticism of oral matters to words. Table manners were another "active source of provocation." At a dinner in Paris she once sat across from the "Countess-----," Byron's inamorata. The countess was then very much "in the sere and yellow leaf," but with "the remains of great beauty," a much patched and mended beauty, however. She possessed, FitzClarence observed, "most lovely teeth—evidently all her own (not by right of purchase)." The countess also wore white, ill-fitting gloves which she did not remove for dinner. During much of the meal, she pursued a piece of bread which "persistently eluded her grasp, drowning itself in the gravy on her plate." Eventually, FitzClarence reported, the countess captured the dripping morsel and carrying it to her lips "devoured it with much gusto." "Not being overanxious to behold the lady's method of cleansing her kid fingers," FitzClarence wrote, "I turned away." FitzClarence wasn't certain who her table mate was until after she asked a young diplomat. He identified the countess then said, "do look at her now." "I obeyed," FitzClarence wrote. "She was using her fork—well, not to eat with. And at that moment two great mysteries were solved in my mind: one, why the countess's teeth were so well-preserved; and the other, why Lord Byron declined to see his fair enslaver eat."

The first time I read *My Memories* I shut the book just after this anecdote. I stopped because Vicki called from the kitchen announcing that dinner was ready. We did not dine in a grand hall in Paris. We have not been to a dinner party or a fashionable restaurant in thirty years. We ate veggie burgers, potato chips, cherry tomatoes, and broccoli in the television room. I drank a bottle of Shiner Bock beer, and Vicki a glass and a half of "Hot to Trot Red Blend" from 14 Hands Winery. For dessert we had rice pudding and a single Milano cookie apiece. I sat in a sagging Naugahyde armchair that belonged to my father, and Vicki on the sofa with Jack and Suzy under throws sleeping beside her. Vicki did not wear gloves. Both of us, though, wore fuzzy slippers and kept them on while we ate. We watched a ripping movie based on the life of Maud Lewis, the folk artist born in Yarmouth, Nova Scotia. Upstairs above our bed hangs one of her paintings. A yoke of oxen stands in snow amid a grove of spruce trees. The oxen have the big, soft eyes of children intoxicated by the approach of Christmas. Around the necks of the oxen swing bells ready to ring out the old and ring in the new year. After the movie, we talked after hearing a sibbolethite newscaster say, "between you and I," a grating illiteracy that makes one consider corking his ears, an infectious barbarism almost excusable if spoken by a foreigner but unpardonable if coming from the mouth of the native-born.

In the "To the Reader," the introduction to *Sylva: or, a Discourse of Forest Trees*, John Evelyn judged that "Men seldom plant *Trees* till they begin to be *Wise*, that is, till they grow *Old*, and find by *Experience* the *Prudence* and *Necessity* of it." Yes, a valetudinarian may plant trees. If he is prudent, however, he will leave his shovel in the garage. Instead of digging, and criticizing, he'll loiter — pulling books off shelves, looking at birds, trees, and other rusticities while almost thinking, wondering about sundry things, what, for example, FitzClarence would say about "grassing him," sibbolethic slang for knocking someone down, or if Arthur Morrison's investigator Martin Hewitt knew what flowers people planted in Coronary Gardens. If experience necessitates an old man's planting something, I hope his doctor urges him to sow marigold seeds in a Coronary Plot. Preserves made from marigold flowers are good for tremblings of the heart, the first of the flutters caused by love, the second by age, these last, atrial fibrillations, one of my ailments.

In 1887 in *Sylvan Secrets* Maurice Thompson described his and a friend's sitting atop a swell of sand "thinly set with tall, slender pine trees." Behind them stretched a primeval forest; before them gleamed a white beach and the pale water of the Gulf of Mexico. Their perch was a weather-beaten log, and while listening to bird song, they mulled Ruskin's descriptions of the natural and the man-made. Eventually, however, reading Ruskin became onerous, and Thompson exclaimed, "Give me something lighter, a volume of Keats or Wordsworth; or–no, give me nothing by nobody; let me lie in this balmy spot and dream and see visions and be free from the cunning of genius and the tricks of talent."

Heredity treated me kindly and avoiding genius comes naturally. But the learned, mockingbird tricks of writing got into my blood decades ago and now flow into my pen despite efforts to staunch them. But, oh, yes, give me nothing by nobody, especially if I am that nobody. "The original and proper sources of knowledge," John Stuart Blackie wrote, "are not books, but life, experience, personal thinking, and acting." If a person has not lived, he declared, "books are like rain and sunshine fallen on unbroken soil." Let me loiter in my study, not thinking about the coming of spring but feeling its warm familiar sights: rabbits in the yard at dusk, titmice trilling, cardinals scratching in the leaves under the lilacs behind the garage, and on the banks of coppery creeks glowing collars of green, the leaves of skunk cabbage and false hellebore, set amid them yellow pendants of marsh marigolds.

As the World Turns Us

Beside the entrance to the Willimantic Co-op stood a wood sign. Painted on it was a replica of the American flag. Instead of stars the words "In Our America" appeared in the blue canton. Printed on the red and white ribbons that alternated and ran horizontally across the flag were statements, all of which were introduced by "In Our America." The first was "All People Are Equal" followed by, "Love Wins," "Black Lives Matter," "Immigrants & Refugees Are Welcome," "Disabilities Are Respected," Women Are In Charge of Their Bodies," "People and Planet Are Valued Over Profit," and lastly "Diversity Is Celebrated." Glued to the door of the men's lavatory inside the store was a six-by-four-inch card. At the top of the card was the emblem of the store, a carrot with a flourishing green top knot. Written on the card was the store's declaration of water closet rights: "The Willimantic Food Co-op is a diverse and inclusive community that strives to provide a safe environment for everyone, including those who challenge gender norms within society. We support efforts to cultivate understanding and acceptance of gender diversity, including an individual's choice of restroom."

The statements meant well, but they were anesthetizing. Inevitably objections to them were also chloroforming although this did not deter Vicki from emending the "Black Lives" line to "All Life Matters." "And all," she said, "includes moths and centipedes, squirrels, oaks, poison ivy, lichens and slime molds, dandelions and durian." "The truth is," she continued, "I value almost every kind of life more than that of homo sapiens." Democracy, Josh argues, so celebrates individuality that man's understanding of his place in the world is perversely inflated. In *Earth-Hunger*, William Graham Sumner wrote, "Before the tribunal of nature a man has no more right to life than a rattlesnake; he has no more right to liberty than any wild beast; his right to the pursuit of happiness is nothing but a license to maintain the struggle for existence, if he can find within himself the powers with which to do it."

People who drum roll pronouncements comparable to those on the flag are on a platform. Usually they belong to cabals, the members of which may look different but who think the same narrow-gauged ideas. They dress in drab orthodox morality and have all graduated, Josh says, from the seminary of the self-ordained. They have a priggish belief in themselves and reek of prosecutorial hubris. "Their eyes lack cone cells and contain only rod cells excluding color and limiting their vision to black and white." "It is so easy to be solemn," Chesterton wrote. "It is hard to be frivolous." The public lives of solemn people become their private lives, and they wax as inflexible as the wooden flag itself. "Did you read the editorial written by a woman in the Midwest which argued that the most effective way to stop sexual harassment was to prevent the birth of male babies?" Josh asked. "That is out-Heroding Herod." Astonishingly, most responses to the article were positive. One woman suggested that parents who allowed male children to be born should be fined. Another announced that she was "Pro-Life, with God, and against abortion except in the case of male births." The next day Josh showed me an article in which yet another legislator declared that guns did not kill people, people did. "If God were real," Josh said, "that is, an Episcopalian, decent, responsible, and rational, He'd sweep guns away in a whirlwind."

"There is a melancholy which accompanies all enthusiasm," Shaftesbury declared in his *Characteristicks*.

Shield me from the zealous. Protect me from the abuses of crabbed virtues. Instead introduce me to the zany who imagined himself a Roman consul one day, a field of turnips the next, Democritus in the morning, a jar of marmalade in the evening. I want to meet the muffin man who lived on Drury Lane and gossiped with the Man in the Moon. Every spring he dressed in black like a beetle and attended the Butterfly's Ball. Point out the verbal inebriate who declared, "When days are good, they're good, and when they ain't, they isn't." He must have been a cousin of the woman who became an opera singer after a bulldog bit two toes off her right foot. She was in eighth grade, and the bulldog swallowed the toes and half a red stocking without chewing. The dog's owner couldn't talk but earned a good living mewing like a cat. Landlords paid him to rid houses of mice, and undertakers, graveyards of rats. According to genealogists, he was a lineal descendent of the eighteenth-century preacher Orator Henley. One Sunday Henley announced that in his sermon the following week, he would unveil a quicker and less expensive way of making shoes. When a large crowd answered the call and appeared, Henley revealed that the best method was to cut the uppers off boots.

If I must be preached at, let the sermon come from Slubey Garts, a minister who rode a circuit through my books twenty years ago. Slubey wasn't a big-mouthed, big-bellied buckra preacher who danced around with his shirttail out hollering for Jesus. Never did he steer parishioners' eyes toward the sky so he could slip under their sight and fondle wives and wallets. Instead he praised the here and now. He urged people to do good deeds and earn their ways to Glory. "Make this life heaven for others and yourself, and Jacob's Ladder will turn into an escalator." Every July 4th Slubey's Tabernacle of Love held a church picnic. For the blessing Slubey preached about food and lauded the sisters who prepared the dishes "in kitchens on this earth, no blue yonders above their heads but hot linoleum floors beneath their feet. There ain't no cornbread in heaven, no grits, no turnip greens or corn on the cob, no beefsteak tomatoes, no fried chicken, sweet potatoes, watermelon rind pickle, or grandma's applesauce. Once you cross the River Jordan, you'll never taste catfish again," he said, "and don't imagine eating a deviled egg. Only in that other place will you find red velvet cake. The spirits you'll see won't be bottled. No, they'll be flocks of winged old girls and boys. At feasts cherubim will serve manna bread and milk and honey. If an archangel is the guest speaker, locusts in olive oil might be on the menu, but otherwise all the dishes will be puréed — suitable for the unweaned and for the forgetful who left their store-bought teeth beside their death beds and now have to gump their meals. There will be nothing spicy for red-blooded repentant sinners." "Thank these Wives of Zarephath then stick your fork into this life and the food on these tables," Slubey concluded, "and when eternal night comes you will sleep on the hillside where the peach blossoms bloom and the wild birds sing."

Recently I saw a man wearing a T-shirt on the front of which was printed "Different Day. Same Shirt." "Different Day. Same Predictable Attitude" encapsulates the thought of many well-intentioned people. The compassionate life is more complex than slogans. Moreover, the gap between words and deeds is cavernous. Writing instructive truisms is easy; living an instructive life is difficult, "probably impossible even for a Methodist," Vicki said. Was it Oscar Wilde who remarked "that it was well good people did not live to see the evil results of their goodness and that evil people did not live to see the good results of their wickedness"? On lawns throughout Storrs signs have sprouted urging passersby to "Love The Stranger." "Not the stranger bearing lollipops who entices children into his car smiling like the Cheshire Cat and promising to take them to the circus," Josh said. Silly and irritating, the signs evoke cynicism because they sacrifice explanation for brevity. In "Galatians" Paul put things better. He suggested that the latitudinarian spirit of Christianity, not doctrine or rules, freed people to love. It shattered tribalism and self-serving identities. It lifted the repressive fear of difference and formed the basis of a true community of Samaritans. In this Christ people were one, Paul preached, saying, "there is neither Jew nor Greek, there is neither bond nor free, there is neither male nor female."

Ill-considered decency is the opiate of the comfortable middle class causing absurd behavior. Recently students at the university disrupted an insipid speech by an unpleasant right-wing puppy. They were too inexperienced to realize that the best way to geld an argumentative speaker is to agree with him. "A third-semester women's, gender and sexuality studies major," the campus newspaper reported, said the situation sickened her. "For me, what did it was when he sipped milk," the student recounted. Whenever the audience interrupted him, the speaker drank from a glass of milk. "Milk," the student explained, "has been used as a motif for white supremacy since over half the world cannot digest milk." Happily, for her sake, the girl's statement caused only a ripple of giggles. She rapidly eddied out of mind, and her remarks faded from conversation being recognized as the sort of silly thing said by a school child flailing through adolescence. However, if a prominent adult declared that he was politically lactose intolerant, the testimonial would be glued to his name becoming Time's tag to his passing. Alas, as Agnes Repplier wrote, "there is no harder fate than to be immortalized as a fool; to have one's name—which merits nothing sterner than oblivion—handed down to generations as an example of silliness, or stupidity, or presumption; to be enshrined pitilessly in the amber of the 'Dunciad.'"

The card on the door of the Co-op's necessary house seemed unnecessary. Only the insensitive would criticize a person on the cusp of being caught short for ignoring a gender-specific sign outside a bathroom. Who could possible care about the sex or the lack thereof of one's temporary neighbor? What sort of person fulminates over where a needy person urinates: whether it be a room for men or for women, lawns back or front, a putting green, a graveyard, the wall behind the chancel of a church, almost anywhere imaginable and practical? Moreover, I suspect that the only folks upset by the possibility of untoward behavior are those who have not, to bring Thoreau to mind, sucked the marrow out of life. In a moment of mellow braggadocio Josh reported that in greener days he was ogled, propositioned, stalked, pinched, tickled, bit, grabbed, groped, and goosed by both men and women. "Indeed, an unexpected goosing sometimes added hop to my step," he said, noting that he discouraged ardent admirers because he wasn't naturally inclined to love the stranger. "Still," he continued wistfully, "although groping is not a proper handshake, I suppose it could facilitate an introduction, one that might lead to fruitful communication." In Josh's case, surprising intimacies ripened into verbal not fleshly matters, becoming the subjects and predicates of humor—tales limited to topic-sentence beginnings and never hindered by bruising middles or ends.

The world resembles a lathe turning and shaping conformity. It locks people in place and rotates them honing cant and grinding off eccentricities. As result speech becomes as bland and predictable as the statements on the wooden flag. The tuition for respectability is high and comes at the cost of delight, foolishness, and harmless folly. Many forces mold people, especially school and family. Most parents want children to genuflect to convention so that they'll fit seamlessly into the jigsaw puzzle of existence insuring that they will become "successful and productive members of society," or in other words, genteel nonentities. Pressures to blend in are various. For example, few things, John Kenneth Galbraith declared, "are so bad for the youngster of impressionable age as team sports. Instead of causing him to think first of his own self-interest, they turn his mind to the problem of the group. He ceases to be an individualist and becomes a mere cog in a social machine." "I believe that a large amount of unorganized time is valuable in life," David Fairchild wrote, describing his boyhood. "My childhood was more casual than that of most children today, who are forced into some sort of regimented play," he recounted. "I can see no advantage (particularly to a young naturalist) in this over-organization of childhood."

I was fortunate to be born with no athletic ability or indeed any precocious gifts. Because I lacked talents capable of being cultivated, no one forced me to bloom out of season. My parents encouraged "boyhood's painless play." They allowed me to roam and grow weedy, trying this and that, exploring and pulling books off library shelves at random. I caught snakes and frogs, and to emend John Greenleaf Whitter, saw how the tortoise bore his shell and discovered where the freshest berries grew. What a blessing it was to be uncoordinated and untalented. I was also fortunate to go to Sewanee for college. In the early 1960s, Sewanee was a small undistinguished school struggling to survive rather than laboring to achieve national recognition by measuring itself against a series of banal educational benchmarks. The faculty thought themselves teachers rather than educators; consequently, their courses were educational. They did not confuse instruction and learning and march into classes armed with study plans. They didn't try to mold us. They knew that giving advice was easier than receiving it, so they simply introduced students to books and ideas. They understood that the path leading to understanding was not straight and narrow. Instead it was a crooked and happily puzzling switchback.

My teachers did not make outlandish claims for the classroom. They steered clear of the prating mumbo jumbo of uplift. They realized, as Sir John Lubbock wrote, that "the important thing is not so much that every child should be taught, as every child should be given the wish to learn." Like the Emerson who wrote "Experience," they were wise enough to be uncertain about the effects and methods of learning. "We do not know today whether we are busy or idle," Emerson judged. "In times when we thought ourselves indolent, we have afterwards discovered that much was accomplished and much was begun in us." They hoped the matter of their courses would someday soften the cares of our lives. To this end they encouraged us to explore and delight in life and other people. They wanted us to appreciate the expected and the unexpected. If a person looked closely at the scraggy and the despoiled, he often discovered radiance. They trusted us and human nature enough to believe we would learn on our own. Only rarely were they dogmatic. They realized, as Douglas Jerrold put it, that dogmatism was puppyism grown to maturity. Occasionally, however, they warned us that a collective rage for virtue was a great danger to virtue. Just as corrupting to character was offering moral support, a placebo, words that cost and risked nothing.

Of course, classes taught me all sorts of miscellaneous things, the most valuable being that people mattered more than ideas. The wisdom stressed was taught in old, recognizable words and was usually assuaging and aphoristic rather than disturbing and mystifying, continuing the familial middle-class schooling prevalent in the mannered South. In a notebook I unearthed in the basement last year appeared a statement by Sir William Temple that I jotted down in 1962. In conversation, Temple said, humor mattered more than wit, and easiness, more than knowledge. Few people either desired or thought they needed to learn. All, however, wanted "to be pleased, or, if not, to be easy." "Antagonism of all kinds," James Payn wrote in "On Conversation," is "inimical to social enjoyment."

Over time I picked up a few lesser social truths overlooked by Miss Manners, among them, not to trust the well-groomed. Such folks were liable to be vain and self-centered. In contrast the slovenly rarely suffered from diseased egos and made better, more trustworthy companions. I was told that a guest should always arrive on time no matter the inconvenience to himself. I learned that the company of a person who tore open correspondence was preferable to that of an individual who sliced open envelopes with a letter opener. Life is disorderly, and people addicted to the sharp and narrow, the geometric, are often unable to cope with the rag-tail ripping of emotions. Similarly, serving ice cream reveals character. One should avoid the permanent company of people who removed ice cream from half-gallon containers by dragging the scoop across the surface of the block of ice cream in straight lines, creating neat furrows. Easier to live with is someone who digs deep into the block leaving behind potholes and caverns and who returns to the container later when dietary censors are out of sight and spoons out hunks melting around the edges of the cartoon. College taught me a great deal about the symptoms of sanity, and the only thing I can think of now that I wish courses had taught was ventriloquism. When I overhear a smarmy oldster asking a little, little girl if she'd like a kitty for Christmas, would that I could throw my voice and answer, saying, "Hell, no! I'd like a boyfriend, one with a chest hairier than a chinchilla. Don't think of giving a babe like me no sweetheart whose head looks like the backside of an armadillo."

I wish that the sign outside the Co-op was a real flag, dangling limply then suddenly blowing and waving in the breeze, being whipped into knots, rain causing its colors to sweep beyond their lines and its letters to wash hither and thither in a confusing, provocative jumble. Pharisaical thought and behavior are too much with us. Some days all the world seems the same stage. Music never stops, literal music, until a person becomes deaf — in cafés, restaurants, gymnasiums, airports, malls — every place is a dentist's office. Nicknames have been sieved out of speech. Where I wonder is my friend from Portland who did well in school and got so many

126

degrees that his boyhood companions fondly dubbed him "Thermometer?" In an ancient story a man bought a goat for a family feast. Afterward he strapped the goat to his back to carry it home. Three thieves, however, saw him purchase the goat, and they raced ahead of the man stationing themselves at intervals along his route. "Why are you carrying that dog — such an unclean animal?" the first thief said when he saw the man. The man paused for a moment, looked at the thief then trudged on. A little farther down the road, the second thief appeared. "What sort of man carries a mangy dog on his back?" the thief exclaimed, turning his head aside and spitting as if to eradicate the sight. The man stopped, and loosening the straps binding the goat studied the animal. After several moments he shook his head, tightened the straps and walked on, his stride slightly tentative. Two bends along the road later, the man met the last thief. "Oh, Lord, protect me from the Devil and his dog," the thief moaned, covering his eyes and falling to his knees. The third time proved too much for the man. With trembling hands, he untied the goat, threw it into bushes beside the road, and ran away kicking up a fog of dust. The first two thieves then joined the third. Together they caught the goat and cooking it with ginger and garlic, coriander, cardamom and maybe a peppercorn, enjoyed a fine meal in a shady wood near the road.

Although primarily a trickster tale, the story illustrates the power of opinion. Too often people defer to a group, not seeing what they saw but what others say they saw and distrusting their own intelligence thinking what others say they ought to think. Students are conformists in and out of class. As a result, frequently their papers are drab and conventional especially those that are autobiographical. Sometimes, however, words slip from the anticipated signage and are so honest that the teacher wonders if the student attended high school, wrote compositions, and played field hockey. The last sentence of a girl's description of her parents made me sigh, "I go home to my mother, and I miss her when I am away. I have not seen my father for years, and it is getting hard to continue to love him." "Nuts," I muttered and laying the paper down stared out the window of my study. Suddenly, a red-tailed hawk landed in the shagbark hickory in the side yard. In its talons the hawk clutched a chipmunk. A salad of green shield lichens curled over the surface of a ledge. In the distance a woman walked three small black dogs along a street. On the other side of the road a man carried a ladder twice his height.

"A good day for seeing and thinking," I reflected and set out for the library. Libraries, however, are not as exciting and unpredictable as they once were. Once upon a time, in the words of Thomas Bailey Aldrich, libraries were the asylums of incurable egotists. No longer do aspiring physicians sketch courses in comparative male and female anatomy on the flyleaves and end papers of books. No longer do the comments of readers festoon margins: "what a fool" followed by "he's no fool; you are the fool" then "if I'm one, you're one, too," end-stopped by an illustration of a male donkey, that is a jack, kicking up his heels and flashing a backside larger than the third largest planet in the solar system. Because so few comments decorated the margins of the books I wrote, I sank to the occasion and rectified the fault, at first writing words and phrases like, genius, brilliant, he's the Socrates of Storrs, and when Pickering says, "let there be light" the sun rises, its rays scrolling cursive across the sky spelling Halleluiah.

It was especially gratifying to discover comments by well-known literati. "Although Iram is gone taking his rose with him, I do not mourn because you, Sam, are left," Omar Khayyam wrote. "No sheik could wish for more." "I thought I heard the garments of the night sweep though the upstairs hall, but then I opened this book, Sam, and my spirit drank repose," H. W. Longfellow wrote, adding, "Forever in your debt." "The Lady of Shalott would not have forsaken her loom if she had discovered the magic sights on your pages," Alfy Tennyson opined. "Even better if you weren't hitched and she'd seen you riding between the barley sheaves, the poor repressed girl wouldn't have tossed herself ass over teakettle into the river." As might be expected because I am innately modest, the litany of compliments eventually embarrassed and bored me, so I changed pens. I jettisoned the administrative fountain pen with its respectable blue-black ink and using a ballpoint pen sloppy with scarlet ink wrote scathing remarks, most of which were hardy and scatological, the stuff of extracurricular barnyard and boudoir doings. Once or twice readers fertilized the sterile margins of my books, causing them to bloom and me to smile. "Pickering," one annotator wrote, "is always right in general." Beneath the comment, a perceptive reader wrote "What?"

Much as I explore the shrub surrounding a pasture before entering a field, so I rummage the hedgerows binding the texts of books. Alas, the stones that once tripped and intrigued readers have been turned and ploughed out. Dedications to academic books, for example, are now as memorable as parsnips, generally consisting of aspartame-like testimonials to the domestic partner of the moment or praise for the long-armed patron with his hands deep in the pockets of grant-giving foundations. Like many of the pastures I used to meander which now grow condominiums instead of hay, so dedications today rarely flourish as memorably as that introducing William Thompson's *Wigwam Wonder Tales* published in 1919. "This book is affectionately dedicated to H. T., who for ten years has been my constant companion," Thompson wrote. "We have travelled together from the Gulf of Mexico to the Arctic Ocean. Have climbed glaciers of Alaska and shivered in the fogs of Newfoundland. Have rocked in the crafts of the North Sea fishermen. Have looked from the Phoenician ruins of Eze to the island of Corsica. Have enjoyed the nature smiles of southern Europe from Italy to Setubal, the ancient Cetubriga of the Romans. Have strolled along the highways and byways of Germany, Holland, France, Belgium, Moresnet, Italy, and romped together in the cork-groves of Portugal and the olive-groves of Spain. We have shared the same room in spooky inns along the trails of Don Quixote in La Mancha and have ridden fourth-class with a first-class ticket hundreds of kilometers . . . because dogs were not allowed in first-class compartments on European railways."

Although people kick against Time's lathe, they rarely succeed in stopping the turning. In the preface to *A Final Reckoning*, G. A. Henty addressed young readers explaining why he wrote "a tale of bush life in Australia" rather than another account of military adventurers and medieval swashing-buckling. "You know," he wrote, "the old story of the boy who bothered his brains with Euclid, until he came to dream regularly that he was an equilateral triangle enclosed in a circle." "Unless I break away sometimes from history," he noted, drawing a parallel to the young mathematician, "I shall be haunted day and night by visions of men in armor, and soldiers of all ages and times." Did Henty succeed in escaping the rack of dreams? I suspect not. The great worry of passengers on cruise ships is being abandoned at some obscure port. They imagine themselves standing on the dock waving frantically as their ship vanishes over the horizon. Vicki and I have taken many cruises. We've spent countless days wandering islands alone, arriving back at ships only moments before gangways are raised. Practically every day during a cruise, even on sea days, we discuss being marooned, our conversation as dismal as that of Stevenson's poor Ben Gunn. We have worried so much about being left behind that now I dream about missing departures. I wake at four in the morning short of breath because I have been sprinting through muddy streets in backwater towns in hopes of reaching the port before my ship disappears. As I don't ever reach the boat before it departs, I suspect I won't be able to break free from the dream. However, I have adapted. Man can master his nighttime fate. Now at the beginning of each dream about cruising I stuff my pockets with money so that, I tell Vicki as we set off roaming, "we'll be able to fly back to Connecticut or jump on a ferry traveling to the boat's next stop if we are deserted."

I occasionally try to escape social conformity. As Henty failed to clean military dress out of his literary wardrobe, so I, too, am unsuccessful. The year after the appearance of *A Final Reckoning*, Henty published, among other roistering books, *The Young Carthaginian, A Story of the Time of Hannibal, With Wolfe in Canada: The Winning of a Continent*, and *Bonnie Prince Charlie: A Tale of Fontenoy and Culloden*. For my part I decided not to vote in recent local elections. I told friends that the baby food dished out by candidates gave me colic. The friends reacted with Pavlovian fervor haranguing me almost as if they heard me deny that "Love Wins." "Democracy depends upon citizens exercising the right to vote," a neighbor said. "My exercise doesn't effect anything," I replied. "My vote will neither oil the wheels of democracy nor throw a spanner in the bureaucracy." "The person who doesn't vote forfeits his right to criticize the government," another man said waxing argumentative and red in the face. "Not voting," a woman said, "is a vote for" and here she named a lickspittle running for the State House. "No—not voting is only not voting," I replied, for the sake of calm of mind swallowing words like dolt and dunce, both prefaced by you. Once acquaintances discovered my antipathy to electoral matters, they telephoned. "Don't abnegate your moral responsibility" and "you will lose respect if Betty and I don't see you at town hall," people said. The earnest chorus was shrill and twice on election day, I almost left home and voted. Although I would have written my name in for the highest office on the ballot, something I have done in the past, be that position senator, president, or first alternate to Planning and Zoning, I remained at home. I raked leaves, picked up sticks, and did not answer the telephone until after the polls closed.

Next year, I'll vote. "In Our America" life is more tranquil if a person cultivates the impression of genuflecting to commandments promulgated by the self-godded. My difficulty is that, in John Masefield's words, "a wind is in the heart of me." The wind is not a nor'easter, but it swirls and blows contrary to the general flow of opinion. When hot air settles heavy and oppressive, the wind turns cold and biting, making me an uncomfortable conversationalist. Then I eschew conviviality and become reclusive, my only companions trivial books. In younger days I read stacks of biographies. My muscles have collapsed, and no longer can I heft a three-decker biography, much less read it. Moreover, most famous people belong on the Lord High Executioner's list of folks who would never be missed and, alas, should have been missed, their doings more destructive than constructive, people whose punishments rarely fitted, as the Mikado sang, their crimes.

Matters that hagiography celebrates as accomplishments dwindle into insignificance. What schoolchildren today read about the admirable career of the "Mill Boy of the Slashes"? An earthquake destroyed the Colossus of Rhodes twenty-three hundred years ago, and today almost no one knows or cares what famous victory the statue commemorated. The man who stamped hard on the world and left footprints on the sands of time doesn't interest me. I am intrigued by what really matters. Did that person's heels crack and bleed in winter? Did he plant iris and what was his favorite variety? Although the biographies I read now are succinct, they delight me, among others, that of the Old Person of Troy who drank brandy and soy with a spoon by the light of the moon then that of his next-door neighbor the Young Lady who on being annoyed by large flies killed some with a thump and drowned others at the pump. I'd rather dine with the octogenarian in whose beard two owls, a hen, four larks, and a wren built nests than with any American president. How I'd like to attend a literary meeting with "X" the cousin of James Fields' friend G. T. who asked

Harriet Beecher Stowe "if she had looked much into the subject of slavery."

In reclusive hours I read mysteries and crime novels, rather I peruse first chapters. Rarely do I finish a volume. After a racing through signature of pages, I fall asleep and the book slips out of hand and thought. Sometimes, though, a paragraph diverts me, for example, Vincent Starrett's forward to *The Casebook of Solar Pons* in which he asks, "What sort of murder do you particularly fancy? I mean, of course, in a book. What is your secret relish in the way of fictive corpses? A nameless body with a jeweled dagger still quivering in the warm flesh? A bullet-slain card expert clutching at the jack of spades in his lifeless fingers? A hideous gargoyle swaying beneath a blackened rafter? Or do you like a still, cold form about whose pale lips the transcendent fathomer detects the familiar odor of bitter almonds?" "How about a sectarian ninny killed by brain hypoxia caused by phrases that suck all the oxygen out of a conversation?" Josh suggested, "'it is what it is' being a particularly deadly example."

People "who blurt out hard and home truths" make mortal enemies, Hazlitt stated. My close friends are aged and civilized. They believe the decalogue Moses fetched from the summit of Mount Sinai was a conduct book containing rules governing decorum and civility. Decades ago they stopped telling the truth, and consequently their lives are not in danger in my presence. In the "almost -true" — I dare not say "in truth" — I prefer comments about murders to the stories and deeds themselves. My favorite is De Quincey's witty observation in "On Murder as One of the Fine Arts," an essay I read at Sewanee. "If once a man indulges himself in murder," De Quincey declared, "very soon he comes to think very little of robbing; and from robbing to drinking and to Sabbath-breaking, and from that to incivility and procrastination. Once begin upon this downward path, you never know where you are to stop. Many a man has dated his ruin from some murder or other that perhaps he thought little of at the time."

I spent forty-five years as an academic cantering through books, hunting sources, and baying print. For my "unmatched assiduousness" in revealing the influence of Arthur Conan Doyle's "The Adventure of the Speckled Band" upon a murder mentioned in P. G. Wodehouse's *Mulliner Nights*, the Modern Language Guild awarded me both a mask and a brush. The Draught Stout was not his usual cheery self when he appeared at the bar parlor of the Anglers' Rest, Wodehouse recounted. His face was drawn and twisted, and he contributed nothing to the conversation until a sympathetic Lemonade and Angostura laid a hand on his shoulder and asked, "What is it, old man . . . lost a friend?" "Worse," the Draught Stout answered, explaining that while on a train he read half a mystery. Unfortunately, in the haste to disembark, he left the book on his seat. Now, he lamented he would spend a sleepless night wondering who poisoned "Sir Geoffrey Tuttle, Bart." Perhaps, he continued, the vicar was the culprit as he was "known to be interested in strange poisons." No, the murderer was the plumber, Mr. Mulliner stated, saying that he had read the entire *Murglow Manor Mystery*. In 1896 Sir Geoffrey wronged one of the plumber's aunts. In revenge, Mr. Mulliner recounted, the plumber "fastened a snake in the nozzles of the shower bath with glue and when Sir Geoffrey turned on the stream the hot water melted the glue. This released the snake, which dropped through one of the holes, bit the baronet in the leg, and disappeared down the waste pipe."

As the World Turns Us, II

Actions generate thoughts, not thoughts actions. Nattering about civic matters tired me and made me tedious, particularly to myself. In November I chopped all notions of wooden flags into kindling and booked two back-to-back cruises in the Caribbean, both with Holland America. The cruises began in December and lasted for a month. I hoped that travel would invigorate me. In gazing at societal matters I'd raised my sight too high. I ignored backyard clotheslines and alders furry in the sunshine wrapping ponds like silver stoles. I hadn't noticed turkey tail covering broken trees like fish scales or the traps of plastic bags and waxed milk cartons that tumbled across yards and roads after trash-day pickup. During the trip I imagined glimpsing the unfamiliar and having fresh thoughts becoming a little less fussy. However, the expectation was illusory. Vicki and I had visited all the cruise-ship islands in the Caribbean several times. Moreover, the actions of people my age are habitual. Unstringing ritual is practically impossible. Indeed, the attempt to slip routine by not voting did not rise to a speed bump in ordinary living.

In an interview recently published in *Time*, a staff writer reported that Wendell Berry's wife Tanya said that her husband's "principal asset as a writer has been" his "knack for repeating" himself. Berry explained that he did so because things were not improving in rural America. My asset as a writer has also been the knack for repeating myself. I do so not for high purpose but because years and pages have worn furrows in my mind. If I could hoist myself out of the cruising rut, I'd purposely slip back. The furrows are comfortable, familiar places. Moreover, my experiences on each trip differ enough from those in Storrs and from those of previous trips to invigorate me. Always I hear a chorus of astonishing remarks. After landing, Vicki's and my flight from Hartford to Florida sat for sixteen minutes on a runway far from the terminal in Fort Lauderdale. Later as I stood at the baggage carousel waiting for our suitcases, a man standing next to me said, his voice burry with irritation, "We parked on the tarmac so long that the luggage should have been waiting for us when we disembarked. That damn Obama is responsible for this delay. Trump will make America efficient again." "What did that man say?" Vicki said drawing close. "Is he an imbecile or just an asshole?" "I don't know," I said, easing Vicki away and pointing at the entrance to the carousel, "Here come our bags. Let's go get them."

That was the single political remark I heard during the journey. When the ship embarked, people ceased talking about newspaper matters. Along with getting sea legs, they got sea vocabularies. On board, "have a nice day" became "keep cruising," this accompanied by a thumbs-up, the digital equivalent of a sextant's index mirror. Tidbits of autobiography accompanied dinner. "When I was twenty-eight," a retired fireman from New York City recounted, "I was overcome by smoke in a blazing apartment. Firefighters from the station hauled me out of the building. They draped a blanket over me, and I heard one say, 'He's dead.' 'No, I'm not,' I said from under the blanket." Many cruisers sailing from Fort Lauderdale emigrated to Florida from the northeast to escape high taxes and cold winters. They lived in retirement communities, and on the ship the main topics of chat were numerical: how many cruises they had taken and how many countries they'd visited. During the shipboard month, I heard but a single pun, and it was an old standby. "How," a woman asked one night at dinner, "are an exhumed corpse and a new opera alike?"

"They both," she said interrupting herself to chuckle approvingly, "have to be rehearsed." Recipes interested the woman. She said she watched every cooking show on television. Food puns have long been a side dish of my gastronomical conversation, and I almost asked the woman if she couldn't obtain a calf's head for mock turtle soup would the meaty parts of a tortoise shell cat be an adequate substitute. However, I remained silent because Vicki glared at me with a silencing basilisk eye.

Occasionally a passenger had a bee in his bonnet, and when the opportunity arose, he doffed his cap in hopes the buzzing would attract auditors. Self-driving cars will change courtship rituals, I heard a woman predict at Happy Hour in a bar on the Sports Deck. The woman was the sort of person who got everywhere early as she'd clearly been at the bar for some time. Lovers, she said, would abandon their lanes, and urban myths about teenagers being decapitated by escapees from prisons for the criminally insane would disappear. "Rural hook murderers would get prostheses, attend college, play basketball, and after majoring in "Giftedness, Creativity, and Early Childhood Talent Development" earn fortunes as inspirational speakers. Parking was destined to become Driving as traffic jams of the hormonal took their endocrine glands to the highway. Front seat passengers would no longer fumble about and risk their lives attempting to undo seat belts. Because of overwhelming demand, car manufacturers would reinforce backseats making them firmer than memory-foam mattresses. Even better highways themselves were bound to improve as courting couples demanded that pot holes be filled immediately. Familial matters would also change. After Sally said, "I'm going for a wee little ride with Joey. I'll be back for dinner. I'll have a good appetite, so tell Mom to make a big pot of spaghetti" then hung her overcoat in the hall closet before leaving home one chilly afternoon, Daddy who usually dozed silently through dusk to dinner would leap from his armchair and shout, "the Hell you say!"

Shortly after boarding, I overheard a man talking to the ship's hotel manager about culture. Everyone, the man said, carried with him a suitcase packed with ideas and thoughts. While some bags were heavy, others were light. Suitcases varied, the man elaborated. A small number were leather; "the majority were cloth or plastic. Many were new while a few were ancient and scuffed, looking beloved." Young people, the man continued, strapped on backpacks; aging hippies dragged duffel bags, and old people pulled luggage that had wheels and long handles attached to them. What the man said intrigued me but not the hotel manager. He rotated his head and looked about desperately. For my part I wanted to hear more about the contents of the bags—how they were packed and what sort of labels or identifying tags and tapes were pasted to the sides or attached to the handles. The man, himself, looked weary. I speculated that he had traveled an exhausting distance to reach Fort Lauderdale, and when the hotel manager's responses were a dull "yes" and a perfunctory "interesting," the man became silent and walked away, going, I assumed, to his stateroom to unpack. Twice more I overheard the man. Both times occurred at breakfast as I stood in line in the Lido restaurant, and on each occasion he was talking about luggage. Rarely is a person able to explain another individual's obsession. But at the end of the cruise as passengers snaked through the customs hall at Port Everglades, the man and his wife appeared accompanied by a porter pushing a castle keep of suitcases on a trolley. I counted seven large suitcases, hanging down from them at least six voluminous tote bags.

Off the ship I met an assortment of people. On Tobago I didn't meet the Old Man "who lived on rice, gruel and sago." But at the Heritage Park in Pembroke a girl served me traditional black cake—fruit cake baked in a dirt oven and christened with rum, not a total immersion soaking but a give-the-tourists-a-taste splash. The girl wore colorful island holiday dress except on her feet. On them she wore flip-flops. Across the top of the shoes a gold-colored Michael Jordan leapt palming a basketball with his right hand. On Boxing Day in Bridgetown Vicki and I attended the horse races at Garrison Savannah sponsored by the Barbados Turf Club. I bet small change on each race. Although I consulted men who looked like touts, that is, seedy guys studying racing forms and swilling beer, all the while keeping toothpicks in their mouths, I did not pocket any winnings until the fifth race. As I stood in line before the pari-mutuel window waiting to wager, a girl holding a baby said, "Bet on 'Stealin'.'" The girl was fifteen or sixteen years old, and both she and the baby were diminutive. Tattooed on the girl's upper arm was a heart. In the middle of the heart was "LOVE." "I couldn't do worse," I told Vicki when I returned to trackside and told her I'd obeyed the girl and put three dollars down on Stealin', raising my wager from the usual two dollars. Indeed, I could not have done better. Stealin' finished four lengths ahead of the other horses, and I more than doubled my bet, receiving six dollars and thirty-six cents.

On Bequia a Rastafarian stared through a splintered fence at the entrance to his yard. Scrap metal lay behind him on the ground rusting and collecting dirt while jerry-built sheds leaned broken-kneed, walls bulging and varicose, their windows plastic bags. On a clothesline hung a T-shirt ratty with holes. On the chest appeared the face of Hailee Selassie, the Lion of Judah. Painted on stepladders of boards nailed to trees were statements, almost none of which made sense to me, for example, "What is transparent skin?" The Rastafarian himself was "The Last Bible Seer," and for two dollars, he told me, I could take his picture. I don't own a camera, so I declined the invitation. On every trip, a new experience occurs. On Gutters Gade behind Market Square in Charlotte Amalie, I experienced my first bump handshake, knocking my fist against that of a man dressed in a black shirt and black trousers and sitting near the road on a front stoop smoking marijuana. I have forgotten what we enthusiastically agreed about. I remember that we both laughed as we bumped hands, and I noticed that on the right side of his maxillary teeth he was missing two premolars.

Years ago, Vicki and I roamed eagerly anticipating the unexpected. Time has made us brittle, and we don't tolerate bruises as well as we did in the past. Now we worry that the unexpected might bang into us, and we didn't wander as carelessly as we once did. We sat more: on a bench in front of the Supreme Bar in Willemstad, drinking two-dollar bottles of Presidente beer. The man who sold the beer wore a gold chain around his neck. Attached to the end of it was half a heart. "My wife wears the other half," he said. "You and your wife should get a heart, too." Upstairs in Mama's Café on Bequia, we ate conch fritters and watched crowds swirl along Belmont Road. We chose a table so small that no one else could join us. At dinner one night near the start of the cruise, a stranger helped himself to Vicki's and my company. He was talkative. After informing us that he was a teetotaler, he began preaching the virtues of abstinence. Earlier Vicki purchased a wine package. On our waiter's sending the wine steward to the table, Vicki interrupted the sermon to select a bottle for the meal, "an ecumenical, nondenominational merlot," she said. The steward then turned to the man and asked if he wanted to purchase any drink. "Yes, a bottle of wine as God made it," the man exclaimed, "a bunch of grapes!" He then pounded the table with his fist and shouted, "Lord bind the devil!" "The man's hitting the table made me and the silverware jump," Vicki said after the meal. "I regret that I didn't recover fast enough to ask him whether he wanted red or green grapes." "What would you have recommended?" I asked. "Red, without a doubt, imported from Mexico, grown on gravelly soil, and with a hint of manure on the skin—a soupcon of horseshit to suit the palate of the presumptuous fool."

On Christmas Eve in Sabor y Rumba in Ponce, Puerto Rico, we celebrated by munching plantains and pork, a traditional seasonal dish. A woman wearing a red cap like those worn by Santa's helpers approached us and leaning over our table wished us Merry Christmas. Afterward she said that for a dollar she'd share her Christmas thought. I handed her a dollar and got my money's worth. Her remark was both unseasonal and unexpected — common sense which seemed startling true. "Cowards make the best generals," she said. "They avoid danger, save lives, and preserve peace." Wisdom was for sale at closing-out prices, and when I gave the woman a second dollar, she said, "If a man works hard, he can make a living, but if he wants to be rich, he has to find another way." In George Town in Grand Cayman we sat on a bench behind Yolanni's Place, a small stand, and ate fried crabs, beans, rice, slaw, and mashed potatoes. At a package store I bought a six-pack of White Tip beer, two of which I sold to another tourist couple. They lived in Alberta. "The proud home of the tar sands, the greatest boon to the environment in North America," the woman volunteered, huckstering like a salesman hawking knives and bibles at a carnival. Vicki and I swam that morning, and I was too fagged to mold my face into an innocuous lying smile. "What!" I exclaimed, rice exploding from my mouth. "That's outrageous! Because the President is an imbecile doesn't mean all Americans are know-nothing idiots," I said turning away from the woman, ending the conversation and acquaintance before either began.

Painted on the front on Yolanni's Place was "Good Times. Good Food. Good People." In the Caribbean slogans decorated stores as often as they did shirts, my favorite appearing on a butcher shop in Hope, Tobago, "The Meeting Place for Meats." In Cartagena's Old Town, the cacophony of selling was as deafening as the clamorous advertising at American college basketball games. Hawkers pushed barrows loaded with mounds of fruit and vegetables. Women stood in doorways and exhibited lace. Wearing red and yellow dresses, balancing pans filled with bouquets of flowers and stalks of bananas on their heads, and looking like advertisements sliced from travel magazines, other women posed for pictures charging a couple of dollars. Panama hats and holiday shirts hung on sidewalk racks. Street corner artists painted waterfalls and seascapes, and coffee sellers invited passersby to sip their wares. To escape the come-hither waves of words, Vicki and I retreated into La Brioche, a French café and drank cappuccinos and shared an almond croissant. "Like Storrs except tastier," Vicki said gathering the energy to breach the street again and buy coffee beans for friends at home.

Along with invigorating and exhausting, the doings of shop and street repulsed. Far from ports, sewers of seaweed flushed past the ship carrying a sludge thickened with plastic bags, cans, and Styrofoam. In Willemstad the buildings along Handelskade facing St. Anna Bay were trimmed and scrubbed. Their fronts bloomed like spring, red, blue, orange, and yellow awakening fancy and evoking sentimental visions of a toy Amsterdam, Delft children in wooden shoes, and rinsing, wholesome fields of tulips. Only a few paces beyond "cute" Smith Bridge on the far side of the Waaigat, however, the city became a ratty Caribbean town. Roofs of houses had collapsed, and the floors below became tips of saplings and toppled privies. Alleys were bogs of moldering rubbish. Below Queen Juliana Bridge streets were impassable septic troughs of garbage. We watched a man haul a trash can into the street and dump it. The filth was so deep that he had difficulty finding a place where he could turn the can upside down. "The waste generated by tourists swarming out of cruise ships like termites is partly responsible for this mire," Vicki said, shaking her head as if movement could erase the sight, "what a nasty suppurating town." "Yes," I said as we turned back to Smith Bridge. On the bank of the Waaigat a gumbo limbo was pink with berries. Across a curb someone planted a row of neem trees, the sight as medicinal as the seeds of the trees themselves detoxifying opprobrium.

The popular and simple beguiles travelers more often than the grand. To appreciate the sublime, one needs leisure to study, something cruisers lack as they bustle frenetically from one port to another. Both the exterior and the interior of the Cathedral of Our Lady of Guadalupe in Ponce were luminously blue and airy. Light flowed honeyed into the nave. If one paused and sat in a pew, the travel day's gray-water vanished, and the moment like Wordsworth's beauteous evening turned poetic. Alas, I didn't linger to appreciate buttresses and spandrels, digital and transverse ribs. Instead I hurried across Degetau Plaza to Isabel Munoz-Rivera. Parked along the street a hundred yards from the entrance to the cathedral was the Barber on Wheels, a white E350 Ford van. I'd seen librarians and nurses on wheels but never a barber, and I looked at the truck more carefully than at the cathedral. Attached to the frame outside the window on the passenger's side of the front seat wasn't a mirror but a barber's pole with its recognizable helix of red, white and blue stripes. In a side window a neon side flashed announcing in red letters that the truck was open. On other windows the barber had painted inspirational statements, among others "God Has Control" and "Why Get Desperate." The statements were in Spanish, and a policeman translated them, adding that the barber was good and that during lunch customers lined up outside the truck. A sign near the front door announced that WiFi was free. To enter the box compartment, one opened the front door on the passenger's side of the van then turned left and walked up two steps. Inside the box at the rear was a conventional barber's chair. Along each side of the interior were big windows, benches on which customers sat, a stand of magazines, and a rack of sundry packets of Lay's Potato Chips. "That's one for the scrapbook," I said to Vicki as we sauntered away from the truck. "Scrap is right," Vicki answered. "But then," I thought but didn't say, "our lives are shreds and leavings. Cruising is a metaphor for life — in sight today, over the horizon tomorrow, then beyond bridgeless Dreamland and forgotten."

Holly cut my hair six weeks before I left Storrs. If she had not, I'd have visited the barber on wheels. "An excursion few cruise passengers have purchased," I said. Although years have put the occasional hitch in our strides, Vicki and I were not as sedentary as I implied earlier. We remained ramblers, exploring out of the way places in which we were the only tourists. Moreover, I behaved thoughtlessly booking a climb to the top of La Grande Soufriere, an active volcano on Basse-Terre in Guadeloupe, at 1487 meters the highest peak in the Lesser Antilles. When I told Vicki about the excursion, I did not give her a chance to express doubt. Instead I gushed ahead and quoted George Linnaeus Banks's poetry: "My home is on the mountain steep, / Far away—far away, / Where the playful Chamois leap, / All the day—all the day."

Banks stated he imagined that climbing every "Alpine height / Led away in Fancy's flight." On the actual hike muscle and grit mattered more than fancy. The climb began at a parking lot in a rain forest and took Vicki and me two-and-a-half hours. The climb started slowly but then turned sharply upward leaving the rain forest and grinding through scrub, carpets of mud, and a rock quarry of slippery wet and moss-covered, pelvis-smashing stones. Winds blew in hard staccato bursts, and rain came and went soaking and slapping us. Fog and clouds suddenly covered us then just as suddenly lifted and disappeared. On some parts of the path we crawled on hands and knees, and on most of the upper portions we tottered rather than walked, leaning against rock faces and grabbing saplings using them as crutches. The top of the volcano was a quarry of tossed boulders, and vents discharging sulfurous steam. I leaned over several vents and breathed in as much steam as I could stand. We returned the way we ascended taking almost two hours, my legs quivering. I fell once, digging a long furrow into the shin of my right leg and knocking my thigh hard against a protruding outcrop.

Vicki and I held up well, however, she because she

is eleven years younger than me, and I, probably because I run five or six miles every weekday in Storrs.
At the end of the climb I would have felt exhilarated if
I'd had the strength. As it was, I bent over like Rodin's
Thinker, flexed my right arm, and said, "You are the
boy." Of course, at 76 I wasn't either *the* or *a* boy, and
the trek almost convinced me to temper my imaginary
wanderings and certainly to cancel an actual wandering.
I'd contemplated joining an excursion in May, walking
for some twenty days six or seven hours a day across
an Australian desert accompanying a train of camels. I
now realized that I lacked the endurance. "Maybe so,"
Vicki said cheery after accomplishing the climb, adding,
"but wouldn't it be better to die in a desert listening to
the grunts of camels and watching wedge-tailed eagles
circling overhead eager to make you a meal rather than
dripping boneless in a hospice?" Yes, it would be better.
Occasionally the grinding of joints and the washboard
wringing of muscles awaken libido moriendi. Not long
ago in the university locker room, I said, "I'm so tired
of pain that I think I'll skip taking a shower and just go
home and douse the lights." "Don't let people hear you
say things like that," a man dressing nearby said. "One
morning at breakfast I dropped my cereal bowl on the
floor and in exasperation said I was going to blow my
brains out, and my wife—former wife—called the police
out of maliciousness. The bitch knew I wasn't serious.
I realized later that she was stock-piling grounds for
divorce. Anyway, the police came and refused to listen
when I said I talked in hyperbole. They stuffed me in the
back of a patrol car and carted me off to a psychiatric
hospital. A psychiatrist quizzed me for two humiliating
hours, and I wasn't released until after dinner." "What's
the big deal?" Vicki said after I described the man's
discomfort. "Outside the Bible Belt the punishment for
committing suicide isn't severe—almost never any jail
time, usually a small fine, a hundred dollars or so the
amount comparable to the penalty for being nabbed
smoking marijuana."

Alpenglow occurs when the rising or setting sun is below the horizon, and its light backscatters turning clouds rosy. I am in my alpenglow years. My sun is setting, but every so often its light deceives me. I mistake the glow under darkening clouds for energy and forgetting age behave injudiciously, for example, climbing La Soufriere. Alpenglow does more, however, than provoke sporadic foolish behavior; it colors my perception of the natural world. As I approach the end of my long journey, things that I ignored in younger days glow with a magnetic appeal. Perhaps they draw me because I like to think that in man's fretful unstable world some things endure. Perhaps the natural functions as an anchor-hold that I can grab and which steadies me as the secular withdraws from my presence. Maybe the glow is merely the residue of a continuum. Since boyhood I've looked at insects and birds, chewed wild berries and leaves, run my palms across tree trucks, and smelled the fragrance of droppings and flowers. I've listened to the screams of dying rabbits and tracked snakes by ear through leaves and high grass. Rarely have I analyzed. Being aware satisfied me. Perhaps I was too lazy to dissect or maybe I took Thoreau's call to simplify too literally, limiting appreciation to surface description. But then, maybe the concept of depth is itself a fiction, and that the superficial is the magical real.

In Tobago, Fort King George overlooked Scarborough and the windward coast. The orange and red bricks in the restored buildings looked like baked loaves. From the fort an eiderdown of land and sea rumpled green and blue across the distance. Yet what attracted me more were nearby trees, great raintrees and royal Poinciana. I had seen such trees on many islands; yet, in my alpenglow years these trees radiated rooted warmth, heat that helped forge the pleasing fictions that tourist moments were abiding and that if my hearing and sight were better, I'd spot Amaryllis sitting in their shade playing his oaten pipe. Above Port Elizabeth the view from Battery Hill across Admiralty Bay beyond to Princess Margaret Beach on Bequia opened like a glossy magazine foldout. Yet what held my attention longer was the glow of scratchy hillside scrub: scarlet fairy dusters, prickly pear, jittering bushes of red and yellow dwarf Poinciana, organ pipe cactus springing from the slope irregular and unkept, then nearby a single papaya, the fruits full and bosomy, hanging down like the breasts of a primitive Venus.

On the islands I did not spot the fabled fiduciary tree, the foliage of which was money rather than leaves, but which turned into leaves when a person tried to spend them. Neither did I notice the most profitable branch of that taxonomic family, the tree whose leaves became money after being washed in goat's milk and carried to the bank. No one pointed out the tree the sap of which blackened the hands of beer jerkers and rum suckers but which soothed the calloused palms of peacemakers and the pure in heart. Although I scanned groves, I did not glimpse any of those fabulous fish that nested in the crowns of trees and hatched schools of golden minnows. And as improbably as this may be to believe because I ate trenchers of coconut meat, I did not run across the tiny flying fish that spawn and hatch in the nuts. Pestiferous coconut mites infest young nuts. After draining a nut's milk, the mites bore through the fiber surrounding the shell. The mites then follow each other in a line out of the nut, leaving behind a single hole. During rainstorms, water drips through the hole into the nut forming a pool. Once pools are formed, fish enter some of the nuts. Scientists do not agree on how the fish manage to reach the tops of coconut palms. Some say they fly riding high winds like gliders, others that they crawl up the trunks of the trees using their fins like hands and legs. The most popular hunch is that storms sweep roe off fronds and perhaps off the surface of the ocean itself. The eggs become enclosed in gouts of water like fish in aquariums, and during downpours some of the egg-laden water drops through the holes into the cavities of the nuts.

Not seeing fabulous trees and the almost-mythological creatures associated with them did not disappoint me greatly. Fabled plants are never as remarkable as actual plants. To take two small examples, Ant Plant and Bull Thorn Acacia. Ant Plant is an epiphyte, that is, a plant that grows on another plant but is not parasitic. Ant Plant's stems swell into gray, rounded woody structures. While the outsides of the structures are bumpy and hard like the rind of Blue Hubbard squash, the insides are tangles of hollow tunnels. Ants live in the tunnels. The tunnels provide shelter. In return the ants defend the plants from herbivores. The ants also deposit their waste in the tunnels. In the tunnels are glands which absorb the nutrients in the droppings and recycle them converting them into plant food. On Bull-Thorn Acacia pairs of spines jut out from the stems then pinch inward curving like the racks of horns that adorn longhorn cattle. The spines are partly hollow and are inhabited by ants. At the ends of leaves on the acacia are small yellow detachable tips. Filled with sugars and proteins, the tips supply resident ants with food. In return the ants protect the acacia from hungry grazers.

No matter what a person misses noticing, in his alpenglow years lonely sauntering waxes alluring. One longs for loose ends and gladly misses the prick and stitch of binding conversation. On Catalina Island off the coast of the Dominican Republic, I wandered the rough coral bush by myself. In losing others I discovered Key treecactus, its trunk medieval and metallic with spines, arms breaking and grappling upward in gauntlets. The limbs of catclaw blackbead twisted through themselves in an impenetrable maze. Over them draped curtains of small green leaves, most splotched by leaf miners. The coppery trunks on a stand of gumbo limbo cast pink shadows on the bark of poison ash. Flowers spilled out in white ribbons from Caribbean princewood after which the petals curled back resembling ornate calligraphy.

As I looked at trees, life itself bloomed. Hatchings

of cabbage white butterflies swirled aloft then toppled down in mating frenzies. While gracile anoles clung immobile to trees, masked curly-tailed lizards wound their tails up over their backs exposing the undersides and forming orange circles. I stuffed bits of coral in my pockets, and as I bent to pick up a lump of brain coral, I saw a gaudy sphinx moth, an insect lovelier than any jewelry sold in the tourist streets of island towns. The moth's body and forewings were forest or fern green, muted and natural. In contrast to the wings of many moths, they were not a mélange of lines and colors reminding one of a modernist "composition." The moth kept its forewings folded back, but if spread their span would have been four-and-a-half inches. Beneath the wings were flashes of yellow and flax while the spiracles along the sides were bone white, as were the tops of the moth's legs, "puttees for the thighs," Vicki said. We Pickerings are, I should add, an insect family, though our second son Edward ameliorates his enthusiasm with a regard for snakes. For Christmas, Francis, our older boy, gave his sister Eliza cicada earrings that he found in New York in an antique shop, good size bugs, two inches long and noticeable as they jangled around Eliza's neck. For her part Eliza sent me a white Chinese cricket dish an inch and a quarter in diameter, its sides half an inch high. Across the bowl of the dish flew a golden-brown scarab beetle, its wings spread looking like waning crescent moons. Eliza purchased the dish in a cricket shop in Shanghai. While in China, Eliza met Annie a successful developer who frequented the cricket market. At the market she purchased "the casualties of fights," crickets who lost matches and were missing antennae or legs. Annie took them home and turned them out to pasture in her penthouse garden. "Better to hobble around a rooftop garden than to live out one's life as a winner in a tiny coffin-like box, tickled into mad rages," Eliza stated.

Accompanying the dish were the innards of Robert Sherard's translation of Tcheng-Ki-Tong's *Chin-chin;*

or, The Chinaman at Home. Eliza found the volume in a junk store in San Francisco. *Chin-chin* appeared in 1895 and hadn't weathered Time's Great Leap Forward well. Its front board, half the back board, and a signature of front pages were missing. "Look at Chapter 36," Eliza instructed. The chapter described cricket and quail fights. Cricket fights were especially popular. "The modest denizens of the grass are terrible fighters," Sherard wrote, "good company as they are." After catching crickets in the field, devotees lodged them in small bamboo cages, fed them a healthy diet of "grains of rice to which a few leaves of salad are added," and trained them rigorously, scheduling intramural conditioning fights. Each fight pitted two crickets against each other, one of the participants often a veteran of the cricket-ring. Gladiatorial rings consisted of wooden bowls the surfaces of which prevented the fighters from "slipping about too much." To arouse combatants "to a sufficient degree of hated and bad feeling," trainers tickled their heads with hairs. The fights themselves were brief. On being released by their handlers, the crickets immediately raced across the bowls and dashed against each other. The collision knocked one fighter over ending the match. While "the vanquished withdraws, ashamed and resigned," Shepard wrote, "the victor, intoxicated with delight, claps his hands, and celebrates his triumph with piercing cries." If a cricket proved a robust fighter, he was promoted out of the training league and into the public ring where he displayed his talents to punters and spectators. Although the amounts wagered were small, betters placed them "with as much interest and passion as in Europe are made about horses."

Vicki and I spent a day in Tobago traveling from Scarborough to Charlotteville along the Windward Road. We rode in a van named Gethsemane after the garden at the foot of the Mount of Olives in which Jesus prayed following the Last Supper and in which he was betrayed by Judas. On the drive I didn't experience the numinous. But when I glanced at trees, moments blossomed. I watched a copper-rumped hummingbird forage through a noni. The bird's green back shined like a gilded shield while its wings were a dark angelic blue, the bird's severe activity bringing judgment and Adam and Eve's expulsion from Eden to mind. As I pushed aside a slab of mystery fish in a seaside restaurant at Tyrrell's Bay, I noticed a tropical mockingbird perched on the limb of an almond tree. The bird's breast was white and full like a wave gathering to break and roll toward a shore. "Such birds are drops for dry eyes and minds," Vicki said. After Vicki and I climbed La Soufriere, we ate at a picnic table at the edge of a wood. Actually, we were too tired to eat. Instead we played with the meal, listlessly turning over spoons of rice and chicken. We were careless, and when we spilled a few grains of rice on the ground, birds appeared, mostly sparrows, but among them, two that brought alpenglow back to the day: a lesser Antillean bullfinch its coat black like that worn by waiters at formal dinners, tucked under its beak not a black bow tie and the top of a white shirt but a scarlet napkin. The second was a brown trembler — an elegant picnic crasher, a bird which I had never seen. Its coat was a subdued rufous-and-gray comforter. Gold monocles circled its eyes, and its bill curved over and down giving the bird a haughty aristocratic appearance, at least until it shuffled its wings downward and raised its tail into the semblance of a folded hand fan. Then the trembler looked slightly goofy, less a source of alpenglow than a table companion who'd laugh at my jokes.

I hoped Vicki and I would return home refreshed — so greened that we could resist the turning of place. That, of course, was naïve as was the metaphor of the lathe. Life is a tangle. Metaphors are useful in teasing out loose threads, but the chaotic knot itself resists tweezering. We landed in Hartford at midnight the day after a storm dropped a foot of snow on Connecticut. For the third cruise year in a row, the doors to our car were frozen and the battery dead. The temperature was six degrees, and as we drove home along the barren highway at three o'clock avoiding ice patches, a red light on the dashboard flashed warning that the car was about to die. "Oh, God," I moaned, words I repeat endlessly during winter. Once home, the car coughed and died, but Francis saved me from self-murder. He had driven across the state and shoveled the drive. The next day he drove Vicki to fetch the dogs and arranged for Marty to resuscitate the car. In our absence he even installed a new hard drive in my computer. Before going to bed that first night, I deleted every email from my computer — unread, something I always do after a trip. Mail, however, covered the kitchen table. I dumped several pounds of catalogues and solicitations in the recycle bin. I did not count the items, but the pile was fourteen and three-quarter inches high. I set aside a rack of magazines to read during next week. The week passed without my having perused a single magazine, so I threw them away also, not bothering to glance at the covers or measure the stack.

The day after arriving home I read the few items that remained. No bills were due, but Vicki and I received new medical insurance cards. I put mine in my wallet and laid Vicki's on the dining room table, urging her not to delay burying it in her purse. An old rowing friend sent a medical column clipped from an underground paper published in San Francisco. Despite the presence of untold numbers of chickens, pigeons, and pigs, flu, the newspaper recounted, was almost unheard of in China's Guizhou Province. The populace wore face masks, but more importantly they recognized that urine was an effective anti-viral. In the morning before eating breakfast people slathered their hands with urine and throughout the day kept the flu at arm's length by sprinkling their fingers. "Another incidence of the advantages of wealth and being able to afford servants to cater one's needs," Vicki said, "the contemporary Chinese equivalent of the British wet nurse."

From South Carolina Edward sent a photograph of a copperhead he unearthed while digging a garden plot in his backyard. The snake lay coiled a foot underground in brumation, Edward said, using the technical word that describes the slowing of a snake's metabolism in winter. The copperhead was cold and did not respond when Edward touched it. Edward couldn't tell if the snake was alive or dead, but assuming it would die if left exposed. he shoveled it up and put it in a cardboard box on his screened porch. "Off the ground and out of the wind in a spot warmed by the sun," he wrote. Edward then went back to the garden and dug for another hour. On returning to the house, he examined the snake. Sunlight had not affected it. The snake hadn't moved, and even though its body "almost glistened," it looked dead. To make sure, Edward picked it up and undid the coils. "My copperhead wasn't dead because it had never lived," Edward wrote. "It was a toy snake — two and a half feet long with a rough wedge-shaped head and brownish red skin marked by scales as distinct as tire treads. It was very realistic, but it was still a toy. When and how did it slither into my garden? To prevent it from crawling outdoors and springing at me when I'm stringing up beans or sowing seeds for squash, I keep it inside the house in the shower."

When Vicki walked into the study bringing me a cup of tea, I read her Edward's letter "He's a little odd," I said. "Huh," Vicki snorted. "The stolon doesn't stray far from the crown." Sliding down from the top of a bookcase behind her was the rubber skeleton of a Halloween cobra. The skeleton was forty inches long and below the head was a chain composed of forty-six vertebrae. The cobra's eye sockets were dark pits. Its hood was spread in alarum, and its mouth hinged and open exposing two sharp curved fangs. I bought the snake at the downtown CVS pharmacy. Before Halloween, the pharmacy sold a haunted shelf of rubber skeletons, among others, those of rats, ravens, giant cockroaches suckled on chemicals, rabid bats spreading their wings, and cats snarling and arching their backs turning their rib cages into pronged reaping hooks. Some skeletons cost twenty-five dollars. After Halloween prices dropped to ten and fifteen dollars. Slowly the skeletons vanished until only that of the snake remained. The price tag had fallen off its hood. "This baby isn't going to sell," I told the clerk, wrapping the skeleton around my neck. "I'll give you a dollar for it, sparing you the trouble of clearing it off the shelf. I've handled serpents since Sunday School, and the snake won't nip me. But if you pick it up you are liable to receive an unforgettable love bite." The clerk studied me for a moment then agreed, and I paid a dollar — well, a dollar and six cents after sales tax was included.

Vicki's and my appearance at home did not go unnoticed. Josh sent me a clipping from yet another op-ed page. The writer noted that revoking honorary degrees awarded to people who later proved miscreants had become epizootic. "But why be faint-hearted and stop with rescinding honorary degrees?" the man wrote. "Universities should act boldly. They should cry 'excelsior' and forging onward and upward revoke graduate and undergraduate degrees as well. Malfeasance and malpractice permeate society. Demanding the return of mobs of sheepskins would be gratifyingly just and endlessly entertaining. Moreover, it would foster stability. By distracting moralists from military adventurism and the failings of government, it would nurture illusions of peace and happiness, and, above all, stimulate the stock market." Before I read the clipping to Vicki, Todd telephoned to inform me that my free wellness package was ready to be mailed. Todd is getting long in the tooth; he has called me since 2013. I told Vicki that his persistence was admirable, and he deserved a reward. "Yes," Vicki said, "a jail cell, the sound of telephones piped in and ringing twenty-four hours a day, twenty-five hours if possible."

After we had been home for a fortnight, Josh sent

a present, this, he instructed, to be glued to the chassis of my lawnmower. In a honky-tonk souvenir store, he purchased a plastic strip three inches tall and a foot long and painted white so that from a distance it looked like a metal plate. Pressed into it were the raised letters of a statement that began, "Beware of Attack." On the plate Josh sent Vicki and me the next word was "Republican." Other plates warned people against assault by a zoo of creatures, these including: Jackass, Waitress, Bee, Frog, Hamster, Mosquito, Asshole, and Democrat. What was discouraging was that the store had sold no more signs alerting people to the danger of Attack Republicans than to that of Attack Democrats.

One of our first callers was a nameless financial Samaritan keen to warn me that my Microsoft license was about to expire. The Samaritan was hyper-benevolent. Hours after calling me, she telephoned my friends David and Raymond and alerted them. The secretary of the local veterinarian also called asking us to update her records for "the darlings of the house." In our absence the snow blower had come down with the croup, and Vicki was outside putting it in the back of the car, so I supplied the information. "I am the house hound and am six feet one in carpet slippers and weigh 185 pounds. I have been vaccinated and have never found tape or round worms in my business. At least twice a year, 'virtucrats' make me feverish, and I suffer from distempered moods," I said, pausing to catch my breath and sentences. "I used to be the handsomest man in Tennessee but now my looks have gone to the bow-wows," I continued before breaking down. "No, Sam, not puppy chow already? We just got home," Vicki said after I described the call.

"Most old people chirp," I replied mixing animal kingdom metaphors, "but until all my feathers are plucked and I am completely addled and fall off the perch, I'm going to yap and scamper, chasing the tail ends of paragraphs and digging up verbicides." That night the telephone rang during dinner. Vicki answered the phone. It was the eighth time in four days that a fundraiser called soliciting money for a conservation group. All the calls came from the 412 area code; attached to them was the prefix PIC, the first three letters of our last name. Vicki began by chirping mildly, saying that we didn't respond to the ministrations of telephone canvassers and suggested that the charity contact us by mail. When the solicitor ignored Vicki's response and battered on into a searing description of the misdeeds of agri-business, Vicki snarled. "Your charity my bottom! Didn't you understand what I said?" Vicki shouted, her voice a bark that would have made a Rottweiler tuck his tail between his legs and slink away. "I'm goddamned tired of your telephone calls! If you call again, I won't give another penny to your fucking charity!" "Well, Vicki," I said after she slammed receiver down in its cradle, "not that kind of language already?" "Yes, and yes again," Vicki said, "and if Todd calls once more, I'm going to tell him where he can stuff his headset. My directions will be explicit and in short declarative sentences that cannot be misunderstood—just the sort of prose you admire." "All right," I replied, "but please don't say anything about his mother." "I won't," Vicki said, "but it is open season on the grandmothers of shysters."

The day after settling in, I wrote notes wishing "Happy New Year" to nineteen people who sent us Christmas cards. I enclosed the notes in cards on the front of which appeared reproductions of ferns painted by William Jackson Hooker in the 19th century. Two days after returning I resumed running and discovered that two acquaintances died. Neither jogged, so the population of Road Widows in Tolland County did not increase. I read the men's obituaries and again concluded that more was less. During the initial week home, I received a letter from Doris, a friend from graduate school. She and her husband Jake lived in Boston. Each year they wintered on Sanibel Island. In November Jake felt poorly, but he refused to let health delay their trip south. "Jake," Doris wrote, "is in a hospice. He looks peaceful. In the spring I will have a memorial service. I will let you know the exact date later." Back-gate exits were on my mind. I had just written a letter of condolence to Mickey whose wife died after suffering from dementia for eleven years. Mickey answered by return mail, thanking me for my letter and saying, "I'm doing well, having had more than enough time to prepare for this loss."

Death's dislocations often ripple beyond family. In my case they often make me aware that the differences between the contemporary South and my old South are so great that no sentimental bridge can link them together. A fortnight after arriving home, I received a letter from Frank, an acquaintance who lived in Columbia, South Carolina. Once upon a time I knew Frank and Harwood his college roommate. Frank wrote to tell me Harwood died. "He had a heart attack," Frank said, then mused, "We have reached the age when friends are sinking out of sight. I hate it, but because of what Jesus did for us upon the cross, I will have all eternity to be with my roomy again. If you know any good jokes, please send them to me. I am making a collection to tell Harwood once I join him." "That's a slice of the entire country's daily bread, not just beaten biscuit from the South," Vicki said when I read her Frank's letter. She then opened her purse and pulled out a magenta pencil. Staggering along the body of the pencil were yellow footprints and white cloud-like words reading "Walk With Jesus." "Handed to me by a man at the entrance to Price Chopper," Vicki said, adding, "it's not my Wonder Bread. I prefer bagels."

In Dog Lane Café, I bumped into Neil, a fellow retiree. As usual Neil had a cuckoo bee in his ear. Neil's preoccupation wasn't wacky because it was irrational but on the contrary cuckoo because it was so rational. In December his former department asked him to teach a course at a branch of the university. Because of the drive, "they" offered him ten thousand dollars instead of the usual seventy-five hundred. I agreed to teach, Neil recounted, "with the proviso that the university offer more equitable remuneration." The school pays the men's basketball coach three million dollars to coach a team that plays thirty games a year, "give or take a quarter of million dollars or a handful of games." "I marshalled my actuarial skills and agreed to teach, selflessly requesting to be paid only what the coach received for one game," Neil said, "sweetening the deal by noting that I'd teach fifty students without the aid of assistant coaches, 'life-skills' counselors, publicists, adjuncts, trainers, graders, physicians, policemen or equipment managers." "How has the drive been to the branch campus?" I asked. "Not tiring," Neil answered, "surprisingly easy."

A week after we returned home, Vicki drove to the Co-op to buy granola. I accompanied her. Winter had not affected the sign, and it was still in place accosting people at the front door. The next day Vicki drove to Buckland Mall in Manchester to look for snow boots. I stayed home and for the third time read J. Meade Falkner's *Moonfleet*. The novel was as familiar as the ports our ships visited, and I assumed I'd spend becalmed hours drifting through pages being entertained by constellation-crossed lovers and romantic smugglers. Alas, the day was not as relaxed as I anticipated. Midway through the afternoon I took a break from reading. I ate a bowl of chocolate ice cream and two Milano cookies after which I checked Vicki's and my credit card account to ensure no bills from the cruises were outstanding. When I did so, I spotted a charge pending for "Sarku Japan." The amount was small, but crooks, I once read, tested purloined card numbers by first making insignificant purchases. If the purchases rolled through unchallenged, a deluge of whopping charges followed. I immediately telephoned Bank of America. "Sarku Japan, probably a suburb of Tokyo," I said when a woman took my call, my voice wobbly because while waiting to talk to someone at the bank I imagined thievery draining our checking account like a doctor opening an abscess. "My wife and I live in Storrs, Connecticut, and an ocean and a continent separate us from Japan," I continued. "Our card number must have grown teletype wings." "Sometimes cards move faster than Olympic athletes," the woman said, "let me look at the charge. Just stay on the line." After a minute, she returned to the phone. "Sarku Japanese Restaurant in Manchester, Connecticut," she said. "Oh — oh, dear," I said, "my wife is in Manchester trying on waterproof boots. She must have bought Japanese takeout for lunch." "I hope she enjoyed the food and that she found good boots," the woman said, a smile light in her voice.

Vicki did not bring home leftovers from the restaurant, and I did not mention my calling Bank of America. The following evening as she cooked dinner, I read her an excerpt from Jerome K. Jerome's *Anthony John*. In the selection young Anthony asked his uncle Joseph Newt why he wasn't religious and why he didn't believe what people in the neighborhood believed. Newt replied that his neighbors were not actually religious and said they attended chapel only in order "to get something out of it." "If they believed all they say that they believe," Newt declared, "this world would be a very different place to what it is." "Is the book good?" Vicki asked when I stopped reading. "The section I read you is very good, but otherwise, the book is ghastly," I replied. "Well then," Vicki said, "the broccoli rabe is ready. Make yourself useful. See if you can find an entertaining show for us to watch on Netflix." "For dessert," she continued. "we'll sample the chocolate rum cake you bought on Grand Cayman. I'll whip some cream and brew a cup of Columbian coffee."

"Yummy," I said getting up from the table, the gospel song "I saw the light" unaccountably running through my mind as I left the kitchen. "I saw the light. I saw the light. / No more darkness. No more night." "Naïve," I muttered, thinking of Newt's statement after which my thoughts fluttered back to the Caribbean. I watched black vultures fan their wings to catch the morning sun at the entrance to the Panama Canal, the tips of their primaries gloved and dirty white. Next, I glimpsed a yellow-headed cara-cara atop a fence post near the Chagres River. "Just out of the beauty parlor, its bangs dyed and looking punk," Vicki said at the time. "Remember the man in Ponce who asked me how much Puerto Rican dollars were worth in comparison to American dollars," I shouted from the study after turning on the television, "and how about the millipede on the rock beside us as we rested under tree ferns in Hunte's Gardens in Barbados? You said it was the color of dark eggplant. I said it looked like an anteater's tongue." "I think I remember," Vicki said, "but anyway dinner's ready. Come get your plate."

Eureka I

For thirty-five years Vicki and I summered in Four Winds a rambling old house in Beaver River, Nova Scotia that her parents bought in 1947. Last summer from the July 31st through the 8th of September family members spent every day and night with us. They brought kayaks, mountain bikes, dogs, spouses, recollections of carefree childhoods, and then scrapbooks of exhausting expectations. Built in the 1860s, Four Winds was a sea captain's house with a backhouse and barn attached. Keeping the house clean was impossible. The roof and windows leaked; ceilings peeled; walls shredded, and molding collapsed. During winter mice and red squirrels moved into seasonal apartments, and in the spring scores of spiders spun webs, caught insects, and raised offspring. Dirt seeped between the clapboards and rose from the basement through the floor. Putting the house in livable order took a month. Trunks had to be unpacked, sheets and blankets cleaned, furniture uncovered, pictures hung, and rooms appointed with the necessary remembrances of years past.

Years wore the design off the linoleum on the kitchen floor and during storms the window frames shook and knocked. At dinner, family sat around a long oval wooden table covered with an oilcloth, its pattern red and white and recognizable to people familiar with nineteenth-century narrative paintings. In the middle of the table sat a Lazy Susan, loaded with spices, honey, and preserves. Vicki cooked on an old wood stove, secondhand when we bought it twenty-two years ago. The stove's firebox was small, and the bricks lining the oven were cracked. As a result, while bringing a pot of water to a boil was difficult, baking was impossible. Preparing a meal for several people was tiring and required agile hands and a nimble planning mind. Organizing involved more than shifting pans, and Vicki had to consider people's dietary preferences: vegetarian, vegan, meat lover, gluten free, sugarless, and a pantry of allergies. After the meal was over and dishes washed and put away, the cast iron top of the stove had to be scrubbed and blackened.

The house had one bathroom. The tub and toilet were ancient and because water from the well was laden with iron were streaked with brown. For its part the hot water heater was over fifty years old. Baths had to be scheduled, and people urged to conserve water. What cannot be accurately described were worries: will the innards of the stove collapse? will the water heater rupture and die? The septic field had not been touched since long before I married Vicki in 1979. Suppose the influx of family overloaded the septic tank — what then? When people visited, Vicki worried constantly about something breaking and ruining their vacations. For the record she did not worry about me. During summers I always limited ablutions and grew rank and moldy. Regarding other Necessary House doings: I had not urinated inside for thirty years, and insofar as the second matter — well, forty acres of field and wood soft with sphagnum moss abutted the house.

Last summer's continual presence of visitors exhausted Vicki, and in September she was eager for her holiday to end so she could recuperate in Connecticut. "We are not going to Canada next summer," she announced. "I want to stay in Storrs and tidy 23 Hillside Circle, and," she added, "you'll have to vanish." I remonstrated with her pointing out that I was 76 with a bad heart and like the wood stove liable to collapse at any moment. Assuming I'd be in good enough health in two years to return to Nova Scotia was naïve. I read her a letter from Joyce, the wife of Abner, a friend from Nashville. "Abner has gotten a motorized wheelchair," Joyce wrote. "Now we can go on walks together." I told her what Rosie told me about Don her husband. Don was a difficult man, always angry and disturbed by a slew of things. Two years ago, he began suffering from dementia. On returning from Four Winds, I learned that he was in a nursing home. "Don has no idea who or where he is, but he smiles all the time," Rosie said. "I didn't know he had such a nice smile. I've never seen him so calm and happy." Vicki is eleven years younger than me, and for her mortality and catastrophic diseases are not imminent presences. "Oh, you'll be around in two years blathering and pontificating," she said. "It's now that I want you gone."

People are their DNA. Vicki was her mother's daughter. Vicki's mother expelled her father from their home in Princeton several times. Often, he rusticated in England, and twice he joined Vicki and me and our children in Nova Scotia. Once he camped in a bed-sitter on Nassau Street around the corner from his house. I was accustomed to Vicki's wanting "space." At her urging in past years I'd spent five months in Australia, four in Scotland, and one at the Writers' Colony at Dairy Hollow in Eureka Springs, Arkansas. I told curious friends that I wanted to give Vicki practice in being a widow, a remark that deflected concern into laughter. In truth I enjoyed the forced absences. I thrived and wrote books describing my meanderings. However, over a decade had passed since the last banishing, and I was older in muscle and brain. Spontaneity now distressed me, and I worried that I wasn't limber enough to transform the unexpected into delight. On one occasion Vicki's father took a month-long cruise. I tried to do the same. Early in July Holland America's *Rotterdam* left Boston on a thirty-eight-day return trip dubbed the Voyage of the Vikings. The ship sailed up the coast of Eastern Canada then over to Greenland, Iceland, Ireland, Scotland, and Scandinavia. I asked Vicki to accompany me on the cruise, but she refused reiterating her intention to spend summer at home. I then tried to book the cruise for myself thinking my being gone for thirty-eight days would satisfy Vicki. Although I'd been a customer for many years, had lectured on Holland America's ships, and despite rooms being available, the company insisted on charging me the price of a cabin for two people, all cabins being doubles. If, for example, the price for each person was $5000 then the single traveler paid $10,000. Sometimes cruise lines adjusted prices either charging the lone traveler the price for one person or an amount somewhere between the $5000 and the $10,000. Because Holland America was inflexible, I remained a Puritan and did not become a Viking. I was miffed, however, and as angry as Grendel's Mother.

Vicki belongs to that select group of wives more sentimental about cars than about husbands. I bought our Volvo in 2005. Although it had been driven only 85,000 miles, I lost confidence in it. During the past four years the electrical system shorted out three times causing three batteries to die. On four occasions mechanical ailments forced us to telephone AAA and ask a mechanic to come to the house. Practically every time, we started on a trip longer than fifty miles, a red warning light seemed to flash on the dashboard, demanding that we "Check Engine." The shock absorbers clattered; the brake pads had thinned, and the axle leaked. Even worse, age made my getting out of the car progressively difficult. The Volvo was low to the ground, and to escape the driver's seat, I had to swing my legs to the left twisting my back into the lumbar equivalent of the child's Indian Burn. Next, I planted my feet flat on the garage floor and pushed myself up, one hand on the headrest atop my seat, the other on the armrest on the door. "In the future the only way I'll be able get out of this damn seat," I told Vicki, "is if I install a derrick in the garage."

The time had come to buy a new car. I assumed Vicki thought like me and could not imagine risking calm of mind by driving the Volvo to Nova Scotia. Here I miscalculated and underestimated Vicki's affection for the car.

For me a car was a household device, to be sure bigger and more expensive that a washing machine but nonetheless a machine, not bone and pulsing blood, but barren steel and aluminum. For Vicki a car was — well, I don't know — something mystical and mysterious. I thought that if I purchased a reliable new car, certainly one easier on the spine, then Vicki might change her mind and decide to return to Four Winds. In June I bought a Subaru Outback and traded in the Volvo. I realized I was in trouble when Vicki wished the Volvo well, told it goodbye, kissed it on the hood, and took an album of pictures of it. When I returned from the dealer with the new car, Vicki was simmering, a condition made worse by my thinking her reaction inexplicable.

Book learning is suspect. But would that I'd read Alexander McCall Smith's *The Saturday Big Tent Wedding* before trading in the Volvo. At the beginning of the novel, after Precious Ramotswe's ancient white van appeared to have suffered its final breakdown, her husband bought her a new blue van. Precious tried to seem grateful but found it difficult. "Her van had been her companion and friend for many years," Smith recounted. "Can a vehicle — a collection of mechanical bits and pieces, nuts and bolts and parts the names of which one has not the faintest idea of — can such a thing be a friend?" he asked rhetorically. "Of course it can," he wrote answering his own question. "Physical objects can have personalities, at least in the eyes of their owners. To others, it may be only a van, but to the owner it may be the friend that has started loyally each morning — except sometimes." Like a person, a car, he declared, "may have likes and dislikes." Smooth and pot-holed roads affected cars differently, he elaborated, the latter provoking "rattles and groans of protest from even the most tolerant of vehicles." "For this reason," Smith wrote, "the owners of cars may be forgiven for thinking that under the metal there lurks something not all that different from a human soul." What became obvious once the Volvo disappeared was that I erred. Instead of ridding the garage of an unreliable car, I sold a friend down the river and had to get out of Storrs. Vicki refused to drive the new car. Devices such as a GPS and side view mirrors that flashed warning the driver not to change lanes — devices that made driving easier and safer — irritated her. "I'd rather watch *The Bachelorette* than read *Consumer Reports*," she said. Meals were quieter than empty confessionals. The only thing we did as a couple was walk the dogs. Then Vicki strode so far ahead that the dogs became confused and exhausted themselves yo-yoing back and forth between us.

Before buying the Subaru, I thought I might be able to creep through summer without having to leave town. I was content at home. Every morning five days a week I jogged four miles with my friend David. During afternoons I rode my bicycle across the campus stopping at gardens and smelling flowers. My small chores around the house gratified me, more, I suppose, than they should have: picking up sticks and limbs, trimming shrubs, mowing grass, digging stumps, hoeing poison ivy, and managing compost and dogs, putting the latter outside at six in the morning then cleaning after them, shoveling and tossing droppings into the wood behind the house. I mulled familiar matters, wondering, for example, if I would have become a more intelligent adult if I'd been a less successful student. I remained ambivalent, a satisfying state of mind because, as I also mulled, conclusions were artificial — psychological artifacts, stoppers that plugged streams of thought before they bucketed upward and swept away serenity.

Every other day I went to the university library. In the stacks I unearthed books which had never been checked out, but which interested me, among them, Rex Beach's *The Crimson Gardenia*, a collection of short stories published in 1916. Born in 1877 Beach had been an athlete, adventurer, and a writer of popular he-man novels, many of which were turned into movies, the most famous being *The Spoilers*. In one version of the film, Gary

Cooper played the lead, in another John Wayne. On December 16, 1916, Beach signed *The Crimson Gardenia* for Amos R. Wells writing "With the author's wishes." Like Beach, Wells was an interesting successful man: initially a professor of Greek then editor of the *Christian Endeavor World*, and the author of more than sixty books, most focusing on moral subjects: devotion, Sunday School, and young people. The book I would have read had I not been forced to decamp was *Grace Before Meat* "a collection of table blessings for all occasions." I suspected Wells did not quote Uncle Remus' pithy observation, "Dem w'at eats kin say grace."

Finishing a book leads to unfinished speculation. The week before leaving Storrs, I read William McFee's *Derelicts*. Born in 1881, McFee died in 1966. He went to sea in the first decade of the 20th century serving as an engineer on sundry ships ending in 1924 when he retired as chief engineer with the United Fruit Company to devote his days to writing. He wrote wondrous sea stories. For two decades his books were popular, but now he and his writings have sunk without a ripple. The only people familiar with his books are library lubbers like me who explore the backwater lagoons of stacks — sections librarians think stagnant with forgotten volumes, books which will eventually disappear into skips beside loading platforms. *Derelicts* consisted of conversations between Mr. Spenlove, chief engineer of the *Sansovino*, and Mrs. Colwell, a Long Island socialite and first-class passenger. Cruising the Caribbean gave the two main characters islands enough and time for anecdotal and revealing talk ranging from allusions to "Paphian courts" to descriptions of villages huddled in the shadowy damp of Mayan ruins. Probably most long-lived people drifting toward the shoal end of their days think themselves derelicts, stranded, happily and unhappily, in places and careers they never imagined. *Derelicts* enthralled me, as it once did patrons of the university library. Inside the front board of the book was a pocket holder containing library check-out cards. Published in 1939, *Derelicts* was borrowed twenty-four times between January 1940 and October 1944 the last due date. Although space remained to record more borrowers, the cards eddied into emptiness. I wondered why. Had the library changed its lending procedure or was the book simply moved out of sight and mind and lost in the stacks? I studied the cards. What I wondered happened to Pratt, H. Dawson, Alcorn, A. B. Crandall, Corey, and J. Lathrop? Were any of the borrowers in the navy during the war? Did any readers become well-known and how many enjoyed happy lives? Did some retire to the Hamptons and meet Mrs. Colwell?

"What do you think?" I asked Vicki. Vicki shook her head, implying that only the indulgently idle considered such matters. I thought I was busy, interestingly so. Vicki disagreed. "Since you retired, you haven't had anything to do," she said in response to my query. "You need to leave for your sake. Change of place will invigorate you. If you stay here, you'll get fat, and your clothes won't fit. Buying you a new wardrobe will bankrupt us, and there'll be no money to leave to the children." "I wrote four books in five years," I answered. "That doesn't count as doing something," Vicki said. "It's the same-old 'same-old.' You wrote books before you retired."

Perhaps I wasn't as active as Vicki thought I should have been, but the sights of summer, not simply books, kept me busy and enlivened my days. Northern water snakes sunned on shallow ledges behind the Gurleyville Grist Mill. In Mirror Lake painted turtles hatched and climbed onto mats of last year's cattails. Hordes of gypsy moth caterpillars chopped the leaves of oaks into sharp slivers of green. From below, crowns of the trees looked like the shattered remnants of cut-glass bowls. Around boles of the oaks, the bodies of male moths clumped like cotton batting exploded through the seams of fraying pillows. Higher on the trunks of the oaks, females clutched the bark and laid swatches of eggs. The patches were cinnamon colored and looked spilled from measuring spoons. Once they finished laying, the females also died. Their grips on the trees loosened, and they tumbled into the batting. Along banks of the Fenton River ebony and river jewel wings swarmed. When the sunlight was behind them, the damselflies glowed blue and green, transforming scraggily shrubs into July Christmas trees. Across the river northern water thrushes foraged rocks tails bobbing, and, if I didn't know better, greeting hikers. When Halloween pennants flew over the fringed sedges wrapping the beaver pond, their wings glowed like burnt gold – richness too beautiful to waste on anything other than sight. In the meadow beyond the beaver pond, flowers bloomed like music: bouncing Bet, her peppery fragrance snapping in castanets, cool clarinets of blue vervain, milkweed its pink fading like an echo, unobtrusive sweet melodious bedstraw, and in the gallery naively enthusiastic monkey flower and at the door just arriving mullein and Canada goldenrod.

After the *Rotterdam* left Boston without me in steerage, I chummed my surroundings in hopes of hooking somewhere to rusticate. Because I traded in the Volvo, I couldn't drive any place. Effrontery almost inevitably leads to embarrassment, but my cheeks redden only when my heart kicks off its diltiazem, heists up its blood pressure, and goes on a toot. I wrote the most expensive resort in Fiji, one featured in *Condé Nast Traveler*. In exchange for a month's room and board, I promised I'd write about an article about the experience. I also said that I'd pay for my travel. The resort did not respond. "An astute manager should have swallowed that proposal like the bait taken by those giant marlins caught by Hemingway," I told Vicki. Despite the apt literary reference, Vicki did not respond either. I then shifted my sight from Fiji to Arkansas.

Sixteen years ago, I spent a month at the Writers' Colony at Dairy Hollow in Eureka Springs, Arkansas, a small resort town in the Ozarks in northwest Arkansas.

Today's town differed little from the town I remembered. The population had not swollen, and Eureka consisted of 2800 people, slightly more than half its population at the beginning of the twentieth century. There were no traffic lights or four-way intersections. Fireplugs were blue and white, the barrels white, caps and side valves or spigots blue. Streets and parks remained cleaner than operating rooms. Every day sweepers scoured roads; caretakers and gardeners plucked trash from sidewalks and groomed the public areas surrounding springs. According to the Bible the hairs on a person's head were numbered; on the streets of Eureka so were leaves. As soon as one fell to the ground, it was swept away. In town roads twisted around, over, and down limestone bluffs. Here and there they broke away only to return suddenly and tangle back together. By necessity and intention, the roads were narrow and slowed traffic, and on several streets the speed limit was fifteen miles an hour. Many houses were Victorian, sentimental and homey with candy cane porches and gingerbread ornaments iced with bright colors. "People around here," a trolley drive told me, "likes to keep things old and ran down." Houses themselves perched under and atop the bluffs. Cottages that appeared to be one-level from the street often extended back then dropped down over bluffs for three stories greatly increasing their size, and upkeep.

Motorized trolleys painted green and red with bench seats plied the streets. Their frames were period piece copies of early twentieth-century electric trollies, and for an imaginative person boarding was not a step off the ground but a step back in time. Because of its elevation in the Ozarks and the innumerable springs that percolated through the limestone the town had long been a resort. In the past it was a health resort, but now it was primarily a vacation spot and a destination amenable to the "gentle people," that is, the once and sometimes still free-spirited. In the town were innumerable rental houses, bed and breakfasts, and hotels. Several hotels were stone, usually limestone. They were eye-catching and foot-stopping. The most impressive was the Crescent a massive and beautifully blond limestone hotel on a brow of West Mountain overlooking downtown. Built in 1886, it was immediately celebrated as the "finest hotel West of the Mississippi." Quite a few of the largest homes in town were owned by deep-pocketed people who did not live year round in Eureka. Fine to visit and racket around in for a short time, especially with grandchildren, the houses were too big and lumbering for daily living. Still, a goodly percentage of the population lived in Eureka because they loved the town. Many residents moved from other places, not because they were migratory American nomads but because the spirit of place seduced them. They were tolerant and humble and did not presume to tell neighbors how to think. Because of them much was easy, and sensible, attitudes toward marriage, for example. The shuffling of genders did not matter; people merely married people.

"My wife and I traveled the country searching for a congenial place to live," a man from Iowa told me. "Then a friend mentioned Eureka. We came here, spent three days exploring, went back to Iowa, took early retirement, returned, and restored a decrepit Victorian." "I lived in Europe nine years. I was very happy, but then I lost my heart in Spain," an art dealer said, her account sounding rehearsed played repeatedly for inquisitive tourists. "Home is where the heart is. I returned to the United States. And eureka! I found my lost heart in Eureka."

When a woman parked at Grotto Spring started her car, the motor coughed. "He has a cold," I said. "No," she answered. "He's healthy and is just being difficult. He's not happy because we went to Missouri today, and he doesn't like to leave Eureka." Topsoil atop the limestone was thin, and people who moved to Eureka were not obliged to change their natures and force taproots deep into an inhospitable alien clay. Instead they settled in houses literally built on rocks enabling them to withstand rain and flood and everchanging cultural winds. They had not allowed the things they owned or achieved to define them. Instead they consciously prevented ambition and possessions from becoming their gods and determining the courses of their lives, or, put in an old-fashioned way, the world from corrupting their souls.

In my initial stay at the Colony, I was the recipient of a fellowship awarded to "Nature Writers." I lived in a bright bed-sitter and ate meals with resident writers. Food was provided, and Cindy the cook prepared astonishingly varied dinners. She kept the kitchen better supplied than a small grocery, and for breakfast and lunch, colonists rummaged through the shelves and refrigerators always finding too much from which to choose. I drove to Eureka from Storrs, 1440 miles, and I spent hours every morning walking the town. Afterward in my car I explored the environs. I canoed the Kings River and hiked the Ozarks. I saw The Great Passion Play at Holy Land and visited the Big Cat Refuge at Turpentine Creek. Every day I got up at five and jogged the four-mile Historic Loop through and around town. The only difficult stretch was Ellis Grade, a curving incline from Dairy Hollow to the Crescent Hotel. The rest of the route bounced softly up and down eventually turning into a sharp drop along Main Street and rounding back to Spring Street and Dairy Hollow. I remembered the springs I ran past: Sweet, Harding, Crescent, and Grotto, among others. Cinched around them were gardens tended and dressed immaculately. The planting domesticated the springs, particularly on West Mountain as gardeners shoveled the chaos of life out of sight and mind. On East Mountain, the other part of town, gardens were not so curried. The lands immediately around the springs retained an uncultivated vitality and made one aware that behind the mouths of the springs lay dark caves and lobes of limestone, water seeping through and around them in sinuses of veins.

I recognized the plants surrounding the springs on

West Mountain. The familiarity was welcoming and made me feel comfortable — at home although Connecticut was far away: boxwood, cleome with its cleansing shower fragrance, butterfly bush, hibiscus, redbud, Virginia creeper and trumpet vine woven into trellises, hyssop its leaves liquorish and smelling like cough medicine, and then a catalogue of everyday household flowers: petunias, lantana, impatiens, coreopsis, phlox, lavender, bee balm, agapanthus, and four o'clocks with their nostalgic heirloom aroma. Usually as I jogged down Planer Hill at sunrise, roads were silent and empty. When light topped the nearby ridges, yellow flowed across buildings and washed through the streets, and Eureka looked like, and was, fairyland. As I climbed out of downtown and ran along Spring Street, occasionally an empty lot opened like an eye, revealing green ridges rumpling the horizon, the creases between them pillowed with mist. Atop a ridge Christ of the Ozarks spread his welcoming arms. Above him low clouds glowed pink and gold, the sight making me wish I believed something other than non-belief.

Immediately after breakfast I sat on the porch outside my room, rocking, waving to drivers, and chatting with walkers. Dogs were the familiars of people who chose to settle in Eureka after living elsewhere. For my part I practiced the high pleasure of talking about nothing. I had been schooled to stir and accomplish, and after half a cup of coffee I wondered how much life I'd missed by constantly doing. Should I have left most things and people alone, particularly myself? I watched hummingbirds waver then dart into morning glories. A skink scooted under a throw of clematis blossoms. A bark centipede curled around the edge of a pressed wooden board. Deer stared at me. Initially they were nervous, but they quickly grew accustomed to my cousinly once-removed presence. Red-headed woodpeckers gabled and cavorted, and Carolina wrens laughed, sounding a little out of control, to the nest not to the country club born. I watched leaves blow and shake in the gathering sunlight:

the glowing Valentine's Day hearts of catalpa, thumbed sassafras, saw-toothed chinquapin, and sycamore almost like maple but in the morning buttery, lightly salted, and dripping yellow.

When I tired of writing or thinking about writing, I roamed, collecting matter for pages. In the lobby of the Crescent Hotel I noticed a man wearing a blue T-shirt. Printed on the back was FAITH RIDERS COWBOY CHURCH, "Riding the Brand with Jesus." The brand was The Cross, and man was from Missouri. "There are lots of Cowboy Churches, especially in Texas," he told me adding that parishioners didn't have to be cowboys. "Many folks come to my church on motorcycles or like me in pickup trucks." I recorded conversations, none of them Miltonic. "Bring your oxygen?" a wife asked her husband as they climbed Spring Street past Ozark Mountain Quilts. "It's in the car," he answered bending and pressing his hands onto his knees turning his arms into studs. I asked a tattooist if customers ever requested tattoos of Porky Pig or Elmer Fudd. "Who?" he said. "You know, Donald Duck's friends," I said. "Who?" he repeated.

I knew I'd be comfortable at the Writers' Colony, and so long as Vicki was peeved, I'd be more at ease than in Storrs. Despite Arkansas's humid summer weather, days would be temperate. One afternoon after Vicki criticized me for shuffling "like someone on day release from a Home," I telephoned the Colony. Space was available, and I arranged a two month stay running from the end of July to the end of September. The cost was modest, $65 a day for room and board. Getting to Eureka was difficult, however. I was too old to drive, and even if a doctor gave me an invigorating monkey-gland shot, I did not have an extra car sagging on its tires and drooling oil in the garage. A bus trip from Hartford to Eureka took 45 hours, and the way was measly with stops and broken by shunting from one bus to another. Insofar as trains were concerned, I could get to San Francisco quicker and easier than to Eureka. My only option was flying. From New

York Southwest flew nonstop to Little Rock. Alas, to get to Kennedy airport from Storrs necessitated taking a limousine. From the airport in Little Rock I could take a cab to the Capitol Hotel, spend the night, and the next day take a slow bus to Eureka. After looking at flights to sundry airports including Branson, Missouri, for example, I decided to fly Delta from Hartford to Fayetteville. Usually I avoided Delta because having to pay $25 to check a suitcase irritated me. "You mean burns your ass," Vicki said. "Right," I answered.

A roundtrip ticket cost $560 plus an additional $50 for a checking one bag each way. I left Hartford at 10:30 on a Wednesday morning and flew to Atlanta landing at 1:00. Fifty minutes later I took off for Fayetteville arriving at quarter to three. I was an uneasy traveler. I worried so much that my suitcase would miss the connection in Atlanta that after buying my ticket I slept poorly until I left Storrs. The concern was real. Eureka Springs was 50 miles from the Fayetteville airport, and a lost bag could not skip quickly to the Colony. Getting myself to the Colony was another problem. Six or seven car-rental companies had booths at the airport. None had a return office in Eureka. As a result, I paid Richard $85 to drive me to the Colony.

I was glad to be carless. That relieved the pressure I inevitably put on myself to do and see. Missing a landmark outside town wouldn't make me feel guilty. Not bound to the wheels and speedometers of experiencing, I was free to revel in lethargy. The only concession I made to travel in Eureka was to purchase a town trolley ticket—$34 for two months, the senior citizen price. When roaming tired me, I rode a trolley back to the Colony. Settling into the Colony took only a single afternoon. I awoke at six o'clock the morning after arriving. Twenty minutes later I was on Ellis Grade running the Historic Loop. Afterward I ate my usual breakfast of a banana, yogurt, and cereal, this last granola or Raisin Bran depending on the larder. I then brewed a cup of coffee and going outside resumed sitting on the porch, the years that elapsed between my stays suddenly themselves elapsing, the distant past seeming another season, part of the natural continuum of spring and fall, winter, summer, past, present, and future. Descendants of the deer that observed me sixteen years ago studied me and decided I was harmless. By the end of September, I was a deer whisperer. When I talked to them as I did to my dogs at home, raising my voice into a lilt and saying "hellyo—hellyo," the deer waggled their ears and stared. Only rarely did they bound off even when I approached within touching distance. A vixen and two kits scampered back and forth across Spring Street. Sometimes they sat in the middle of the road looking at me unsure whether I was threatening or friendly, or maybe edible. The kits were full-sized but thin. Their legs resembled wooden slats, and when the kits ran, they looked like movable sections of a picket fence. As I had done throughout my life, I looked at trees. On a broken slope across from the Colony, I noticed a single royal paulownia. Initially I thought it another catalpa, but then I spotted its fruit—dangling mustardy clusters of seed capsules. "Good for you, Sam," I thought growing comfortable with my porch self.

After I reached sixty, repetition ceased to discourage and instead reassured. Every morning I talked to passersby: Jane who moved to Eureka from New Orleans after hurricane Katrina and Joyce who was a widow. "I always wanted to be an artist," she said. "After my husband died, I left Kansas City and moved to Eureka. My sculptures are not very good, but I am getting better, and I love doing them." A pair of Barlows jogged toward Harmon Park. "Brothers," I said. "No, husband and wife," one said. A few walkers were short-time visitors, people who lived tabloid lives, "poor Casuals of the way-worn earth." Bill was spending a week with his granddaughter. He told me he'd had 141 different addresses, most when he was in the army and the air force. "When I was in Cambodia flying with Air America, I did not have an address or a passport," he said. "I didn't exist." Quinn said he was passing through. He didn't reveal his destination, only that he was on the way. He informed me, however, that he urinated only once a day. He interpreted my rolling eyes as another sort turning, that of a knob opening the door to an extended nephrological discussion. When he began citing statistics delineating the amount of water necessary to continue "the existence of a healthy young male weighing one-hundred-and-forty-two pounds," I excused myself from the conversation. "A call of nature," I said, a statement that at first chagrined me but of which I am now inordinately proud.

Couples walked their dogs early in the morning, she, striding after their pet, he often limping and lagging. No dog roamed free. With one exception all dogs I saw on the street were leashed. The exception was a small brown and white terrier that roamed a porch roof nearby. Whenever he saw me, he raced along the roof and barked. "Do his feet ever touch dirt?" I asked his owner. "Never," she said, "the roof is his yard." The dogs were obedient and didn't pull and jerk their leashes. Some owners were less well-behaved and didn't remove droppings from sidewalks. In a yard off Ridgeway stood a sign mounted on a stake. Printed on the sign in black letters was "BEWARE." Below *beware* an arrow pointed toward the ground. Written under the arrow was "Neighbors Dog Shit." At the foot of the sign lay a turd. The sign left, if I may be so inelegant as to say so, a bad taste in my mouth.

Happily, the world of dog owners was more sentimental than excremental. I met Charlie and Karma, his King Charles spaniel. Karma was a rescue. She wasn't pure bred, but she was literally rescued. Every year Charlie surveyed telephone poles stored in sparsely populated areas of Nebraska. At one forsaken spot he noticed fur sticking from the end of a metal pole and discovered Karma. She was stuck head first in the pipe. Her long ears locked her in place. Charlie began attempting to free her by reaching into the pipe and pulling the hairs out of Karma's ears. Charlie hoped that once her ears were bare they'd be slippery, and he would be able to move Karma's head. After stripping her ears, Charlie worked an hour more to free Karma. "I thought about driving to a garage and purchasing some grease. I even stood up and started toward my car, but I could not bring myself to leave her. She never nipped me, and when I finally lifted her out of the pipe and held her in my arms, she licked my face." The local humane society told Charlie that nobody had reported a missing spaniel, adding that their kennels were full and that they couldn't take her in. "Someone dumped her on the roadside," a woman said; "What a shame. She looks like such a nice dog." A vet told Charlie that Karma would have died by the end of the day if he had not rescued her. "It was karma, and she became Karma, and we have been together for eight years," Charlie told me. Charlie lived on a road that pitched steeply off West Mountain toward town. Because Karma "isn't as energetic as she once was," early every morning he drove Karma up the hill, parked, and walked her along on the flat tabletop of Prospect. During my runs, I often met them, Karma sniffing and wagging her tail like a brush, and Charlie following at the end of her leash, smiling and happy.

When walkers thinned out, I started stories like those agents urged me to write forty years ago. I didn't write them because I knew that eventually the characters I created would bore me. The world was an alluring place in which everyday doings stirred my curiosity, endlessly surprised me, and as a result were rarely jejune. Besides, Vicki and I didn't need the money I might earn writing. I'd inherited enough to see us in and out of the cemetery and to cover admission fees to the Great City in the Clouds. I suspected there'd be even enough remaining for us to purchase a carriage, and certainly not a cheap pagan Roman chariot in which a person stood and maneuvered a whip, a skill more difficult to master than shifting gears. I consulted *Corpse Reports* and decided we could afford The Clarence, not a new but a pre-owned model. The Clarence used twice the horsepower of a chariot, but "over time," *Reports* said, "money saved by The Clarence's springs would reduce repair costs and justify the purchase." We might even have enough talents left to hire one of the lower ranked Seraphim to chauffeur us around, take us, for example, to visit the hatchery that manufactured wings or the paving company that patched pot holes in the golden streets.

I started my most recent story on a bright morning. My coffee cup was full, and on a platter on the table beside me was a slice of corpuscular watermelon. "The drive to the graveyard had been long and dull, but trip home was short and sweet," I began. "'Oh, so very sweet,' she thought as the Murine dropped into her eyes. 'Forcing out crocodile tears makes a person's eyes unfashionably red,' she muttered while she spooned out a helping of the chicken tetrazene sent to her by her next-door neighbor. 'I should stop at four. I am flush with cash. I could live in Paris, drink champagne, and eat escargot every night, but murdering aged husbands is just so much fun. Still, my good looks won't last forever. A little variety might spice up my life. I wonder how titillating it would be to murder a young husband.'"

A hundred miles away a slender handsome man thirty-five years old with soft brown eyes and hair graying around the temple removed a black band from his arm. "Why," he thought as he peeled back the cellophane and looked at the contents of a dish on the kitchen table, "why do country people always season potato salad with pickles? Why do they invariably send widowers potato salad? Why not foie gras for God's sake?" How much longer, he wondered, "can I do this? Six should satisfy a normal, decent murderer. I've been left vaults of money. I could live in Paris. I could wear a beret and sit on the banks of the Seine. I could be debonair. I could chaperone wealthy tourists and take them to cafés that served Champagne and escargot. But, oh, murdering

aged widows is just so much fun, and the supply is unlimited. But still, self-help books all preach the virtues of
reinventing one's self. Maybe, I should try marrying a
young widow."

And right here the story and I stopped. A man walking a fuzzy brown dog leaned over the railing of the
porch. He noticed the sign in front of the Colony. "Are
you a writer?" he asked. "Sometimes," I answered.
"Where are you from?" he asked. "Connecticut," I said.
"*A Connecticut Yankee in King Arthur's Court* is one of my
favorite books. Do you like it?" he asked. "You bet," I
said. "Good," he said. The man was wearing a gray T-
shirt. Printed on the front in red was a razorback hog,
logo of athletic teams at the University of Arkansas. "Do
you like football?" he asked. "Not much," I said. "I don't
like it either. But my wife gave me this shirt, and to keep
in her good graces I wear it sometimes. I cringe when
strangers notice it and think I'm a fan. They get such a
wrong impression of me." "So go the lives of husbands,"
I said. "Too true," the man replied. Then he looked at the
sky. "I don't see any clouds," he said. "But the weather-
man says it is going to rain today. It's raining in Tulsa
now, and what happens in Tulsa usually happens in Eureka, so I guess I better go. Jimmy here," he said looking
at his dog, "doesn't like to get wet." "Maybe it won't
rain," I said. "We'll see," the man said hurrying after
Jimmy who was tugging on the leash.

Unless a dog plucked his deerstalker from a hook in
the kennel and was on a Holmesian quest to identify previous canine passersby, dogs were friendlier and more
affable than their owners. Jimmy's master was an exception. While ambling dogs paused and sniffed, some
owners resisted visiting. They kept their heads down,
eyes pasted to the road. Maybe domesticity was drowning them, and they didn't want to waste free moments
exchanging saccharine nothings with a stranger. On the
other hand, most dog owners were past their middle
years, and perhaps they realized that if they broke stride,

they might be caught short before reaching home. Occasionally a lone walker appeared, her body sloping like a shadow away from my porch, head tilted looking wrenched out of hope. Such people needed pets, I thought. I realized dogs were not emotional antibiotics and I was only an amateur GP. But if a medical school diploma were hanging behind me on the porch, I would have prescribed a regimen of foundling-home canine. "There is no better cure for the painful lesions of melancholia than a tail-wagging dog," I'd have said.

Changing place also changed time. As Jimmy and his owner walked into Harmon Park, I remembered that in 1970 I spent two months in Tulsa and two years later wrote an essay entitled "Taking the Night Plane to Tulsa." I liked the title, and the essay was reprinted twice. I recalled that it was good-natured, but that was all that came to mind. My return to Tulsa was brief. I hurried back to the porch and thought about a conversation I heard two days earlier in a souvenir shop. "How are you today?" the owner of the shop asked a man as he entered. "Wonderful," the man replied. "Every day is wonderful." "I agree totally," the owner responded. "Every day I can get up and put my feet on the floor is a wonderful day." "Yes," the first man said echoing himself, "every day is wonderful." "That's so true. Every day is wonderful," the owner said.

My reaction to the back and forth of greetings wasn't as good-natured as my essay on Tulsa. Practically every time I climbed into a trolley and started to sit down, someone asked, "How are you doing today?" The greeters were pleasant, but after smiling and responding a litany of times, I began to think them inquisitors. Not only that, but I fretted that strangers inquired about my health because I looked like I had one foot in the grave. Shortly after I arrived in Eureka, a man driving a pickup and towing a carrier laden with two riding mowers stopped beside me as I walked along Prospect. "You look thirsty," he said, "would you like some water?" Running lubricated my bones, and the only thing threatening to dry them was the desiccating wind of genial palaver or so I thought for a moment. But then one day a policeman appeared to track my early morning run, driving past then reversing direction and returning, only to turn back around and pass me again. By the fourth drive-by, we were practically cousins, and I waved.

Initially I suspected that a concerned citizen spotted me, and worried that I might be a malefactor casing empty houses, notified the police. "How exciting to be thought burglarous," I mused titillating myself. "I wonder what the county jail serves for breakfast?" Of course, that was a silly fantasy, one, though, that so diverted me that I finished the run without fretting that my knees would sprocket sideways or that my bosom would come unhinged and falling off, disappear down a culvert. Alas, the truth probably was that the police were the concerned citizens. Bent like a coat hanger, wobbly and staggering despite taking baby steps, I would not be an alluring frontispiece for *Men's Health*. Yes, the police tracked me, not because I was a modern Raffles, feline on my feet and simian on fire escapes, but because they worried that I might suddenly tremble, collapse, turn up my toes, and finish my run by sprinting up the grand Hill of Zion. "No, no, and no," Vicki said later when I described my Ten Most-Wanted celebrity. "Writing personal essays has turned you into an egomaniac. The policeman was making his morning round and noticed you only because you waved at him."

The saving grace of porch meditations is that they are fleeting. As if synchronized with rocking, my thoughts pitched forward with the chair and disappeared before the movement reversed itself and rolled backwards. In an advertising weekly, I spotted a notice for "Funeral Service." "Honoring Traditions & Creating New Ones," the notice declared. With services offered in three towns—Eureka, Berryville, and Green Forest—business must have been lively, but what, I wondered, were the traditions, new and old, especially the new, and how did undertakers create them? Did casketeers wrap "morgue-aged property" in mauve slumber robes? Did they replace Black Masters with Slingshots and strap Western Travelers onto the hoods for their journeys to six-foot bungalows? Did they print red memorial cards on the front of which appeared pictures of the defuncts swallowing their birth certificates? Possibilities were unlimited, transforming lights out into lights on, death rattles into symphonies, and cold-meat parties into neighborhood barbeques.

Some mornings as I started my run a barred owl flew into a mimosa across the street from the Colony. Several times during runs I saw mink, armadillos, and families of racoons. Bats had disappeared from Connecticut and Nova Scotia. But in the evening bats jiggered above Eureka. The sightings pleased me. Even more pleasing were efforts to protect local bats from "White Nose Syndrome," one of which was closing the entrance to Cave Spring. Still, I missed seeing goldenrod explode like fireworks beyond the beaver pond at the edge of the university forest. But then in Eureka crape myrtle bloomed beside the springs and the porches of countless houses. Colors were as various as those in stained glass windows, my favorite being blackish scarlet, a shade sinfully complex and evocative rather than ornamental.

When I arrived in Eureka buxom bouquets of naked ladies bloomed in medians next to sidewalks and across almost every yard on Spring Street. Their petals were delicate and pink, and their fragrance subtle and bewitching not cosmetic but natural. "It makes me want to take the lilies to church, clothes or no clothes," a man working in his yard said. "If religion were that soft, how fine life would be." "I love them," a woman told me. "They and zinnias are the only flowers in my yard that deer won't eat." By the middle of August, the lilies' petals browned, shriveled, and collapsed into wrinkles. Eventually the stems broke. The flowers vanished, and a stranger wouldn't know that earlier in the summer naked ladies transformed ambles into dances. The person who cultivates flowers simultaneously nurtures a sensible awareness of mortality. "We and they come and go," an old man said; "the good gardener weeds and helps flowers and youth bloom." Also, planted in medians and along the borders of yards were bushels of purple coneflowers. By the middle of August, their central disks dried into spiny fibroids, and their petals withered and turned liverish, evoking an unexpected association with cancer. For a watcher of gardens, summer's changes were not melancholy. They simply were. In July black tiger swallowtail butterflies swarmed around the springs: eastern, pipevine, and spicebush. They wavered and darted so quickly that distinguishing them was impossible. Once my eyes would have swooped them out of flight and pinned them to a field guide. No longer—my focus shifted slower than in the past, and colors drifted and like those of rainbows vanished one into another. Later in the summer as the wings of black swallowtails faded and shredded, yellow swallowtails hatched and fluttered around the springs bright as daffodils.

Familiarity fosters calm, and my walks were generally serene. Only rarely did my pulse skip at the sight of unfamiliar flowers, among others, a spurge across the emerald leaves of which wing-like bands of pine green flapped lyrically, and then night blooming moon flower, a datura related to jimson weed, its white lucent and hallucinatory, the purest white I'd ever seen. The roots of habit both dug deep and spread broad within me. No matter where circumstance transplanted me—Canada, Australia, the Caribbean, or Arkansas, I noticed trees. With my eyes shut and nose stoppered, I could identify magnolias by the crackling sound their dried leaves made underfoot. But then who would plug his nose and miss the lemony perfume of a great magnolia and the fantasies it evoked, provoking a person to shed scratchy polyester and don soft graciousness, magnanimity, and kindness based on touch rather than perfunctory bank checks?

In the middle of an abandoned field near the Colony towered a dead white oak. Its limbs were massive and raked upward into the sky. Dryads hadn't abandoned the oak but had metamorphosed into vultures, their once-comely maidenly appearance compacted into the rounded comma-like hunch of the black birds. For youth virginal dryads are emblems of the sensual offerings spilling from life's cornucopia. The vulture is better suited for the aged who no longer feared ceasing to be. After a person's ripened grain has been harvested or tossed aside mildewed, how appealing it becomes to imagine riding high winds far above regret and achievement. On every walk, big trees raised my sight and spirit, making me glad to be ambulatory: oaks and sycamores and black walnuts. The leaves of these last billowed like ferny sails, the blue sky behind them smooth and azure. My favorite trees were short leaf pines. The trunks of mature trees were towering and muscular. While plates of brown and reddish bark, sometimes tinged with orange, pressed hard against the heart wood like cuirasses, crowns of the trees broke into loose flails. Sight hastened on to sight—on the leaf of a post oak a small praying mantis, its abdomen red and spotted with white dots, sunning on a ledge behind a sycamore a fence lizard, and on the bark of a black oak a jittery brown creeper—jewels to string through the hours of a day. Musicians played in Basin Park on weekends. A couple of times I went to hear them, but generally I stayed at the Colony after dinner and sitting on the porch let music come to me. Tree frogs appeared on stage first. At times they were shrill, but shortly thereafter rain often began to fall. Creeping through the trees and lightly tapping leaves, the rain softened the high trills of the frogs. Later lightning bugs started flicking their radiant batons, and the chorale of crickets, cicadas, and katydids began their modernist zithering. Sometimes an overture of thunder preceded them; other times a high wind whisked through trees like a drummer's brush.

Eureka II

Most visitors to Eureka traveled from Arkansas itself and states nearby: Missouri, Oklahoma, Kansas, and Texas. Many came from cultural rungs below the middle of the middle class. Those who were not motorcycle tourists drove new model SUV's and massive pickup trucks; yet many dressed in clothes too soiled, a shopkeeper said, "to pass as work clothes." No matter the place — in restaurants and joints, in the lobby of the Crescent, in shops on Center or South Main Street or on a bench in Basin Springs Park — men wore dungarees and T-shirts, the women baggy dresses and blouses big as tablecloths.

The exceptions were troops of motorcycle tourists. They left cars and trucks at home, and both men and women wore utilitarian cycling outfits, leather jackets and trousers or chaps being the highway equivalents of club ties. Most also wore Harley-Davidson shirts. I thought about buying a shirt before I left Eureka. It would have been the only such shirt in Storrs, a fashion statement to rival my son Francis' shirt which commanded, "Stop Being Poor." A billboard outside a beery eatery welcomed "Christian Bikers." On seeing it I almost said something regrettable, but before I spoke a man sitting near me in the trolley volunteered, "My uncle is a Christian Biker." "Good for him," I said temporizing as usual. Would I ever see a sign, I wondered, welcoming Christian Christians, the caveat, Josh remarked later, "being that almost no Christians are Christian." When I was young, members of the Fellowship of Christian Athletes visited high schools. As an Episcopalian I was immune to proselytizing. But why not Christian Bikers? I suspected that hedge fund managers welcomed, probably solicited, the interest of Christian cardiologists and gynecologists.

Obesity was normal in Eureka, and feedlots of four-hundred-pound men and three-hundred-pound women lumbered walkways made for slimmer times. Hordes had tattoos, including elementary school children—on their necks, shoulders, hands, backs, calves, arms, under their hair, everywhere in sight and likely out of sight, too. Some tourists were so tattooed they looked like aliens. Arms were sleeves of tattoos, greaves covered calves, and torsos were shadows of blue or purple although a smidgen of pink, a petal of a flower that had blossomed into cellulite sometimes resisted wilting and glimmered, a remnant of healthier days past. While game legs limited physical prowess, tattoos imposed an ink ceiling. What corporation would hire a woman over whose back, neck, left shoulder, upper arm, and breast draped a blue sheet web? The spider itself lurked in a retreat under the woman's left ear lobe, its two front legs hanging down, the tarsus and claw on each curving like a meat hook. Wrapping the right arm of one man like thick red, yellow, and black bracelets was a coral snake; around the man's left arm coiled a rattlesnake, its head atop the man's hand, mouth opened, fangs exposed, ready to strike.

Tattoos disabled. By restricting opportunity, they crippled. "I expect," Josh said, "that the grotesquely tattooed will eventually apply to Social Security for disability benefits. They'll call it blue skin disease." On one occasion in Basin Park, I mumbled "too bad" when I saw a young girl hideously disfigured by tattoos. "She'll be all right," the man next to me said overhearing me. He was from Oklahoma, and his pastor told his congregation that Jesus had tattoos. Jesus got his first tattoos before he was ten years old. I asked the man what the tattoos were. He didn't know but said, "maybe a cross or something or maybe since Joseph was a carpenter, a hammer and a saw." "How about a hammer and sickle?"

I said. "No," he replied, "maybe a bow or coping saw, but not a sickle."

Crowds of people in Eureka smoked. Escaping the gagging smell was impossible. Some houses on Spring Street reeked, and even when I stayed off sidewalks and walked down the center of the street air outside them was noisome. Downtown men stood on street corners and smoked while their wives explored the shops. Between puffs men between, say 35 and 48, were eager to chat. Almost invariably they called strangers "bro." I was startled when a man soliciting advice on cafés addressed me as bro. Never had anyone applied that honorific to me or for that matter its sibling appellation "sis." Cigarette butts filled the humidors on the grand front porch of the Crescent Hotel. Frequently when I sat there unconsciously delectating in the shimmering crowns of walnuts, someone, usually a woman, walked out of the hotel lobby and lit a cigarette. Even if she did not smoke, she stank despoiling appreciation. High above Eureka and facing West Mountain, the East Mountain Overlook was a popular spot for wedding pictures. Scattered around the green gazebo were cartons of cigarette butts. Without rotating my head, I once counted 58 then became repulsed and stopping started walking back down and around the mountain. Not a single person I knew in Connecticut smoked. In fact, I haven't noticed an adult smoking in Storrs in a decade. On the university campus, only Chinese graduate students smoked. Initially women smoking in Eureka so surprised me that the sight seemed obscene, comparable to that of the intoxicated women I saw in Leningrad forty-five years ago lying crumpled across sidewalks or slumped into doorways, their clothes knotted and bloody.

After leaving the gazebo, I noticed there was more yard art on East than on West Mountain, much the detritus of barbeque and deck living: overturned grills, bottomless chairs, and picnic tables collapsed into firewood. Doves, ducks, and geese wearing sombreros waddled about in mixed flocks. Elves, dragonflies, tailless rabbits, grinning honeybees, cherubs, and mysterious rotund Chinamen studied passersby. Carved wooden cornucopias spilled orchards of fruit, and trees of life spread like capillaries across broad coppery plates. A metal cat stared through oil-gauge eyes while plastic owls perched on limbs. I wondered if the cat was related to the tuxedo cat that sat outside my flat early in the morning and stared through a window at me, studying me as if I were a mouse.

Of course, Eureka was much more than day-trippers and weekenders. The town was Vermont in Arkansas, in part because of the mountains and rivers but also because year-round residents were liberal and well-educated, lovers of nature, advocates of Thoreauvian simplicity, thoughtful and appreciative. They also drove older, smaller cars and trucks than tourists or at least I think they did. In any case I wanted them to do so, probably because I kept every car I owned at least ten years, including the Volvo, the experience convincing me that maintaining a car for a decade was socially responsible. Clearly, however, more townspeople drove with their windows down than did visitors, the better, it seemed, to wave and nod. Throughout the day tourists passed the Colony hermetically sealed in metallic exoskeletons protected against unexpected greetings.

Despite the pleasure it provided, roaming Eureka saddened me — for myself rather than for the cultural and, maybe financial, poverty of so many weekend tourists. Examining the unexamined life doesn't lead anywhere — maybe to weariness but not to truth or self-knowledge. Still, Eureka provoked me to wonder about myself. Had I become overcivilized? Certainly, my sympathies were imperfect. Did this occur naturally because of age and the withdrawing from others that accompanied time's passing? Or was it the effect of living half a century in New England? When I spotted a mock orange lying on the ground above Jacob's Ladder on East Mountain, I saw myself on Love Circle in Nashville pulling a wagon overflowing with mock oranges. What treasure! What joy! When a man to whom I was talking said "ah, shoot" not as a euphemism but only as an expression, my heart bounced. I was ten years old and back on grandfather's farm with James and Henry, my best friends and playmates. I had not been schooled out of believing that catching cicadas was life's greatest pleasure and that snake doctors were dragonflies. As could be expected, my associations were simultaneously meaningful and meaningless. While the warty bark on hackberries evoked memories of mornings in Nashville when flakes of soot fell from the sky, the leaves of tulip trees were only leaves, not chasubles green with summer.

In general, tourists were good spirited, genial people. They talked southern vernaculars I did not speak but which I recognized. Listening to them should have made me nostalgic. But it did not. Women quacked and shrieked, and their conversation rambled on roller coasters of exclamation marks. Men ground syllables out of words, and both sexes neglected grammar. Like morality grammar is not static, and whether a person uses the preferred English of the moment should matter little. And it doesn't except to individuals like me drilled into believing correct usage the verbal equivalent of good table manners. I talked to people on the streets, in shops, and aboard trolleys. Their decent effervescence cheered me; yet, I couldn't escape caviling when I heard poor grammar. I asked myself, "What sort of person judges people on the basis of speech?" I didn't like the answer. In New England differences in regional and dialectical speech were to my uneducated ear no more than differences in speech. In fact, people in Connecticut used my Middle Tennessee accent to pin me to a board laden with preconceptions. "Look," Vicki said when I talked to her later. "Being misjudged has never bothered you. You enjoyed untold advantages — money, but not enough to blind or corrupt, education, a wondrously stable family, and good health among untold gifts from your DNA. You entitled a book *Deprived of Unhappiness*. You grew up so confident that you've never cared what anyone thought about you. So, quit agitating about what you thought about others. You didn't really judge people. You simply did not understand them. Are you trying to burden yourself with unearned guilt in name of some fraudulent fashionable sensitivity? Be thankful for your good fortune. Whatever you are doing is unbecoming. Stop!"

Vicki was right. Understanding was often difficult, in part because I no longer hear well but also because there are a multitude of accents in Arkansas. One morning a man walked past the Colony swinging a bamboo pole, letting it waggle across his neck, moving from the right shoulder to the left and back. Because the pole puzzled me, I thought the man's dress odd: a blue baseball cap and a blue wife-beater, both with gold script staggering across them. He also wore cutoff blue shorts and blue sneakers with gold laces. If I had readily identified the purpose of the pole, I wouldn't have thought the clothes strange — heavy on blue but ordinary. "Why are you carrying that pole?" I asked. "Do you carry it everywhere you go?" "Winjums," he answered in an unknown tongue. I repeated my question and received the same mystifying answer. On the third try, I understood his reply. "Wind chimes," he said. He planned to saw the bamboo into different lengths and make wind chimes. "Nifty," I said. "Thank you for asking, sir," he said, walking along, the pole swinging lazily from one shoulder to another.

Two things undermine nonfiction: truth and personal reflection. Sometimes the two conflict. The truth was that I did not mull my reaction to Southern speech for long. I thought about it for a few minutes early one morning as I sat rocking on the front porch of the Colony. I'd finished running the loop immediately before a thunderstorm roiled across the mountains and broke over the town. I had eaten a banana, blueberries, and low-fat peach yogurt for breakfast, and as I rocked I sipped weak coffee — dreary coffee, I suppose, to mirror the dark morning. Thunder drifted away then bounced off ridges and rolled back roughly, lightning sparking around the sound. I listened to a pair of hawks calling, a mother and her fledgling. While I didn't understand every word, I understood a few, specifically those referring to an after-breakfast refection. I watched rain falling through trees. While leaves on a red maple trembled palsied, those on mahonia waggled, almost giggling.

Rocking is stationary movement and lends itself better to mulling the past than to contemplating the present. The previous night I learned that my cousin Katherine died in California. Katherine was very bright, the only person I knew whose intelligence matched that of my father. Katherine went to Radcliffe. After graduating she became a migratory Pickering like me and returned to Nashville only to visit family. She lived in New York and after college ghost wrote books for South African politicians. She inserted disruptive liberal thoughts into the manuscripts, but they were always discovered and cut out. She eventually married, had three children, and became a lawyer after which she retired to California. Katherine and I drifted apart separated by time and distance and the natural busyness of family life. We did not completely lose track of each other, and once every decade one of us wrote the other. As I thought about Katherine, I recalled bits of things: the log house in which she grew up, the cuckoo clock on the wall in the living room, her father overweight and dozing in an armchair. Every year at Christmas he gave friends a datebook bound in leather and consisting of 365 blank pages on which recipients could write notes. Printed on the binding was *What I Know About Women* followed by the year, 1953 for example. Katherine was imaginative and outspoken, and she died grandly, better than she could have dreamed. She died in a movie theater accompanied by her daughter Anna and Anna's son. Before the film, the three ate what turned out to be Katherine's last supper at a McDonald's. Despite two of them being vegetarian, they ate heartily. The movie was *Christopher Robin*, and Katherine died during a preview during which Dumbo the flying elephant soared across the screen. Katherine said "Dumbo, ohhhh" and appeared to fall asleep which she generally did during movies. She was 83, had a weak heart, and had made family promise not to resuscitate her if she collapsed. "'Dumbo, ohhhh,' wonderful, wonderful," I said aloud. "Katherine's last words were the finest I've heard," I thought. "Nothing said by any president, general, patriarch, king or queen, saint or demon, nothing fictional or nonfictional can better them. To sail out of life on the wings of an elephant not a dove—how very fine." Nature agreed. The thunder applauded then left. The hawks cried "Brava," and the sun came out.

Later I walked downtown, and I saw things that were unbecoming. A mother jerked four children, all girls, down First Street. Her right hand was clamped like a manacle around the forearm of the youngest child. In her left she held a cigarette. She wore a brown T-shirt. Printed on the front in exaggerated white letters was, "Friday Is My Second Favorite Word Beginning With F." "There are many nice people in Eureka," a shopkeeper told me, "but there is also a lot trash. Half a dozen garbage trucks couldn't haul them all away." "I liked being a policeman," a man said. "But I'm glad to be retired. I couldn't be one today. The drugs are terrible. You cannot imagine what policemen have to put up with now." Older people generally compare their pasts favorably with their presents. Even if Time moved them from basement bed-sitters under Hard Rock Candy Mountain into chateaus gewgawed with indoor plumbing and hot and cold French water, they often sentimentalize the bad old days, especially as small things they once accomplished easily became chores: buttoning shirts without forcing buttons through the wrong eyes, opening milk cartons, or inserting one's legs into trousers and hoisting them up without losing balance and tumbling over.

If the Dispatch Desk published every week in the

Lovely County Citizen was accurate, matters demanding police attention in Eureka Springs were not too serious. At 11:02 on August 6, "An officer responded to a report of two large, white dogs running in traffic and chasing cars. The officer spoke with the owner, who had already put the dogs back inside a fenced yard." One evening at the end of the month, "a caller advised of a couple yelling. Officers responded and discovered that their dog had slipped through its leash and they were yelling for the dog." Four days later at 9:52, "an officer responded to a local restaurant in reference to a female subject screaming. Officers checked the area and advised it was children playing." One afternoon in mid-August, "An officer responded to a report of a vehicle parked behind an area hotel. The officer made contact with the owner, who moved the vehicle." Three days later at 2:14 in the morning "A caller reported his wife missing. An officer located her. All was well." Would that this account had been longer although in both the larger and smaller schemes of the universe differences between a straying dog and a rambling unfenced spouse are miniscule. However, a second chapter may have occurred a week later at 10:30 P. M. as "there was domestic upheaval which drew the attention of constables. The couple went separate ways for the night." Sometimes medicines don't work. At 2:10 in the morning "Another domestic dispute and the couple separated for the night."

As I watched the woman drag her children along the sidewalk, a man crossed from Spring to First Street. He also wore a black T-shirt. On the front was a gold box; in it was written "Caution Darkness Ahead. Shine Your Light." On the lower back of the shirt a flashlight shone upward. Its beams fanned out over the man's shoulders forming a gold triangle. Printed in the triangle in capital letters was, "In the same way, let your light shine before others that they may do good deeds and glorify your father in heaven." "Be Strong for Jesus" commanded print on a sweatshirt worn by a high school girl. Across the street two girls her age studied the window of a shop selling lingerie and "curiosities." Displayed in the window were tubes of Coochy Shave Cream "Oh So Smooth." Parked beside the courthouse was a white van. Painted on the side was "PRISON VAN." Tourists lined up to have family members take pictures of them leaning against and facing the van, legs spread and hands raised, palms flattened on the panels of the van. The young son of one of the parking lot thespians was a convict in training. He caught a swallowtail butterfly and tore its wings off. An adolescent boy strode past the courthouse. He wore an orange shirt. Stamped on it in blue was the rallying cry, "Put Your Armor On." "What armor?" I asked. I shouldn't have inquired because I recognized the words of St. Paul. "The armor of Jesus, brother. It will save you. Read the King James Bible," the boy shouted. "Are the voices of Pentecostals ear splitting," I thought, "because they spend hours hollering and shouting, wrecking their vocal cords, attempting to yell their way to God?" My musing was evanescent. A bumper sticker on the tailgate of a car from Oklahoma distracted me. "Nothing Fails Like Prayer," it read. On getting off the trolley, a passenger said to me, "May God take a liking to us." On my looking startled, he added, "But not too soon."

The closer a person observes a place, the more he realizes that he knows little about it. Writing distorts. In smoothing life into clarity, writers lose life itself — actual life that sprawls and runs, days with doings and non-doings that could mean everything but don't, meaning being a convenient imposed fabrication. "That lawyer," I heard a man say in the Main Street Café, "is butterfingered." Writers are also slippery. For writers, the only truth is not legal truth but page truth, and page truth is often fiction. When a man sitting beside the individual who used butterfingered paid his bill, I asked him if he knew the precise meaning of the word. "No, I'm not a lawyer," he said. "But I'm going to Portugal."

Marriage was easy in Eureka. Scattered through the

town were marriage chapels as well as clumps of for-hire ministers. Most purchased their credentials online without the inconvenience of theological study or knowledge. To obtain a license at town hall, couples needed drivers' licenses or birth certificates and to know their Social Security Numbers, as well as having sixty dollars in cash. They also had to be over eighteen. For people under eighteen there were other requirements. These did not intrigue me as I have reached the rational age at which the sane find the thoughts and doings of youth mind-numbing if not repellant. At one time marriage was big business in Eureka. During the past decade, however, the number of couples pledging allegiance before kitchen altars seemed to have decreased. I didn't know the reason, but when in doubt blaming the stock market is always good strategy. Resting on a bench beside the courthouse was a couple who had recently bought their license. A blue sash hung over the woman's right shoulder and fell across her midriff. Printed on the sash was "Bride To Be." The couple were middle-aged. They were a widow and a widower and had long known each other and each other's spouse. Most people marrying in Eureka whom I met resembled them. They married as much for friendship and convenience as for affection. No one suffered from the spontaneous combustion of hormones and rushed blazing into a fire-extinguishing coupling. Interspersed among the vintage couples was occasionally a pair of blushing varietals. "We're from McAllister, Oklahoma," a boy barely out of swaddling clothes said. "Our baby is due in three months," his new wife said. "It's a girl, and her name is Camille."

Aside from a Barnes & Noble and a consignment shop there are practically no stores in Storrs, and most restaurants are inexpensive eateries, generally fast-food franchises which cater to the wallets and tastes of students. Shopping is almost nonexistent. Students wear T-shirts almost all celebrating colleges or athletic teams. I'd never seen aggressively patriotic shirts like those on racks in Eureka. "If This Flag Offends You," writing scrolling around an ineptly-drawn American flag read, "I'll Help You Pack." "GEEZER formerly known as STUD MUFFIN," print on a second shirt stated, ostensibly identifying the wearer. I'd never read a recipe for baking studs or for that matter tie clasps, cufflinks, lapel pins, earrings, or arm garters in muffins. "Hard on the teeth and epiglottis," I imagined, "and probably not dandy for the colon." For the record my favorite ingredients of muffins are walnuts, cranberries, apples, raisins. and, if fresh from the bush, blueberries.

On a stand in Hippie Biker Chick, the Biker Boutique, were shelves of baseball caps. None of the caps urged people to make love rather than war. Hippie times had changed, and all celebrated military and xenophobic patriotism. Sewn on the crowns and brims were phrases like "Army Defending the Faith Since 1776" and "United States Marine Corps. The Few. The Proud." The caps were brightly colored. A Vietnam Veteran cap was green and yellow while the Air Force cap was blue as the wild blue yonder. On the crown of the 2nd Amendment cap appeared a skull. Clamped between its jawbones were a pair of pistols—a sketchy representation of flintlocks—"America's Original Homeland Security." "Too old to be fired," Josh said later, "and less dangerous than the caps for sale in Storrs mindlessly celebrating athletics."

The vulgarity apparent in some shops depressed me. The first things I noticed in the window of Blackie's Backyard were sentimental gravestones. Blackie's sold Gifts for Pets and Pet Lovers, but not pets themselves. In the middle of a heart engraved on a marker was a paw print. Below the print, an epitaph said, "You Are My Favorite HELLO and My Hardest GOODBYE." "You Left Paw Prints On Our Hearts And We Are Forever Changed," another epitaph stated. Buried in my side yard at home are two dogs. Atop each grave is a rock, not engraved, but with the dog's name painted on it: Penny and Binky. "Oh, dear," I thought remembering dogs, and indeed years, buried elsewhere: George, Pup Pup, Fritzie, and Heinzie I, II, and III, all dachshunds. But then my mood changed. I noticed a collection of smutty signs hanging on a shelf inside the store. On each sign a black dachshund stood in a patch of grass. While the caption under one sign read, "The Grass is Greener Under My Weiner," that under a second sign asked, "You Want to Hold My Weiner?" "What a poor advertisement," I thought turning my back on the window. No matter how much a person sees, he'll never know any place thoroughly, not even the basinet in which he spent childhood. Morris suddenly appeared beside me. Morris was a familiar sight in Eureka. As I looked at him, my mood changed. Instead of censorious, I became admiring. Morris was afflicted, and townfolk tended to him. He rode the trolley free, and restaurants gave him lunch. When crossing a road, he looked to his right but forgot to look left, so people shepherded him from sidewalk to sidewalk. "We take care of him," Eric a trolley driver said. "That's what we do here." "How decent to be a member of the Safety Patrol fifty years after leaving grammar school," I thought.

Often, I wonder if what I put on paper is ever right. Weeks later I wandered beyond the store window into Blackie's Backyard. The dachshund signs were fibrillations out of rhythm with the rest of the store. Blackie himself had been a border collie. Suspended from the ceiling was the cart in which Blackie rode after he lost the use of his hind legs. On the wall behind the counter was an album of pictures of Blackie. The Weiner dog signs led me to misjudge owners of the store. In truth, they were good-natured and pleasant and remained so even as I marveled, and scoffed a little, at some of the items for sale. Along one wall hung tutus. People who owned Yorkies bought closets of them. Fluffy with crinoline, decorated with shiny ribbons, and dyed red, blue, and pink, the dresses looked like the fanciful rigs worn by participants in baby beauty pageants. Best sellers were sports jerseys donned by pets eager to show solidarity with their masters' favorite professional athletic teams. The most popular jerseys for football teams were the Steelers, the Packers, and the Patriots; among baseball teams, the Cubs and the Cardinals. Also hanging on the wall was a wardrobe of dog life preservers, all orange and in different sizes. "There are rivers everywhere hereabouts," the owner explained albeit he shook his head slightly when he told me that attached to one brand of preserver was a beer bottle opener. "Understandable," I said, "clearly to open Bowser Beer for dogs." Doggy matters make me garrulous. I almost said more about Bowser Beer which, for the record, is brewed out of meat and barley with a touch of yeasty glucosamine, but then two real customers wandered into the Backyard, and I unleashed the owner and scooted out of the way.

Still, soiling humor was common in commercial Eureka. Attached to the wall above the cash register in a clothing store was a placard reading "Don't Forget To Wash Your Butt !!!" "That sign is terrible. Take it down now," I said to the two clerks at the counter. "I wish we could," one of the clerks answered, "But we can't. The owner put it there, and he likes it." I knew nothing about patrons of the store. Maybe they erupted in gaskinslapping hee-haws when they read the placard, kicked up their pasterns, tossed the bits of financial restraint, and galloped off on buying sprees. I was not a potentially valuable costumer. I have never been an impulse or really any species of buyer. When I travel, I purchase nothing for myself only presents for family and octogenarian friends. Once a year I buy a pair of running shoes online, always Asics Gel Keyano's and only when the price drops below ninety dollars and shipping is free. My second day in Eureka, however, I slipped out of character. Perhaps it was more accurate to say I drifted back into adolescence. In a fun shop I bought a Cookie Roach, a plastic imitation oatmeal cookie two-and-a-half inches in diameter. The cookie was really a hollow cap. A snippet of fishing line under the cap was attached to a rubber roach. The cap covered the roach, and when someone lifted the cookie, the roach popped out squiggling. I would have bought other things, but the traditional items that appealed to me had vanished from fun shops: ice cubes with flies frozen in them, flies themselves especially ravenous horseflies, drinking glasses that leaked, monstrous warts, and swollen rubber fingers wrapped in imitation gauze and scabby with dried blood.

In a sense the roach bit me. I succumbed to the buying bug and searched for presents for family. In a china shop I found a platter that I thought would appeal to Vicki. Before purchasing it, I chatted with the shop owner and discovered that she "carried." Arkansas was a carrying state, and she told me that she kept a pistol handy, volunteering that she and her husband went to a shooting range twice a month. I laid platter on the counter and turned away. "I can't buy from you. You are not my kind of person," I said. Sadly, there were times in Eureka when despite my Southern upbringing, or maybe because of it, Arkansas was foreign, and I recognized that I was a citizen of another country. I shrugged and walked down to Center Street. Displayed in a window was a big poster, two by three-and-a-half feet. Depicted on the poster was the night sky vibrant with color and swirling with stars and suns. Although Vicki was earthbound, the poster mirrored her mood when I left home. Printed on the poster in capital letters and signed by NASA was the declaration, "I Need My Space." The poster made me smile, but I never considered purchasing it. Why buy a present certain to bypass the attic and go directly into a tag sale? More to my funny bone was a poster announcing a "Lost Unicorn." "If Found," the poster advised, "Please Lay Off The Drugs."

Most shops in Eureka were hived along Main, Spring, and Center streets. Their cells were narrow but often deep, and their windows were cluttered and colorful—honey to attract swarms of tourists. Downtown reminded me of shopping areas near Caribbean ports where cruise ships docked. In Eureka touts were inside stores hawking business rather than outside. But the bustle was similar, jostling and invigorating, tiring and distasteful if one were feeling splenetic, but withal fun, so much fun that people wanted to buy and participate in the commotion. The stores sold everything: food, clothes, toiletries, semi-precious stones, jewelry, watches, new antiques and old, porcelain, high and low art, folk and sophisticated, handicrafts from abroad and locally made, and caissons loaded with knick-knacks that appealed to people surfing through days on waves of euphoria. I suspected that if Josh poked about he could find a WhooHa, a mythical item he has mentioned for years, maybe even a newer and enhanced variant, a WhooHaHa. "Here in Packrats," a manager said, "I deal with at least fifty vendors. They market everything."

To my embarrassment I bought a fist-sized wooden frog at Natures Treasures. The frog hunkered over, all feet on the ground. A ridge of corrugations ran from his head down his back looking like the froggy version of a Mohawk haircut. Running a small wooden baton over the corrugations produced a frog sound. Little wooden frogs sounded like spring peepers; mine, like a bullfrog. Rana now resides in a storage drawer in my desk, his companions, eyeglasses abandoned when prescriptions changed, and clumped together like leaves of American Pondweed raked and dried, medallions given to runners who completed road races. Rana came down with a permanent sore throat shortly after arriving in Storrs, and his singing days ended immediately after his audition.

Sauntering through shops was good carnivalesque entertainment. Instead of bumper cars and carousel horses, a tourist could wheel through the Jewel Box into Trading Post and on to Just Between Friends, Granny's Place, All That Glitters, Dreamweavers, Fantasy & Stone, Sweet's Fudge Kitchen, Crystal Waters, and Hats, Hides & Heirlooms. Lazy One sold pajamas and loungewear, and Babes 'N Blades specialized in women's dresses and knives, these last more of the eviscerating rather than the kitchen block variety. Outside Wilson & Wilson Folk Art, a sandwich board urged passersby to "Please come in. This is a frown free zone." Inside Bob Marley assured customers that everything was going to be all right. A few stores up the street in Rowdy Beaver Den & Store, Johnny Cash had a different take on life. Confined to Folsom Prison, he hung his head and cried whenever he heard a train whistle. Window displays turned walking into ambling. In the window of White River Tobacco was a selection of ornamental license plates and signs. All had aged literally and metaphorically. "Hippies Use Backdoor," one read, "No Exceptions." There were wastrels in Eureka but no hippies. People who once wore flowers in their hair now tended gardens. Instead of dreaming about going to San Francisco, they worried that if their hearts deflated they wouldn't reach Little Rock before the only sounds they heard were those of silence. For me the stores were entertaining side shows. In the Nut House stood ranks of barrels brimming with pistachios. These were not ordinary salted "sit in front of the television and nibble" pistachios. They were, among others, garlic and onion, hot onion and garlic, jalapeno, lemon, barbeque, Cajun, chili lime, hickory smoked, and red-hot habanero pistachios. A notice in front of the barrels said, "Don't be a NUT MUNCHER! Ask for samples at the front." I am a hetero-gastronome. I looked but didn't taste.

Deep thoughts are fabrications, generally slapped together by people who cannot express themselves clearly. While clarity can be remarkably discerning, obscurity is often trivial, cosmetic rather than natural, and so uninteresting it poisons thinking. Describing what one sees is difficult. Describing the unseen is easy. Eureka's tourist shops were kaleidoscopic with objects — things to be noticed and enjoyed for themselves, not because they awakened krakens dozing in the psyche. In most shops, an item made me pause. The Secret Garden was a mosaic of artifacts. What attracted my attention were two lard cans on a shelf above a row of display cases. Each can cost $245 and once contained fifty pounds of lard. Cooking has changed. Today suburbanites don't keep lard on the kitchen stove as Mother did when I was a boy. Mother kept two cans, both Maxwell House Coffee cans, one for lard, the other a spittoon for Wilna, our maid who dipped snuff.

One of the cans in the Garden had contained Fisher's Lard distributed by Fisher Packing in Louisville, Kentucky; the other BB Lard produced by The Braun Brothers Packing Company in Troy, New York. A ribbon of bunting decorated the front of the can containing Fisher's Lard. "Fine for Frying. Fine for Pastries. Fine for Cakes," it said. "Fifty pounds!" Mechelle who worked in the store exclaimed. "I couldn't use that much lard in a lifetime. But the ribbon explains it. People once used lard for everything." "Yes," I agreed. "Today folks don't even spoon lard into the pot when they cook turnip greens." Also depicted on the Fisher can was a slice of cherry pie. "My favorite pie," Mechelle said, "especially when rhubarb is mixed with the cherries." "Pies with cherries and rhubarb or strawberries and rhubarb are the only desserts worth eating," I said. "I'll bet you will never sell one of the cans," I said. "You'd be surprised," Mechelle answered. "We have a couple more cans, and I sold one last month—to a man named Fisher."

Much surprised me in Eureka. Maybe leaving the snug and often deadening familiarity of home always surprises. Maybe life surprises when people have leisure enough for their attention to wander promiscuously. In a nook next to Basin Springs Park at the curve where South Main became Spring Street was a red wooden kiosk, really an expanded storage shed. Robert sat inside behind a small counter at a cashier's window. Throughout the day he sold funnel cakes, corn dogs, and lemonade. One morning when business was slow, I noticed that he was reading Kazantzakis's *Zorba the Greek*. "I'm also reading *Walden*," he said reaching up to a shelf and pulling out a copy of Thoreau. "I alternate the books I read. Switching back and forth prevents my attention from lagging. That way I won't doze and miss things." Even though I knew people were always more various than pages made them appear, I was surprised. Robert himself was a mechanical engineer. He owned the kiosk, his wife a nearby pizzeria, and his two daughters a coffee stall. "We like Eureka," he said. "We want to help the town, so we each bought a business." Robert and his wife had been married twenty-five years and had three children. Robert, however, was one of seventeen children. His father married six times. Robert's mother was his fifth wife. She was twenty-one when she married Robert's father. He was fifty-eight. "I was an only child," I said. "Very different," Robert said. Online Robert bought my autobiographical account of childhood *A Comfortable Boy*, and before I left Eureka I signed it for him, the only book I autographed in Eureka.

As might be expected, writers at the Colony rarely startled me. Most lived on pages, shaping arresting plots and images. People ate dinner together, but by six o'clock writing had tired them. They were often absent presences, and when they talked, they chatted about families and related autobiographical anecdotes. Rarely did they discuss writing, and never did they mention inspiration. Only neophytes talk about inspiration. Writing is an uninspired, lonely endeavor. The experienced writer reads, thinks, and plans. Day after day he writes. In conversation I minimize the importance of writing in my life, in part to take a vacation from my desk and dank hours spent wrestling with words. The preoccupations of age have exacerbated this inclination. In contrast many people, particularly the young and those who have written little, treat writing as a matter of consequential, almost spiritual seriousness. Only rarely does the author of a small number of pages treat writing as cavalierly, and as refreshingly, as did Norinda at the Colony. "I specialize in Haiku," Norinda announced over dessert at dinner. "I don't like spending time writing. I get exhausted. Haikus are short and easy, and I can write them quickly and get on with my life."

Dwayne was the only other person at the Colony who surprised me. He lived in Akron and was a want-to-be writer. At dinner he was fresh, full of words, and eager to mount his hobby-horse, the curse of plastic bottles. "They are," he maintained, "a greater threat to civilization, to nature, to everything than nuclear weapons." The oceans, he said, were already ruined. I agreed with him. The ships on which Vicki and I cruised sailed through Sargasso Seas composed of plastic bottles rather than brown seaweed. Dwayne enjoyed his stay at the Colony, and the morning he left, he brought a tattered cardboard box into the Colony's office. He put it on the counter. "Enjoy," he said. "It's a present. Open it after I leave."

Inside the box lay a heap of broken Christmas ornaments—discards that failed to sell at a tag sale. On top lay a headless Santa Claus; by his side, an armless plaster of Paris Virgin Mary. Next to her was a small snowman. His body was a stack of three white balls. The middle ball was a snowglobe containing water and white particles or snow. Once shaking the snowman swirled the snow inside the globe. Those winters had ended. The particles remained inside the globe, but the water through which they stormed had evaporated. A few flakes from another gale clung to one side of a plastic wreath two-and-a-half inches in diameter. The rest had melted, and green had leached off the fronds turning them gray. Amid the other items were decorations for small presents: two plastic roses stapled to a green bow, and a match box, a scrap of red cloth wrapping it and on top a green cloth folded into a triangle and looking like a roof. A safety pin tacked both the roof and a snippet of paper to the box. Printed on the paper in miniscule letters was "Merry Christmas." Also in the box was a ceramic Momma Bear holding a Baby Bear. They had immigrated to Eureka from Sri Lanka where they had been manufactured or, better perhaps, born. They must have arrived in summer because while Momma wore a green dress and a servant's white apron and cap, Baby was naked. At the bottom of the box lay two small cards. On the front of one was a candle, a ruff of holly at its base and a golden halo circling the wick. Written inside the card was "A Dickensian Christmas Stocking—A Reminder of Eureka Springs Centennial 1979." Inside the second card was a snapshot of four girls perched on a fence and the words "To Mary Ellen from Lucille." "Well, what a what," Marsha said when I showed her the contents of the box. "A real surprise. What are you going to do with it?" "As the old man said when he walked out of the liquor store and dropped his bottle of whiskey, 'Christmas done come and gone.' I'll get rid of it," I answered.

Late in the 19th and early in the 20th century, Southern mountain villages became popular resorts and health havens. In the middle of the 19th century, Simla on a spur of the Himalayas in Northern India became known as the summer capital of the British Raj. At the start of summer colonial families moved to Simla to escape the miasmas percolating through India's humid lowlands. Similarly, businessmen in Southern cities often sent wives and children to getaways, higher, cooler places, healthier and uncontaminated by urban effluvia. Nashvillians migrated to Monteagle, Tennessee, perched on the Cumberland Plateau, nineteen hundred feet above sea level. Especially popular were springs. People suffering from wards of ailments filled the dozen large hotels and sundry boarding houses in Red Boiling Springs, Tennessee. They rested and drank the mineral waters of which there were five kinds, the most famous being the Red and the Black. Years ago, I tried the Black. It packed a viscera-wringing wallop. Similarly, Eureka Springs was a medical destination. Tourists bathed in pools and drank the waters. As churches now feud over which denominations save more souls, so rivalries existed between the springs, the supporters of Basin Spring, for example, once asserting that its waters were responsible for ninety percent of the cures effected in Eureka.

Panaceas weren't confined to the water. Early in the 20th century for some twenty-five years the Crescent Hotel became Crescent College, a conservatory. The college was open during the entire year excepting summers when the building functioned as a hotel. Dora Maxwell, one of the college's students, drank deep of the healing waters. She married a William Estep, and they traveled to India. The experience transformed Dora, and on her return, she became "that noted lecturer, teacher and healer of Super Science Mind, Madame Price." She and her husband became acclaimed snake-oil salesmen. By 1935 they claimed to have two thousand followers. So long as the devotees followed Estep's teachings, they would "never suffer an illness." Later in Kansas City the couple founded the Gland-Estemeter Corporation which produced machines guaranteed to cure anything. Along the way they lured marks to invest in a Mountain of Gold. In 1949 they perfected Atom Water Treatments, a broad-spectrum wonder regimen which simultaneously cured cancer and provided protection from the explosion of atomic bombs. Although the Esteps have been forgotten, the FBI once labeled them the "most notorious medical and religious fakers" the agency "ever caught up with."

Hucksters are born every day. On November 6, 1937, the headline in *The Daily Times-Echo* read, "Eureka Springs Extends Greetings to Norman Baker and Staff and the New Baker Hospital." The Crescent Hotel folded, but a medical carnival settled in the building. Baker was a smart eccentric. He painted sections of the hospital lavender. He drove a lavender colored Cord automobile and "wore white linen suits with lavender silk shirts and ties and wrote on lavender stationery." Tricksters obscure and bumfuzzle. They wave capes, pull rabbits out of hats, and divert attention from commonplace, and dull, reality. Atop the Ozarks in "The Switzerland of America," Baker Hospital was "Where Sick Folks Get Well." Baker promised to cure cancers and tumors without using knives, radium, x-rays, or serums. The show lasted for three years after which Baker moved to Leavenworth Prison. He received a four-year sentence. In 1944 he was paroled after having his sentence reduced 236 days for good behavior.

Eureka's medical past was in small part its present. The big top departed, but puppet shows continued. Such matters interested me. I had reached the age at which health became a mainstay of conversation. Friends slowly lost words or died suddenly. Forgotten relatives rose from the grave dragging their fatal symptoms behind them. In the pantry at home next to the telephone sat a clutter of pills, elastic bandages, and blood pressure monitors. A holiday was a day in which neither Vicki nor I had a doctor's appointment. Perhaps because I unconsciously secreted sympathy for folks enduring medical problems, shortly after I arrived in Eureka strangers described matters that sickened their days: the wife dying from an inherited neurological disease or the husband who refused to die despite his heart stopping twice, the rupture of a major artery, and two last-resort helicopter flights to specialist hospitals. Outside the Crescent a man showed me a forearm big as a ham and swollen with a staph infection, and a woman described her daughter's heart transplant. The heart came from a man taken off life support in South Carolina. He'd driven his car into a tree. "More than likely," I thought, "he had the South Carolina vanity plate that proclaimed, 'In God We Trust.'" I imagined relatives weeping tears of thanksgiving and saying, "God loved Otis so much that He promoted him to Glory." The same religious sloganeering appeared on a Tennessee vanity plate. The insurance industry lobbied against its adoption. But the money it ladled out on Charlotte Avenue in Nashville was only a drop in the collection plate compared to the shekels with which Pharisees blessed far-right thinking legislators. "Pious pills are always effective," Josh says, "if money is their primary bactericide."

Yesteryear's snake-oil was often viperous. Today's wasn't fanged and smacked of garter and green rather than rattlesnakes. In Eureka fortune tellers raised the spirits of the melancholy, and smiling barkers peddled amulets, crystals, rings, and bracelets. These probably did less good or harm than a sanctified quack's laying on hands and shouting "Heal" or "Get thee hence, Satan." At best they were placebos. "Putting a ring on your finger or through your nose," a man said to me, "isn't going do much for liver cancer." "Or, an ingrowing toenail," his wife said. Still, salesmen implied that their jewelry could alleviate some of the unpleasant aspects of a nursing home of maladies, including among others, the Shakes, Gout, Edema, Poor Balance, Fibromyalgia, Sciatica, Joint Pain, Prostate Ailments, and Poor Blood Flow. "Frequency Infused Jewelry," one company explained, harmonized "the bio energy in our bodies by eliminating high energy electromagnetic interferences to re-establish the bodies [sic] natural frequencies." At the end of its webpage, the company noted that the FDA had not evaluated its products. Moreover, they were not sold as medical devices. "Consult a medical professional before wearing this product if pregnant, lactating, allergic to metal or alloys or if you are using a pace maker or other medical device."

When I resisted her initial pitch explaining that I never wore jewelry, an abnormally pleasant woman tried to sell me a thermos that converted normal water into Structured Water. I left the store. The time had come, to paraphrase Lewis Carroll's walrus, to talk of actual things, "why the sea is boiling hot and whether pigs have wings." However, as I climbed the hill past the Basin Park Hotel, I met a young couple on the sidewalk. They both wore turquoise T-shirts. Stamped on the chest was the phrase, "Hope Dealer." I asked the boy the meaning of the words. "We're from Kansas," he said, "and our church handed these out. I think it means that our faith offers hope." I asked if the church had a large membership. "Yes," he said. "Several hundred — lots of shirts." The boy's wife was pregnant, and I asked when the baby was due. "In four months," she said. "It's our first, and we are so excited." Hope and souvenir dealers—that's what people selling bracelets and telling fortunes were. If quackery didn't undermine a person's health or cost much money, it wasn't dangerous. In fact, occasionally it seasoned bland days.

Several stores sold essential oils, rejuvenators for mind and body, inessential seasoning but to me appealing. Some wellness treatments had exotic names, at one shop, Zyto Compass, Aroma Dome, and Vibrational Raindrop Technique. Most treatments featured a massage. I pondered getting one, but what, I wondered, would I do next? I was by myself, and I'd be all greased up with nowhere to go. I'd be limber, perhaps lissome, but who'd watch me do cartwheels and applaud the new acrobatic me? Some visitors referred to Eureka as Chiggertown. Chiggers in Eureka were not flatland, you-all drawling, cotton-boll chiggers. They were mountain chiggers hardened by scratching out livings in coves and hollows, "the species probably," an entomologist speculated, "a wrong-side-of-the-limestone descendant of the cave centipede." After a week in Eureka, my hide looked like a lumpy quilt all the stuffing gathered in great red welts: around my waist, under my arms, behind my knees, down my legs, across my back, and in places, quite frankly, that I assumed were inhospitable to bugs. They even dug between my toes producing blistering sores. "I moved here from Manitoba ten years ago," a woman told me. "Now I dream of returning. I don't care how cold winters on the prairie are. I can't tolerate chiggers any longer."

Although I ran and walked at least eight miles in Eureka every day, I didn't go to the pharmacy beyond downtown on Route 62 in hopes of finding an ointment to stop itching. Plodding highways unnerved me, especially if they twisted and slanted almost hard-balling cars toward their shoulders. Consequently, I explored oil patches downtown. The owner of one store recommended a comfrey salve produced by Ozark Mountain Goodness. "I've heard," he said, "that comfrey reduces itching" Hearing was only hearing. The salve smelled like fresh air and would have cooled smoldering callouses. But insofar as chiggers were concerned it was a failure. They chewed it, got angry, and escalated the itching. Next, I bought a spray "Bug Off!" sold at Soap Stop. This was another local blend, containing witch hazel, glycerin, citronella, lemon eucalyptus, and other essential oils. I don't know whether Bug Off! was effective because it was a spray or because high chigger season ended. Nevertheless, after I sprayed it on my ankles and calves, fewer chiggers settled around my waist. Moreover, the welts raised by those who dug in were modest — inclines rather than hills. Perhaps I developed immunity. When I was a child despite my roaming wood and field, my parents never discovered a chigger on me. In contrast chiggers ate Mother alive. "Goddamn this grass," I remember her saying as she stood in our driveway in Nashville looking at the yard.

Eureka was home to one real elixir, a magical decoction, overlooked by the FDA but warrantied by me, a phylactery certain to banish spleen, resole shoes and heart, and to make the mute stand and shout (oh, dear) "Eureka." Sixteen years earlier I had a double-chocolate soda at Ice Cream Delights on North Main. Not since childhood had I enjoyed a pure soda — glacier-thick with ice cream and chocolate syrup bubbling in soda water. Order a soda today and one receives that product of bovine mastitis, a milkshake, or, worse, ice cream doused in gum-curdling ginger ale. During my first week in Eureka I walked down North Main lamenting that Ice Cream Delights had closed. I was wrong. The Durhams remained where they had been for thirty-five years, and for $3.50 Richard Durham still dispensed rejuvenating natural wellness — "just what the doctor ordered" served in a waiting room bright with soda fountain tiles black and white on the floor, creamery chairs with heart-shaped vanilla backs, and walls red and white displaying Coca Cola memorabilia: among others, posters depicting girls peppy as cheerleaders toasting life with Cokes in their hands. In the wall at one end of the room was a stained-glass window showing a mother and daughter sitting across from each other eating ice cream. The mother held a cone plump with two scoops, on the bottom pink, on the top yellow, lemon on strawberry, I assumed, not my favorites. The daughter's taste was more to my liking. In front of her sat a dish of chocolate topped with whipped cream.

Every week while I was in Eureka I had a medicinal double-chocolate soda. As a result, not once during the two months did gout turn my toes the color of plums. Never did I suffer from wind colic. After I washed in sandalwood soap made from goat's milk, I didn't baa. Never was I costive or bilious, and only rarely did I call jackasses fools. Having but a single soda each week nurtured both imaginary and real delectation. The former occurred when I pushed back from my writing desk and mulled a chocolate break, the latter, when I lifted the iced tea spoon out of the soda glass, its bowl heaped with chocolate, flakey around the lip with frozen droplets of sparkling water.

The sodas aside, I lived like an ascetic. I don't know if genes, age, or devotion to writing were responsible. A study in the rear of a house isn't a cave in a desert. But people who are modestly prolific occasionally retreat from the bustle of doing and live like anchorites. Excepting one stormy day and then two mornings when I could not stop coughing, I jogged every morning before sunrise. Not once, however, did I watch television, listen to a radio, read a newspaper, drink alcohol, or eat a meal other than at the Colony. My behavior in Eureka resembled my behavior in Connecticut. No matter the ardor of their disclaimers, people are their habits. At Judge Roy Bean's "Old Time Photographs" tourists posed for pictures in unfancy dress. In the most popular pose they donned wild-west rigging and looked like celluloid bar floozies and their gunslinging boyfriends. Despite the costumes and forced smiles, however, the people came across as sheepish, aware that clothes didn't make the man or woman and that they were still salesmen and mechanics, that they worked in an industrial plant outside Houston or that they drove through days selling medical supplies in Kansas and Oklahoma.

At home I do not subscribe to the *Hartford Courant*. At breakfast I don't turn on the radio in the kitchen, and I generally watch television only while Vicki and I eat dinner. As did my mother, so I have lost my tolerance for alcohol. More than a half a glass of wine nauseates me. Although I knew Eureka had many notable restaurants, Jana's dinners at the Colony were too good to miss. Moreover, I was by myself. Eating alone focuses a person's attention on the dishes served, forcing him to treat them sacramentally, something that I, a nonbeliever of most truths, think irreligious. Habits make the man. In Storrs I camp in the university library. In Eureka I haunted the Carnegie Library and read books written by long-time bedside companions: Alan Furst, Lee Child, Martin Cruz Smith, John Sandford, and M. L. Longworth. When I tired of spies and cutthroats, I didn't roam fallow fictional pastures. I stayed home and reread old friends, dear hearts found in familiar places, Isabelle Dalhousie's Edinburgh and Kaye Gibbons's North Carolina.

I didn't regret not straying from Eureka in pursuit of the exotic. Early one morning a resident at the Colony saw a wild pig trying to overturn a garbage can on Spring Street. For a time, I was envious, but soon afterward I had a better porcine experience. One night during an after-dinner stroll, I met a woman outside her house exercising Fat Boy her pet pig. Fat Boy was young and friendly and very obedient. After snouting me, he did a trick on my behalf, spinning in a circle and chasing his "tailet." Later he scratched his back against a tire on a Hyundai causing the car to shiver. The woman also had a dog named Buster and in the house Princess, another pig. Princess weighed 300 pounds and loved to dress in party hats, tutus, and, despite the size of her poitrine, necklaces. Princess and Fat Boy were picky and would not eat pig chow until after their mistress sprinkled Cheerios over the top. I regretted not being quick enough on my trotters to ask their favorite flavors: Very Berry, Honey Nut, or Medley Crunch. Fat Boy looked like my kind of pig, however, and I knew his Cheerio of choice was Chocolate Peanut Butter. Moreover, I suspected that before Princess slipped on glad rags she took a spoonful or two of Frosted Cheerios to goose her into a high-stepping mood.

In Eureka I led a porch life. Sometimes I left the porch without getting up from the swing in front of my room. Other times I strolled a nearby trail or road; I didn't wander far. One afternoon I walked down Grand to the Eureka Springs & North Arkansas Railway on North Main. Bull thistles bloomed beside the road. While the blossoms were purple and as alluringly fragrant as powder puffs, the thistles' stems and leaves wound through each other fencing off the shoulders. "Like so many things," I thought, "simultaneously enticing and forbidding." Buzzards had left their roost behind a nearby ridge and were riding thermals soaring and waltzing the air. The sky was cerulean and cloudless. "The country version of *The Blue Danube*," I thought dreamily until a box truck rattled up the hill, wobbled, and tilted toward me, its motor thudding and coughing expectorant smog.

The railway was a tourist attraction. People took short excursions along the tracks traveling to that vague but always present destination memory. Others ate lunch or dinner in the dining car. A diesel engine pulled and pushed the Pullman and dining cars. The engine had done yeoman service for, among others, the Missouri Pacific, the Chicago and Eastern Illinois, and at Granite Mountain Quarries. The deep thrum of the engine was a soporific, not lulling me to sleep but effacing the present and awakening recollection of my childhood love of trains. Engineers took me for short rides when I was a boy, and in Eureka in the train yard I climbed into Engine 201 and sat in both the engineer's and fireman's seats. I tugged levers, and although 201 did not move and was almost an immigrant having spent distant years working on the Panama Canal, off I rolled through Hanover and Ashland, Virginia. If the day had not been humid, I would have traveled from Nashville to Richmond by way of Cincinnati. Water steamed off me, and although I needed to stop at a water tower, I chugged ahead and climbed into a caboose built by Pacific Car and Foundry in Renton, Washington. I hoisted myself into the crew's raised lookout seats and waved from the windows. "If the boy I was could see the boy I am now, what a treat that would be for him," I thought.

Painted above the doors at both ends of the caboose was "Watch for Slack Action." My porch days were often slack. From the depot I walked up Main to downtown. On the way I stopped at EureKan Art. I'd overheated, and the gallery was a cool place rambling across the first story of a large old house. Ken, the owner, took art on consignment, and the contents were various, hanging on walls and partitions, arranged on tables, filling shelves and a museum of glass-topped exhibition cases: pottery, sculpture, jewelry, fanciful knick-knacks, oil paintings, watercolors, and carvings. "At least once a month, somebody comes in, looks around, and asks, 'Did you make all this?'" Ken said. "Can you imagine?" Yes, I imagined. Tourists were often mind and foot weary. Nonetheless, classrooms of people rarely read or observed carefully. For them speaking was easier than pondering. In the lobby of the Crescent loomed a massive fireplace. Printed on it were six lines of verse: "Although upon a summer's day, / You'll lightly turn from me away. / When autumn leaves are scattered wide, / You'll often linger by my side; / But when the snow the earth doth cover / Then you will be my ardent lover." "All day long guests ask me what that means," a bellhop told me looking at the fireplace. "Even when I explain it's a riddle and tell them that the answer is fireplace, they don't understand."

At moments porch life was dizzingly active. At the end of August, the 26th annual three-day Volkswagen Festival took place. On Saturday Volkswagens paraded. They passed in front of the porch, 263 vans, beetles, kharmann ghias, and customized models — some lowered, others raised, still others welded out of shape into homemade mechanical costume jewelry. While many were zoot-suited, a few were rusted and barn-stalled. While some passed in a whisper, others racketed like motorcycles. Strapped to roofs were surfboards, bicycles, and duffel and leather bags. Through the open roofs of vans children stood and waved. Drivers were old and young, groomed and ungroomed, pretend hippies and car folk. Horns blared and played tunes, the favorite being calls to the post. A couple sat on the steps of the Colony and watched the parade. They drove from Missouri in a new Volkswagen. They owned twelve Volkswagens, "maybe more," the husband told me. The number didn't decrease. "If I sell one," he said. "I'm not happy until I buy another." From the cars people tossed necklaces of Mardi Gras beads and bushels of candy — enough Tootsie Rolls to cause every squirrel in town to become diabetic. Three strands of beads, two gold and one blue, landed in the false dragonhead or obedient plant that had begun to bloom at the corner of the porch. At the end of the parade I picked out the necklaces. One thing leads to another. I'd spent hours trying to decide if the agaricus breaking through the grass across from Grotto Spring were flat top or horse mushrooms. But I hadn't noticed the slender gothic spikes of false dragonhead budding and swelling into bloom in front of the Colony. Instead of resembling reptilian heads, the flowers looked like tapered horn-shaped flagons, their rosy mouths dappled with the spumy remnants of an elfish bacchanalia.

Bluegrass Weekend also took place in August, and I spent two hours on a Friday at Basin Spring listening to

The Crumbs from Fort Smith. They were accomplished. At least two of the group taught music while another evaluated petroleum reserves. The picking plucked at my emotions and attracted me yet simultaneously thrust me away. Days are more tranquil in Connecticut amid the surround-sound easy-listening that plays everywhere endlessly but which one never hears. Still, I enjoyed the bluegrass, especially the twanging narratives akin to hokey tales that appear in my essays. Amid recognizable standbys, The Crumbs played a selection of their own songs, a verse of my favorite recounting, "She tore my heart right out of my chest / And stomped that sucker flat. / She's gone with her boyfriend to Budapest / And left me working at the laundromat."

"If I were teaching, I'd recite that in class," I thought. Because people like me could do so little with our hands that we might as well have been armless, we fashioned the self-aggrandizing fiction that writing was an art, difficult to master and to understand. As a result, our classrooms became solemn insignificant places when instead they should have been raucous with smiles, places where a person wanted to be, not where he was required to be. "Poetry should entertain and delight," I thought, my mind whipping into spin dry. "Certainly, poetry can teach, but then what lessons? Not those, I hoped, pushed by "Inquisitors sticking *God* on license plates at the exhaust pipe end of automobiles." "It's not the office of the poet," Josh said to me later, "to show us how to live our lives." At the concert I sat next to a man from Berryville. The music affected us, and between sets, we chatted about corny matters, literarily so: hominy and cornbread then biscuits. "My cornbread and biscuits were the best in Arkansas, but I can't make them anymore because I've gotten fat," he said. "The doctor told me if I didn't stop eating cornbread and pinto beans my heart would break and worms would eat me." The man said that giving up cornbread was so afflicting that he didn't have much heart left to break. He also said his doctor was tough and outspoken and so frightening everybody obeyed his orders.

On returning to the porch, I eavesdropped on a telephone conversation between the doctor and a new widow. The woman's husband was obese. He suffered a stroke at church while forcing himself off his knees to sing "Stand Up for Jesus." The organist rushed him to the local hospital where he died even before a nurse verified the insurance card in his wallet. Because she felt poorly, his wife did not attend church that morning and didn't learn about her husband's stroke until the doctor telephoned. "Oh, dear, my word, a stroke," she exclaimed. "I'll be there as fast as I can. As soon as I change clothes and bring the cat in, I'm on my way." "No, ma'am, don't take any chances. You shouldn't hurry. It isn't an emergency. Don't run a stop sign and have an accident or get a ticket," the doctor replied.

"I've got to get there for his sake — don't you know?" she said. "No," the doctor answered, "ten minutes or even an hour won't make any difference to him." "Oh, yes, it will. For fifty-four years that man has hovered over me studying everything I do like one of the damn humming-birds he puts feeders out for every spring. They are the meanest birds — always fighting. How'd you like to have them quarrelling outside your kitchen all day long? I'll bet you wouldn't like it at all especially if you were cooking a casserole. No right-thinking Christian cook would. I told my husband that if he'd take those birds off that sugar water they'd calm down. But did he listen? Oh, no, he never listens to anybody. He drinks soda and eats pie all day long. I told him if he didn't stop sweets would be the death of him. Anyway, I'm pulling my girdle up and am practically out the door."

"No, ma'am, take your time," the doctor said. "He won't know whether you get here today or tomorrow or next week. No matter when you arrive, he's not going to sit up and say 'how-do.' He's dead — dead, dead, dead. Dead with the big *d* and the little *d*." "What's that?

What did you say?" the woman responded. "I'm a little deaf, and sometimes I don't hear so well. Last week in the grocery when the butcher asked if I wanted pork. I thought he said something else, and I gave him what for. I told him I was too old for that foolishness, and even if I wasn't, I asked, 'who wants to get up to hot stuff in a cold meat locker. There's no telling what might freeze and break off.'"

"Ma'am," the doctor began. The time for getting words in edgewise had passed. "Doctor, should I bring Cowboy the cat?" the woman continued. "My husband is really fond of her and he'll want to pet her, sort of like that butcher wanted to pet me. Cowboy used to misbehave something terrible before we had her fixed — oh, my, just terrible, but doctor, I guess you don't pay no nevermind to such goings-on. Well, that's finally zipped — too much ice cream. Doctor, I'm all dressed, and I'll be on the way as soon as I find the goddamn cat."

Porches aren't always the quietest and safest places to sit. Sometimes stories hop off swings and wander farther than they do in books. What I have never understood was what made stories appear as siblings — fiction and nonfiction side by side, paragraph to paragraph. Two days after the Bluegrass Festival I talked to a woman whose husband recently had a heart attack and died. She returned from the grocery and discovered him in front of the television sitting in his armchair. A football game was on, but the woman said that in the excitement of the moment she didn't notice if it "was pro or college." She said she thought the game was college because her husband died on Saturday and most professional games were played on Sunday or Monday. "When the doctor examined my husband, he said he'd been dead a long time and frowned implying I should have been at home to save him, pound his chest, when he collapsed. I told that fool doctor I'd spent the morning at the grocery. He had no idea the time it takes a good shopper to fill a cart. A woman has to check her coupons and read flyers printed the day before and put in the rack at the front of the store that morning. She compares prices and read labels. She squeezes cantaloupes and samples grapes. She must decide whether white or green asparagus would be better at dinner. Then after all seems done, if she's a responsible housekeeper, she's obligated to study her receipt and be sure that the check-out girl hasn't made a mistake which she has and which she always does." "I'll bet," the woman concluded, "that doctor's wife buys frozen ready-to-eat meals. While he puts them in the oven, she mixes a drink for herself, flops down on the sofa, puts her feet on the coffee table, and watches Fox News. No wonder the doctor is so irritable. Poor man to be married to such a bitch."

As the railings in front of the porch did not fence me in, so they didn't prevent the unwanted from joining me. Unlike wives who bloomed into wit and flexibility as they aged, husbands lost hearing and often sank into lackluster intransigency. Their conversations smacked of formaldehyde and scotched the liveliest prose. After entombing the two husbands and putting the suffering and insufferable doctor into a folder perhaps to be resuscitated later, I fetched another cup of coffee from the kitchen. I planned to rock on the porch and dozing pencil-less, let days creep by until I returned to Connecticut. Unexpectedly, bronchitis joined me, bringing her unholy family: fever, night sweats, sore throat, plugged nose, galloping sinuses, throbbing head, and ceaseless coughing. The first cure I tried was visual and holistic. Glancing through the crowns of the sycamores surrounding the Colony always lifted my spirits, so I stood in the middle of a fairy circle of sycamores and looked upward along the clean white trunks past the melting green leaves into the rinsed blue sky. "If sight can wash impurities from the mind, then," I thought, "it might scrub the body." It did not. Looking up only made me woozy. In a fairy tale, exposure to Beauty caused Bacteria to mutate into a gentler, kinder pathogen. I needed a realistic not fanciful remedy. How complicated final wrappings would have been for Vicki had the bronchitis turned into pneumonia, "the old man's friend." Still, that would have provided the opportunity for her to discover the new traditions being established by Eureka's morticians. On the other hand, I was old-fashioned, and old ways were good enough for me: the fire, the ashes, and the little box delivered overnight by FedEx.

Becoming sick made me aware again that the country in which I lived differed from that inhabited by Eureka's citizens. Much, of course, was similar. Storrs and Eureka were small, and people in both places were good-natured, accommodating, and equally friendly. However, the availability of medical services diverged remarkably. Even after granting that Eureka was rural and Storrs almost urban and close to medical schools and hospital complexes, differences in the ease with which I and people in Eureka obtained care were startling. At home I could visit a family practice shortly after telephoning for an appointment. Moreover, three hundred yards behind my house was downtown Storrs. The university medical school staffed both a branch and a walk-in clinic on the square. Twice a week, to choose but a single specialty, cardiologists from the medical school saw patients at the branch—a matter of importance to people like me with fibrillations. Four years ago, when I fell off my bicycle late one Saturday afternoon and broke an arm, a doctor at the clinic set it. The following week an orthopedic surgeon from the medical school came to the branch and re-examined my arm. In Eureka medical wheels ground slower. "The hospital here can handle small things," a woman told me. "But for real emergencies, one must see a specialist, so I have medical-evacuation insurance that will fly me to Little Rock. I think the insurance costs sixty-five dollars a month."

Emergency rooms are for emergencies: the aftermath of car wrecks, stabbings, shootings, snake bites, bone-splintering falls, and hearts that inexplicably decide that the beat should not go on. I had never been in an emergency room, and to go to the Eureka hospital complaining of bronchitis struck me as whiny. Linda, the director of the Colony, volunteered to drive me to a walk-in clinic. In Eureka walk-in's were "here one day and gone the next." The organist at St. James Episcopal Church on Prospect told me that during the past year twelve couples left the congregation and Eureka. "We are a small church," she said, "and for us that is a lot of people." The people moved for the expected reasons. They aged and wanted to be closer to their children or to live where medical services were readily available. "I have to move to Fayetteville. I was in a car wreck years ago, and my back is terrible. I have already had four operations," a man said, "but I'm having trouble selling my house."

Hanging on pegs in the vestibule of St. James were four small cloth shoulder bags. Depicted on the front were a boxy, yellow car drawn by a child and the St. George Cross, a red cross on a white field, in the upper left quadrant nine small white crosses in the form of the Saint Andrews Cross. Each of the little crosses represented one of the dioceses that met in 1789 in Philadelphia to adopt the constitution of the Protestant Episcopal Church in the United States. Besides perking up the bags the colors were symbolic: the red for the sacrifice of Christ, white for the purity of the Christian faith, and blue for the humanity of Christ. Printed at the bottom of the bag were "Faith. Hope. Love." All the bags contained a drawing tablet and a box of crayons. "What nice idea," I said to a man in the church, "a good way to occupy children if a sermon goes too long or too high." "Yes," he answered. "But there are no children in this congregation. The average age of our communicants is seventy, maybe more."

I liked St. James. The building was modest and had once been a school. Its stained-glass windows were blocks of calming blue, and the ceiling was a quiet grove of wood slats. Moreover, church members served the community. I saw them cooking meals at The Little Chapel food bank and providing lunch to anyone who stopped — rich or poor. "How decent, and how right," I mused. Often my own thoughts about religion were not always decent. On Spring Street one afternoon, I met tourists from Louisiana walking their dog. The dog growled at me, and the man said, "Scot is harmless. He doesn't bite." We chatted. When I revealed I lived in Connecticut, the man shifted the conversation from dogs to politics. He asked my opinion of the president. I told him then quoted a sticker I saw pasted on a window, "I Miss Bill." "You are wrong. Clinton was a sinner, and this president is a great man," he said, gnawing into indigestible ideology. "I'm a Republican, and I know. I'm a Christian. I don't smoke, and I don't drink and . . ." At *and* the conversation ended. "Rubbish," I said and walked away. "Poor Scot," Vicki said when I wrote her. "How terrible to live with distempered people."

Eureka's most famous church was Fay Jones's Thorncrown Chapel a short distance from town and built on a hillside. On one side of the chapel were thin woods spindly with oaks, hickories, and maples, these last suffering from withering anthracnose; on the other side rose a layered limestone bluff. Between the ledges creases where water washed through sandstone flared like nostrils. The face of the bluff was bearded with moss, and over its forehead locks of ivy hung down unkempt. Here and there leaves had gathered in wrinkles between stones and rolled into damp slides. Some 425 windows and 6000 square feet of glass opened the nave so that the chapel seemed more pantheistic than Christian. The chapel floor was stone forming another ledge, polished and stable in contrast to the unshaved face of the bluff. Beams inside the chapel crossed in lattices ordering the profusion of nature, similar perhaps to the way faith imposes order on a person's life. In the chapel, I recalled Wordsworth's appealing lie, that an "impulse from a vernal wood" could teach more about man and moral good than the writings of the sages. Age calloused and protected me from blistering impulses. "Inspiring," I thought as I stood in the chapel, sunlight dappling through the windows and playing over me. The moment was nice, but it didn't last. How, I wondered, would visitors, react if a cement factory loomed on one side of the chapel and a school bus depot on the other.

I cannot explain the attraction of churches. Perhaps I explore them simply because they exist and because they often stand alone. Immediately below the porch of the Crescent Hotel was a garden of boxwood, canna lilies, and beds of red vinca. Beyond the garden the hill sloped manicured down to the Saint Elizabeth of Hungary Catholic Church. In the evening I often sat on the porch and rocked while the church carillon rang the time. The church itself was small. The interior was light and poetically airy, zephyr-like, and its stained-glass windows were pastel and easy on the eyes and mind, kindly as religion ought to be. If the religious statuary had been removed, the chapel would have seemed more Congregational than Catholic. On the floor of the rotunda was a mosaic of the American eagle, a corset of red and white stripes binding its breast, clutched in one claw an olive branch, in the other, arrows. Waving above the bird's head was bunting reading "Pro Deo" and "Pro Patria." I believe linking religion to nationalism sacrilegious, something that in the chapel failed. The head of the bird did not resemble that of an eagle but that of a dove, a bible bird, rounded, cooing, and appropriate for a church. Outside the church building gardens bloomed in ruffles. In one section, however, stood a white stone on which was engraved in capital letters, "In Loving Memory of the Victims of Abortion" and "I Will Not Forget You. I Have Carved You on the Palm of My Hand." "Let's go. Let's get out of this damnable place," Josie a resident at the Colony said when she saw the stone, turning and starting back to the Crescent. Later we sat by ourselves on the porch and rocked. Reddy Fox and Lightfoot the Deer drifted across the lawn, and as blue faded, yellow and gold streaked the sky. "This," Josie said, "is God's plenty."

What was more than plenty was Christ of the Ozarks, part of a Christian Adventureland including the Passion Play, the Holy Land, a biblical museum, and gift shops. The statue stood at the edge of Magnetic Mountain looking out over Eureka toward the Crescent. I liked seeing it at dawn when I ran and at evening when I walked. Christ was sixty-seven feet tall. His arms were spread, and the distance from fingertip to fingertip was sixty-five feet. His face was fifteen feet long, and the weight of the statue itself was approximately two million pounds. He was inhumanly white, and his robe rippled down His body in four wrinkles. "If Christ had been that big, those sons-of-bitching Romans wouldn't have screwed around with Him. They'd have left his ass alone," one of the Jesus People gazing at the statue said to me. The statue stood in a mowed green field trim as a fairway. Woods curled below and around the statue like roughs on a golf course. Looping through the woods were mountain bike trails named Genesis, Atonement, and Exodus. "Don't wander in the Desert," a sign marking the entrance to Exodus urged.

The statue did not make the present seem wanting or make me imagine a better place. Instead it made me long to wander the woods and the soiled sandy now, and the next afternoon I walked the trails for five hours. As my muscles ached and perspiration on my shirt dried into salt, I thought reverently, almost religiously, "life doesn't get better than this." No one else was on the trails, and I saw only beautiful ordinary things, a three-toed box turtle, droppings I could not identify but wanted to believe were those of a bobcat, a buckeye butterfly, and then a female Diana fritillary, the blue in her wings so iridescent that I gasped. A tangle of purple passion-flower vines spread across an exposed slope. The blue and white blossoms were so intense I could not study them as I did the statue. "The Holy of Holies," I thought, "beyond measurement."

The first two clinics Linda and I visited had shut. The third, Mercy, was closed, but a secretary said it would open the following day at ten o'clock. The clinic was open two days a week, Tuesday and Wednesday. It was staffed by a nurse practitioner, a good sign as practitioners were often women who had risen in the nursing ranks through experience, diligent study, and sheer intelligence. Friends in Storrs said that I had a medical degree from Walmart as I treated all my aches with exercise and advised them to do likewise. The next morning, I dosed myself with my own advice and walked to the clinic taking a roundabout route, perhaps two miles. I thought the exercise would expand my lungs and make breathing easier. It didn't. But no matter, Cathy, the practitioner, was splendid, and an hour later I left Smith Drug, the only pharmacy in town, with three prescriptions and my spirits rising pulling my health along with them. I felt so good that I hailed a trolley, rode down North Main to Ice Cream Delights, and treated myself with a sweet rejuvenator, a double-chocolate soda.

Sodas alleviate spleen and melancholy, but they don't affect bronchial tubes. For the next week I slept poorly and feeling tired rarely gallivanted about mentally. I was the only writer at the Colony, and I spent hours in my room pondering matters I had strolled past for years. Why did writing usually fail to capture the ordinary niceness of nice people without distorting, that is, making them characters and thus other than they really were? Most of life was flat, and people grew accustomed to and comfortable with it. But if pages were dull readers closed books. The receptionist at Mercy was quick and competent, but she only became interesting when one noticed how rapidly she spoke. "People where I am from in Arkansas talk fast," she said. "Quick on the drawl," I said — alas. "Maybe," she said, "but I was also a 911 operator for years and that probably influences the way I talk." Terry cared for the planting surrounding the springs in town. He and I chatted every day. He collected seeds from impatiens, cleome, and cypress vine, among others, which he gave to passersby. In front of the library he planted blue swamp milkweed. One morning I counted nineteen fully-grown monarch butterfly caterpillars on two stems. Terry was part of the fabric of my Eureka but in his unalloyed niceness not suitable for owning a cat named Cowboy.

One afternoon during my last week an old man (probably younger than me) boarded the trolley at Fain's Herbacy. He was humpy with weight and pulled himself laboriously into the trolley. Once safely inside he looked around nervously then addressed the driver and me. "My wife will have to catch the next one," he said. "She's run down to the bathroom." The remark was common-place, and I wondered why I jotted it down. "What do you think?" I wrote Vicki. "Come home," she wrote back. I did not describe the other passenger sitting at the back of the trolley. Professional football players who refused to stand during the national anthem enraged him. "They should be booted out of the country," he inexplicably announced to no one and everyone. High blood pressure turned his face red, and veins throbbed explosively across his forehead. "Send them to Mexico," he yelled. It was the fourth time I'd heard criticism of football players who knelt during the anthem.

I looked out the window. Boneset and white crown beard bloomed in the broken soil along the road. A comforter of sweet pea slouched listlessly over a wall then gathered backward into a second blooming. English ivy swallowed trees, and cabbage whites bobbed about cleome like marionettes. Titmice foraged the scrub bracketing the springs, and nuthatches jerked across hickories like broken pinwheels. The next morning at dawn as I ran past the Palace Hotel, a young raccoon climbed out of a gulley and followed me "cheerrupping" piteously. Either the raccoon associated me with his mother or confused me with someone who fed him scraps. Only by weaving eights across the road was I able to draw the youngster to back to the gulley where I clapped my hands and frightened him into scampering into the brush. Afterward I felt sad, probably because the animal's cries were wrenching or maybe because I'd reached that time of life when life itself made one sad.

Regrettably, I occasionally think, sadness like happiness is ephemeral. Five hours later I was on East Mountain sitting beside Keith in a swing on his front porch. Earlier I waved at him as I walked past. He waved back and invited me to join him on the porch. Keith was 92 and had farmed and delivered mail. His wife was at work. She was 91, but her doctor advised not to retire. Keith described his children, his family's homesteading in Arkansas in 1832, and his years in the Air Force during the Second World War. People today complained too much he opined and repeated an anecdote that he said had made the local rounds. "A woman in a restaurant complained to her waiter because the cook put the pickles on her hamburger upside down." The ambling talk seemed to make me approachable. A woman active in the Native Plant Society noticed my looking at flowers and showed me two plants I had not seen before: beautyberry, its stems beaded with purple berries and to the eye cheeky and jangling, and Texas green eyes, a daisy-like flower with scratchy leaves and eight yellow petals circling a green disk. As always flowers broke my stride. Morning glories bind me, and I cannot pass an orchestra of blue trumpets without hearing the bells and gazing in inarticulate delight.

Beside stepping stones to a house grew a bed of red salvia. From the side the flowers looked like miniature ducks, the anthers sticking sharply ahead like bills, the lower lobes swinging down and trailing like wings. The seed capsules of red buckeye were small reddish pears. The blossoms of rattlesnake master had dried into scratchy seed heads while on the shoulders of gravel roads perilla grew in low blue-green thickets. I crushed a handful of leaves and smelled them. I liked their fragrance, but oddly they made me think of linoleum. I chewed a wad of hairy mountain mint leaves and washed the aroma out of my nose. Near Little Eureka Spring, I met a woman walking two dogs. The dogs were the homely sorts of pets owned by purebred people. They were rescues, literally so. "Three years ago," the woman told me, "when I was driving on a state highway, the car in front of me slowed down. A passenger opened a back door and threw the dogs onto the shoulder of the road. The driver then sped away. I pulled off the road, opened my door, and called the dogs, and here they are." Later Terry stopped his truck and asked about my cough. On the trolley an old man talked about his life. When he was young, he left the United States and spent two years searching for Paradise, wandering through Afghanistan, Nepal, Iran, and Pakistan. "The things I was escaping from — that I wanted to get rid of," he told me. "They all wanted."

On the trolley another afternoon, I caused a stir because I wasn't familiar with Little Debbie snacks. Sitting across from me was a young family, a man, his wife, and their baby girl. They lived in Gentry, Arkansas, "a really nice town of about three thousand people." The town's biggest employer was the Little Debbie factory hiring 1500 people from Gentry and the surrounding area. Passengers on the trolley reacted with disbelief on my saying I'd never heard of Little Debbie or tasted any of her snacks: cakes, brownies, pies, muffins, snack bars, amid sugar beet fields of others. Among Little Debbie's cookies were fudge rounds, peanut clusters, jelly crème pies, chocolate marshmallow pies, and star crunch, this last a blend of oatmeal and crisp rice. Among her mini donuts were frosted, glazed, powdered, strawberry, and double chocolate. The trolley driver shook his head then announced, "I'm going to Dollar General tonight and buy some." "I'll keep them handy, and the next time you get on the trolley," he said to me. "I'll give you a couple." "You will like them," the young man said. What, of course, I liked were the young man and the trolley driver, an unexpected affection that increased my feeling like an

229

alien—a southerner companionable with other southerners, yet someone whose tastes were different and who didn't belong.

The day I left Eureka, John stopped the trolley beside Colony. "I will miss you on the trolley," he said. "Have a good trip and be sure to come back." Several people urged me to return. "Artie will wonder where you've gone," Jay said, Artie being Jay's dog. When people asked when they'd see me again, I said "never." If the past determined the future, sixteen years would elapse between visits and I'd be 93, rather my ghost would be 93. Behind Harmon Park, Fuller, a gravel road, ascended West Mountain climbing to Prospect. A deep ravine paralleled the road. Buzzards roosted in trees growing on the slopes of the ravine. Some mornings I stood on Fuller and watched the buzzards leave the roost exploding out of trees that looked bare. In the evening I watched them return. The numbers were large. Two or three hundred, one man told me. At dusk when they floated and swirled like motes, I often counted fourteen or fifteen at a time. "I'd come back if," I told a poet, "after I fell into the dustbin, people would dump me into the ravine. I'd be buzzard bait. The birds would eat me. I'd become part of them, and bits of me would then live and fly."

In a way, Eureka accompanied me back to Connecticut. "Because of climate change," Fred a university entomologist said in an interview, "lone star ticks and chiggers can now be found in Connecticut." Hot or cold, I did not expect to see the number of walking sticks I spotted in Eureka. Walking sticks fed at the tops of trees. Built on the tops of bluffs, many houses in Eureka were shaped like corner braces. Entrances faced roads, and first stories extended backward over the bluff. From the back edge of the first or top story of the house two or three levels descended the face of the bluff to the ground below. As a result, top stories abutted crowns of the trees growing from the ground bringing walking sticks close to hand and eye. "What about that?" I said to Vicki. "Fascinating," she said crumbling feta cheese over lettuce and not looking up. I brought a handful of dried paulownia seed pods back to Connecticut. Their inner surface glowed golden brown. I didn't show the pods to Vicki.

Although I was a poor tourist, I bought Vicki a present. From Ken at the EureKan Art, I purchased a ten by thirteen-inch painting by Tom Henrichsen a local artist. I got the painting because Vicki loved clouds. In the painting clouds shimmied across a blue sky almost massaging it. Below stretched a green pasture. On it were six rolled bales of hay. They looked radiant and made me dream of walking across the field to the horizon. Of course, the field was chiggerless as were the fields in all the paintings Vicki and I owned. Our fields were quiet places — sentimental but always awakening reverence.

The day after returning from Eureka I wandered wood and field. I hadn't missed goldenrod. The field behind the beaver pond was a tempest of yellow. Growing on a shoulder of a sandy road was white lettuce, a flower I rarely noticed. Along shady, damp paths blewits gleamed like amethysts. As the mushrooms aged, orange spread from the bell-shaped centers of their caps like aureoles. Clustered over a stump in a pine wood were red rider mushrooms, their caps purple and red, densely covered with scales. Or I think they were red riders. Maybe they were yellow riders. So many hickory tussock moth caterpillars blundered across the kitchen stoop that the steps looked as if someone sat on them and shredded a sweater. "You'll miss the people in Eureka and their stories," David said the first morning we ran together. David was wrong. That night I dreamed about Benny. He had never been to Eureka, but I knew a lot about Benny's life. Immediately after his birth he was handed over to an adoption agency. Three years later a woman adopted him. Unbeknownst to the agency the woman was Benny's natural mother. Moreover, she was an alcoholic. Some years later she tried to kill Benny by running over him with her car. He escaped and killed her, the dream did not explain how he did her in. Benny then returned to the adoption agency. Shortly afterward a couple in Dallas adopted him. The agency did not realize the couple were the parents of Benny's mother. They were also alcoholics, and eventually they tried to kill him. The family was not imaginative, and they, too, attempted to run him over. They failed, but Benny did not fail — again.

"How he killed them is important," Vicki said. "No," I said leaving the room to answer the telephone, "life is full of mysteries." David was on the line. "You probably haven't watched television yet," he said, "but when you do, you'll notice advertisements for an antipsychotic drug Halol and the eyedrops that I use Duresol." "Well," he continued, "I forgot to tell you that during your absence I invented Damitol. It will make me a rich man. The drug causes people to fly into apoplectic rages which stir the blood, raise metabolic rates, burn off calories, release tension, and leave people relaxed and euphoric. The possible side effects are minimal, including only the loss of friends, alienation of family members, accumulation of enemies, and eternal exclusion from all properties beyond the Pearly Gates."

Yes, stories appear in pairs. That afternoon I remembered a mean-spirited teacher who taught at Dartmouth during the years I was there. How I forgot her I do not know. But then I never talked to her. In any case she died many years ago. She hated her parents and in classes excoriated family ties. Rumor said that after her parents died, she had them cremated and kept their ashes in a bucket in the trunk of her car. On snowy days when her driveway was slippery she sprinkled the ashes under her car's rear tires. "Finally," she supposedly remarked, "my parents are good for something." People also said that when her dog and goldfish died, she had them cremated and added their ashes to the bucket. Additionally, a former colleague of hers stated that she harvested road kill. She was instrumental in his being denied tenure. Consequently, he rarely missed an opportunity to malign her. For the record his accounts of her doings were not always accurate.

According to him, she kept a shovel and a pail on the floor in front of the backseat of her car, and no matter how mushy they were, she scooped a wildlife refuge of small creatures off the asphalt. She took them home and reduced them to ashes, cooking them on her deck on a hibachi that she paid a welder to adapt to her purposes. "Over the course of a year," the man said, "she barbequed treehouses of squirrels, warrens of rabbits, dens of snakes, and aviaries of birds." She left moose and deer alone; they were too heavy for her to lift, except, of course, the occasional fawn. "Blessed highway offerings," she called fawns. When her neighbors lost dogs and cats, they suspected that she ran over them and fed them to her hibachi. Suspicions, of course, were not proof, no matter how reasonable the circumstantial evidence. Still, neighbors kept their pets inside when they noticed that her car was not in the garage. "All that can't be true," Vicki said when I stopped talking. "Is it?" "Probably not. It doesn't matter," I said. "I just wish that you and I were not the only dog walkers living on Hillside Circle."

Allergies

I have been stung by honey and bumble bees, paper wasps, bull ants, and swarms of bald-faced hornets and yellow jackets. I have stepped barefoot on the stinging hairs and spines of slug and saddleback caterpillars. Rarely have I explored wood and scrub without being jabbed into a jump and exclaiming, "Oh, shit!" I've inhaled the setae of flannel caterpillars, and the hairs of gypsy moth caterpillars have raised ridges on my arms. I have fallen over and been submerged beneath waves of nettles hotter than boiling oil. Poison ivy grows faster on me than it would if farmed hydroponically. Often, I returned from wandering the outdoors having been stung so many times that my face resembled a knobby cluster of red grapes. Mysterious bites and stings have made my legs bloat and look broiled. Twice I munched berries that made my throat swell and almost blocked my breathing. In the spring when I mow the lawn, grass pollen makes me cough, gag, and eventually throw up. In the fall when I rake leaves, mold doubles me over, and I throw up again. In lakes I attract leeches; in the ocean, ill-tempered jellyfish. Yet, not until recently have I thought about allergies. As a child I lived on peanut butter, and instead of making me break into hives, penicillin saved my life. I could eat a salad of ragweed, and the only time I sneezed as a child was when I tickled the inside of my nose with a straw.

Age has changed my tolerance of and fondness for welts and jabs. Once upon a time after the pain and swellings passed, showing and telling took over adding zest to my days. This year pollen from birches and red maples turned my nostrils into unruly creeks, and two weeks ago, a mystery insect stung me on the little finger of my right hand. The finger turned purple and doubling in size looked like the outside finger on a child's baseball glove. For six days the finger throbbed, and my hand sweltered. I wondered if a harvester ant stung me, but I have never seen a harvester in Storrs. "Maybe a cow killer," I said to Vicki, a doubtful attribution because I did not spot the wasp. Vicki urged me to see a doctor. I refused. Much as I'd aged beyond susceptibility to the pricking of all lusts except that of the Platonic variety, so my allergy to stings had clearly worsened. It had not, however, reached and never would reach the anaphylaxis and epinephrine stage. "Gone," I muttered later as I looked at my little finger wondering if the skin would split, "gone are the hardy boyish days when eight or ten stings led only to bad language."

Taxonomies simplify living by defining and separating. Some people, Chesterton wrote, identified the lower classes as "humanity minus ourselves." Retirement has given me the leisure to overindulge observation. Rarely, alas, does a closer walk with a stranger foster tolerance and active benevolence. Often it induces distaste and causes a person to distance himself. I am now allergic to a superfamily of humanity, an Apoidea of types, exposure to which blisters, particularly educational drones collecting money for universities that are hedge funds with hives of classrooms attached. I am also allergic to the allergies of other people, for example, both that of the wealthy for the poor and that of the poor for the wealthy. Complicating the diagnosis of an allergist is the fact that I'm occasionally allergic to consistency. For example, I avoid spirits and the conversation of topers. But then a mixologist stirs a story into talk and turns demon bourbon into a mint julep. In his *Reminiscences and Recollections*, "anecdotes of camp and society 1810 to 1860," Captain Gronow described Twisleton Fiennes, the Late Lord Saye and Sele, a legendary epicure and bacchanalian. "I shall never forget the astonishment of a servant I had recommended to him," Gronow wrote. "On entering his service, John made his appearance as Fiennes was going out to dinner and asked his new master if he had any orders. He received the following answer, 'Place two bottles of sherry by my bedside and call me the day after tomorrow.'" Such a tale is worth a hot flash of mental cirrhosis.

Additionally, I've never admired politicians. Do they run to avoid the self-knowledge that comes to every stationary person? Do they run to escape thought? Do they ache to embrace the assuaging fiction that they are not so flawed as others? How can anyone repeat the old lie and proclaim he is campaigning to serve other people when the truth is that his ego rides him, spurs jabbed into his flanks and whip hand raised above his conscience? Do many adore flowers? Flowers are "the expression of God's love to man," Joseph Breck said. In early summer do politicians saunter across sandy neglected meadows bristling with wild raisin? Do pinks and black-eyed Susans make them stop talking? Do they notice the blossoms of potato vine bleached and looking like sea shells? Do they lose themselves in the lavender mist rising from the anthers of Timothy? Do they believe that anything they accomplish can rival the blue of chicory or the yellow of bird-foot trefoil? Can they appreciate the potpourri of milkweed balls or have the malodourous fumes oozing from putrefying integrity destroyed their sense of smell? Do any ever sing, "Oh, to be beside a beaver pond now that June is there, and white tails are clipping through the air"? Presidential gardens would serve people better than presidential libraries. Obviously, I don't know much about politicians. I have never met one. During campaign season when political worker bees stream through my neighborhood, I shoo them out of my yard. Slightly less noxious and more easily avoided are sports disciples. Imagine attending a dinner at which all the other guests spent Saturdays and Sundays praying in football stadiums. Even before the aspic appetizer, a person would find himself in "The Mind of Darkness," quoting Joseph Conrad, and moaning, "The horror! The horror!"

At the end of life, a person's allergies become him. Rhetorical matters make me dropsical with bile. In two successive days last week, three people encouraged me to "Have a Great Day!" Because of their eructating, formulaic triteness, the remarks lacked the zing of a sweat bee's sting. Yet, they provoked a self-inflected response, not a reaction immediately painful with wasp kinin but instead delayed and gloppy with nausea-producing self-loathing. "Thank you," I responded to all six speakers, "that's so very nice." As my allergies to verbal and social matters have waxed, so my tongue has become waspish. At times I think everyone I have ever met, not simply people my age hastening toward their grand climacterics, visits a physical therapist. I have never talked to a therapist. I refuse to allow anyone to grope my muscles and joints. "Hands-on experiences cause callouses if not blood blisters," I explained to Vicki.

Putting socks on over damp feet is tedious and exhausting. A fortnight ago in the locker room at the Community Center when a sock pasted itself to my right heel and sprouted Velcro preventing me from pulling it above my ankle, I said aloud, "if a therapist tried to put on this sock, lumbago would knock him to the floor." Two other men were in the room. On noticing them, I continued, "not that I'd let a therapist work on my footsies. That feely stuff is a medical racket." "I'm married to a physical therapist." one of the men said. "And," the second man continued, turning the first man's simple sentence into a compound sentence, "my older son manages a firm that specializes in physical therapy." "Oh," I said, realizing the time was ripe to change the subject. "What do you think about Argyle socks?" Neither man ever wore Argyle socks, and that conversation ended before it started. I am easily deterred unless I don't want to be deterred. "Have you noticed," I then asked the men, "that people who use this locker room never groan or

237

moan? Perspiration to the tune of silence isn't exercise. What do you guys think?" A friend told me that moaning, if not whimpering, was an integral part of physical therapy, and I chose the topic to appeal to the men. My friend was wrong; the men did not respond.

Age has changed my literary taste. Nowadays I prefer Emerson to Faulkner. I like mulling Emerson's sententious wisdom, statements like "Words are finite organs of the infinite mind. They cannot cover the dimensions of what is in truth. They break, chop, and impoverish it." I have grown allergic to Southern gothic and books that depict the grotesque antics of the usual extended Southern fictional family, cousins of the Snopes, twice embraced, not removed, folks called Big Bubba Borax and Sweet Baby Tail-Tail. Becoming allergic to place and the best-known literature of that place disturbs me, and occasionally I spade into my library and exhume a book I once liked. Invariably I conclude the book should have remained buried. Last month I re-read Harry Crews's novel *A Feast of Snakes*. The *Feast* featured a carnival of feral scenes of the kind that naïve outlanders once expected in Southern novels and in the South itself. If a woman "would not come across," Sheriff Buddy Matlow locked her in his jail in Mystic, Alabama. If she continued to resist Buddy's affection, Crews recounted, Buddy turned a rattlesnake loose in her cell. "Ain't it a God's wonder what a snake can do for love," Buddy declared after a successful seduction. Buddy would have fared better had he given Lottie Mae, one of his inamoratas, a box of pralines. Sight of the snake unhinged Lottie Mae, hexed her, Lummy, a friend, said. Happily, and memorably, Lottie Mae rid herself of the hex. During a rattlesnake roundup Buddy purchased a snake condom adorned with two small fangs. The next time he courted Lottie Mae, he put on the condom. When a snake rose "straight as a plumb line" in Buddy's lap, Lottie Mae saw the mouth and fangs at the top of its body. "It was the snake she had been waiting for." She pulled a straight razor out of her shoe, and "in a single fluid movement," struck at Buddy's lap "and came away with the snake in her hand, its softening head with the needle fangs still showing just above her thumb and forefinger." Emerson never imagined the mincing which Lottie Mae practiced. For my part the scene made me erupt in spotty allergic laugher. Afterward I reinterred the novel.

"Literature in its highest forms," Richard Holt Hutton wrote, "almost always requires a certain amount of solitude, of separateness of spirit, of imaginative brooding." Hutton's requirements are boons to most writers, be they producing signatures of high or low pages. At their best allergies insulate the aged scribbler not only from the bacterial but also from the vagaries of his times. Although the anchoritic life has some appeal, I am sane. Despite my allergic reaction to the world with its wasps, caterpillars, nettlesome people, and books releasing cadaverine and putrescine, I am unable to remain reclusive for longer than a snip of time. Since childhood I have been a meanderer, and habit is stronger than allergies. "To the quietest human being, seated in the quietest house, there will sometimes come a sudden and unmeaning hunger for the possibilities and impossibilities of things," Chesterton wrote. "He will abruptly wonder whether the teapot may not suddenly begin to pour out honey or sea water, the clock to point to all the hours of the day at once, the candles to burn green or crimson, the door to open upon a lake or on a potato field instead of a London street."

On that street or in the potato field appear sights which immediately make me forlorn. Most are so trifling that they don't rise to the level of allergy. Nevertheless, because schooling civilizes, the sympathies of educated people are imperfect. Shortly after graduation I saw a student walking across the campus wearing a mortar board, black gown, and as a scarf an albino Burmese python. In Florida Burmese pythons have become an invasive species. In spring or summer females lay hatcheries of eggs, almost ninety at one count. I associate people who buy pythons from pet stores with beer cans, burgers, French fries entombed in salt and ketchup, the use of questionable medicinals, cars missing hubcaps, and pickup trucks festooned with rude bumper stickers. I suspect most purchasers are young like the boy I saw. They have rattletrap minds and hope to shift attention away from their prosaic characters. By wearing snakes, they imagine appearing adventuresome thereby attracting admirers. In truth the boy was a visual soporific less interesting than the linguistic short-order cooks who season talk with "Have a great day" or the insultingly-reductive "Have a good one."

If I sprayed myself with an antihistamine and rid myself of allergies. I'd become sleek, reverent, prudent, and in my anonymity respectable, admired, and popular. I'd be recognized as good social mayonnaise. I'd be the sort of all-purpose spread who because he didn't care about anyone or anything never criticized a raw or underdone thought. In sum or rather in subtraction, I'd be a politician. Happily, someone with allergies cannot shed his spots. Moreover, such spots spread and drift into each other like run-on sentences. Within twenty minutes of noticing the boy with the python, I overheard a man haranguing a woman about religion. He believed God created the earth for Man. "Isn't that a little presumptuous?" the woman asked diffidently. "No, haven't you read Genesis?" the man responded almost shouting. "If you were a Christian, you'd know that you and all the other daughters of Eve are responsible for evil and man's expulsion from Eden." Such talk makes my thoughts burn like shingles. If I listened to more of the conversation, I knew the sores would burst, and in viral language I'd urge the man to see a psychiatrist. I like creation stories, but I am allergic to the inhumanity Calvinistic divines have bled out of Genesis. On the wall of my study hangs a painting of Ngalyod, the Rainbow Serpent. The painting was produced by an Aboriginal artist living in Arnhem Land, and I bought it in Darwin fifteen years ago. Ngalyod can be male and female. While female she was the mother responsible for the creation of mankind. She or he also causes wet and dry seasons and can nurture as well as destroy life. In my painting she is coiled protectively around five eggs. When I look at the painting, I imagine that one of the eggs contains humanity's first ancestors. In the other eggs are flowers and trees, clouds, words, the great oceans, herds of beasts, the firmament—everything and all things, all equal and beautiful. What a soothing contrast to the allergenic biblical assertion that the earth and its denizens, vegetable and animal, rooted, feathered, real and fabulous were created for man.

Many things I notice are placebos. Neither do they cause or cure allergies. Occasionally they puzzle or delight. Deciding which can be difficult. Instead of becoming the slave of definition, perhaps it's better to keep Emerson in mind and admit that words "cannot cover the dimensions of what is in truth." My friend Josh recently sent me snapshots of four photographs mounted on a Wall of Remembrance in a community gymnasium in Louisiana. "Four pictures," Josh noted, "selected from many." The pictures were matted and encased in black fourteen by twelve-inch wood frames. The photographs depicted community members who died while exercising at the gymnasium. Under each photograph was a small oval brass plaque. Engraved in cursive on the plaque were the name of individual in the picture, dates of his birth and death, cause of death, and equipment being using when the person died. Thus, Sally Bruckner Brinker was born on April 3, 1927 and died on May 8, 2012 of a stroke while using a rowing machine. Pegram Royce was seventy-three years old when he dove into a pool after hours and drowned. Culpeper Bowman died at fifty-nine after being bowled over by a medicine ball and hitting his head on the floor, suffering an intracerebral hemorrhage. On February 13, 2016, Adelaide Bogusky died prematurely at forty-two when she got entangled in Battle Ropes and snapped her neck.

Accompanying pictures of the wall were two other photographs, the first of the motto stamped across the top of an Oklahoma license plate, "Fracking for You." In the second picture appeared a sticker pasted to the bumper of a Dodge Ram from Texas. Printed on the sticker was "Don't Fence Me In." A thick black X ran like rails through "Don't" leaving behind the imperative "Fence Me In." On the left side of the sticker was a cameo depiction of the Texas state flag with its single white star; on the right the American red, white, and blue flag. The truck was parked on the curb in front of a shop selling essential oils. Side by side in the store window, Josh wrote, were two books: *Healing Oils of the Bible* and *Lucy Libido*, "A Girlfriend's Guide to Using Essential Oils Between the Sheets." "Sam," Josh said, "in idle moments you sometimes mention leaving Connecticut and returning to Tennessee. Fifty years of living in New England have compromised your immune system. Two days after settling in the South, you'd have a massive allergic reaction and sink into a fatal catatonic stupor." Josh may be right. Next to the essential oils shop was a knife store. "Toys for Men" a sign declared. The store on the other side of the shop sold leather goods. Hanging on a rack inside the door was an assortment of Gun Pocket jackets. Manufactured by UNIK Leather Apparel, the jackets were on sale for $149.99 each. Inside the jacket was a pocket in which the wearer could conceal his 1911 forty-five caliber pistol and an extra clip of bullets. "Carry laws have really helped business," a clerk told Josh. "You should see the Concealment Purses made for pistol packing mamas." "Their prices ranged from $59.99 to $94.99, not exactly Louis Vuitton," Josh concluded. "Praise the state legislatures and pass the ammunition."

"All things are artificial," Thomas Browne wrote in *Religio Medici*, "for nature is the art of God." If that is true, mankind's aesthetic sense which neglects appreciation and concentrates on exploitation is blasphemously perverted. If it is also true that the world was created for man and that, as Genesis states, God gave man dominion over all the earth, then man is an unconscionable ingrate. Nevertheless, as a cure-all for my social allergies, a panacea common enough to be labeled patent therapy, I often roam wood and field. In contradistinction to the gospel song, the dew is not still on the roses. I walk alone, and no voice whispers in my ear. Sometimes a bee startles me, but another person's whims or opinions do not determine my pace. I am free from monosyllabic agreement and disagreement. Alas, the suspension of allergenic thought is temporary. Experienced people realize that shucking allergies is impossible. Pessimism cannot be excised and is a fact of everyday life. If an aged individual claims to be an optimist and isn't consciously lying, then he is suffering from an incurable poverty of mind. I'm allergic to such people. When I meet a goose, I imagine someone cramming a pipe down his throat and force-feeding him, fattening his liver before grinding it into foie gras. Of course, the result would be so tasteless that its best gastronomical use would be as cat food.

In the woods, the only geese I see are Canada geese, and I am silent. Words do not break out and impoverish, and my allergies ease into charmed remission. On walks all I hear and see are familiar and domestic: yellow iris in a marsh, red-winged blackbirds nesting amid cattails, overhead the high burring of gray tree frogs, and nearby the fragrance of wild pink azalea spilling over the banks of a creek. The fiddleheads of royal ferns roll into green marbles then suddenly turn brittle and begin to shred into fronds. At dusk chimney sweeps chitter and rise and fall like motes across the sight. In shadowy light the bark of northern white cedar looks pinstriped, reddish and brown, elegantly smooth but also worn into informality, fibers pulling loose here and there. The heartwood of double-file viburnum is sienna and smells berried and roasted. While the songs of vireos jump nervously like a bad conscience, those of rose-breasted grosbeaks are gay and welcoming crying "cheerio, cheer, chee." One morning I slipped off rocks loosely wrapped in algae and tumbled into a stream. Water soaked my clothes, and that night bruises bloomed along my arms and over my knees; yet, the fall was pleasing. I was dirty and cold, and in the soiled, uncomfortable moment, I was happy, my crankish allergies forgotten. As I walked home I found a newly-hatched snapping turtle withering on a dry path. I carried the turtle to a quiet inlet of the Fenton River. I held the turtle in my hand and pushed my palm under water. For a moment the turtle didn't move then it shook and wiggled off my hand into life.

At night when the dander of the world makes me cough and sneeze, I strap on a headlamp and roam the yard. Rabbits freeze immobile in the grass. While their eyes gleam silver in the light their fur spreads loose and foggy, and their bodies lose definition. Raccoons cling to the trunks of red oaks. Five or six deer trail through the woods, their eyes gold and flickering like candles carried by a procession of cowled monks. Across the ground the tinny blue flowers that make shafts of bugle seem rough and vulgar in the day soften, and the color becomes dreamy and sleep-inducing. "Crossing a bare common, in snow puddles, at twilight, under a clouded sky, without having in my thoughts any occurrence of special good fortune," Emerson wrote, "I have enjoyed a perfect exhilaration." No one with strong allergies to humanity can enjoy a perfect exhilaration. But in the woods the stings of civilization become almost unnoticeable. "If a man would be alone, let him look at the stars," Emerson declared. Today skyglow tossed upward from cities makes seeing the stars difficult. But if a man would be content let him stand under a fringe tree and inhale the absolving fragrance of its blossoms. Let him watch yellow warblers flit through alders or study the slow dance of a walking stick. Let him breath the musky spray of foxes and listen to the cocky shrilling of northern flickers. Let him cradle one of the chalices blooming on a tulip tree and let him drink deep of the orange lapping the bottom of the bowl, slowly and thoughtfully as if it were communion wine.

Let him also be aware that contentment on the moldy above-ground side of the grave is evanescent. There is no land of pure delight. On both banks of the Jordan flowers wither and the living green dries to straw. A person's winged thoughts, as Thoreau put it, inevitably turn into poultry. The next hour, the next day, I will blurt something regrettable or a cloying acquaintance will say, "I'm praying for you." I will be tempted to respond, "I hope you mean to the Rainbow Serpent?" But I won't say anything. Consequently, an allergy to my own cowardly respectability will break out, and I'll retreat to the quietest room in my quiet house. The retirement won't last long. Home is where the heart dies. "You should be as a pipe for any wind to play upon," Robert Louis Stevenson advised walkers. At home I'll sit and read. Too often the winds that play upon me are fetid. Two days ago, I started a novel but kicked it into the waste can when an insane girl adorned her hair with a barrette of her own feces. That afternoon the mail brought the photograph of another picture hanging on the Wall of Remembrance, this of Carter (Duke) Sudduth who committed suicide after losing his bearings on an elliptical trainer and becoming a liberal was shunned by his devout friends. Folded inside the local newspaper was a flyer inviting me to join a literary group on the town square on Saturday and explore my "inner creativity." On the radio a gosling honked endlessly about "the transformative effects" of the mid-life crisis. "Listen to the voice of your inner angel and lay your head upon her manly shoulder." Such inanities cause headaches even to mechanical men with aluminum ears. The prating forces listeners to swallow objections to gagging commonplaces. It almost drives them to the extreme of dosing themselves with life-long learning in hopes of exhuming courses that teach knotting necks and extension cords.

Four times during the day a solicitous robocaller

urged me to take advantage of a special promotion promising "peace of mind twenty-four hours a day, seven days a week." The offer consisted of a medical alert system. Purchasers hang little buttons around their necks and press them if emergencies arise. Instantly they are connected to advanced care specialists. During the fourth call an allergic flush spread over my face. Although I knew that I was addressing a machine not a person, I raised my voice and described the barnyard activities of the caller's mother in scarlet round-heeled detail. By the next morning I calmed down and went to Dog Lane Café to have coffee with friends.

Elderly people reminisce and look backward with complacency. They don't live new lives. They are at ease with their mediocrity, and their conversation soothes. They tell good tales and are canny enough to appreciate anecdotes. "My Uncle George died last month," Larry recounted. "But it doesn't matter. He didn't leave me anything." "At the family dinner last Christmas," Belle recalled, "I was seated next to my ten-year-old grandson. An absolute horror! The prospect of schoolboy conversation inflamed my diverticulitis." "What did you do?" Larry asked. "I behaved sensibly," Belle responded. "I funneled wine down the urchin's throat and made him tipsy. When he banged his head on the table, my daughter was forced to remove him from the room and take him upstairs and put him to bed. He did not return." Age itself is the source of much conversation. John's wife Martha bought him an electric lawnmower at Home Depot. John unloaded it from the car then took it to the side yard and assembled it. After adjusting the handle to his height, he pretended to fiddle with the machine, examining its parts, turning it onto the side, and lifting it off the ground, every so often shouting an expletive peppery with exasperation. "Honey," he eventually said going into the house and addressing Martha directly. "What kind of lawnmower did you buy — some sort of Chinese mechanical tangram? I can't start the damn thing. Where in the hell do I put gasoline and oil?"

John thought his remark hilarious. Unfortunately, Martha didn't laugh. She believed he was serious, and nothing he said later convinced her that he was joking and wasn't simply an old guy who had slipped another notch closer to the ground.

Between rows of reminiscences my friends sow remarks about human nature frequently transplanting aphoristic reflections from wise books to clear the fuliginous hours. "If a man must needs be conceited," Henry said quoting G. K. Chesterton, "it is certainly better that he should be conceited about some merits or talents that he does not really possess." "Robert Lynd wrote something almost as perceptive in *The Cockleshell*," Belle noted. "I can scarcely recognize a blessing in disguise except when it is bestowed upon somebody else. The theory that blessings in disguise are constantly happening to other people I find consoling," Lynd said, "it enables me to bear their troubles without feeling too miserable." Earlier in the year, Larry cited Agnes Repplier's criticism of overly-assiduous editors whose notes interrupted reading. They, Repplier, wrote, build bridges over raindrops and "put ladders up a pebble."

In the eighteenth-century Edward Young criticized people who quoted excessively, writing, "Some for renown on scraps of learning dote, / And think they grow immortal as they quote." My coffee mates quote frequently and often discuss death, but they don't believe in immortality. They know words molder quicker than flesh and recognize that all ends are full-stopped. However, if forced to choose between resurrection of the body and that of the mind, they'd choose the latter, especially if its temporal lobes were tumescent with wit. Recently, Albert announced that he had written his obituary. "If I list it as forthcoming, can I include it among the publications on my resumé?" he asked. We agreed unanimously that he should include it. We also concurred that it was unlikely that he'd see it in print. Larry then interrupted saying he agreed with Clarence Day's Father who supposed that all people had to die and "said he wouldn't mind if people died only once in a while, as they used to." "But," Father continued, "he didn't know what the matter was nowadays, somebody died every month."

Only rarely do we talk about local doings, but occasionally happenings astonish us. Last fall, a Human Resources administrator went to a pharmacy in Vernon to get a flu shot. The store's computer was broody, and after entering the administrator's name and date of birth, the clerk had to massage the keyboard before the machine consented to bring up the man's medical record. The machine preoccupied the clerk, and she didn't notice that the man had only one arm. He'd lost his right arm years earlier in a car wreck. Once the insurance information appeared on the screen, the clerk asked, "in which arm would you like the shot?" "I don't think that's funny," the administrator responded. "What kind of horrible person are you? You aren't blind. Use your eyeballs." "Huh?" the clerk said looking up from the computer. "Oh, my god!" she exclaimed when she saw the man lacked an arm. "I am so sorry," she said staring at the stump of his right arm. She was so flustered she confused right and left. "Clearly you'll have the shot in your right arm since that's the only . . ." She didn't finish the sentence. "You insensitive lump! You vacuous imbecile! You'll pay!" the man said raising his stump, jabbing it at her as if his missing hand was filled with graveyard dirt, and shouting repeatedly, "Take that." The clerk took it poorly. She went home in tears and didn't return to the pharmacy until the following week. Even so she resigned shortly thereafter. She could not sleep after coming back to work. Every night she had a nightmare in which a one-armed man chased her though a dark house, carrying her coffin under his left arm.

For the record we do not discuss politics. The subject is bumptious and oozes urushiol. Nevertheless, occasionally one of us slips. Last month before we shushed him, Henry opined that in present-day America "civil obedience is moral disobedience." Henry is verbally trigger-happy and is fond of shoot-from-the-lip maxims. He is also a retired lawyer. "If you want justice in the United States, you have to buy it," he once declared. On another occasion he quoted the old saying, "He who preaches war is the devil's chaplain." "Never trust a man who doesn't mow his own lawn," he said last Friday. "I don't know about that," Larry responded. Larry's mowing ended years ago. He almost amputated his left foot shortly after disobeying his wife Peggy and buying a chainsaw. On most days we disperse after we've had a cup of coffee or if we are feeling adventuresome two cups, one of which our cardiologists advise us ought to be decaffeinated. Twice outside the café on the sidewalk we sang a benediction, not a canticle from Morning Prayer, but a verse from an old music hall song: "We're all growing older, older every day, / Older and older, so the people say; / Some are growing uglier, and some are growing gray, / But we're all growing older every day." At the end of the verse we didn't bow our heads and whisper "Amen." Instead we grinned and shouted a rhyming "hurray."

When I left the café on this occasion, I was alert and in good spirits. Behind a rack of pamphlets on the town square stood two Jehovah's Witnesses. Passersby avoided them, and the men looked forlorn, so I stopped and chatted. At the end of the conversation, I said, "Be seeing you." "Do you live nearby?" one of the men asked. "Yes, on a side street not far from here," I answered. "Well, then," the man said, "We'll be seeing you first." Later as I sauntered home along a state highway I watched a chipmunk scoot under sweet fern then noticed a damsel fly clinging to an autumn olive. The wings of the fly were gray and modest and hung down over its back like a veil. A doe stood on a ledge above the road. She looked posed. Her skin glowed in the sunlight, and muscles rippled across her flanks in currents. Bunched along the shoulder of the road were bouquets of yellow hawkweed. Ox-eyed daisies had begun to bloom and were so bright and spirited that I smiled. Sadly, the smile disappeared quickly. I spotted a painted turtle in the road, but on darting onto the asphalt to rescue the turtle, I discovered that someone had run over it exploding its shell. The turtle was on the center line, and the driver who crushed it strayed out of his lane on purpose. "Damn," I exclaimed, but I didn't limit myself to one expletive. Exposure to the human mongrel makes me fester into words, and I described the driver's phylum, class, order, family, genus, and species, this last, rancidulus filius canis or for the urbane cosmopolite, schweinehund.

Breakdown Years

When I was forty-one, a doctor warned me that unless a surgeon operated on a disk in my lower back I'd be unable to walk in five years. I like doctors. Some of my closest childhood friends became doctors. My friends were smart, and the advice they and other doctors have given me has been unfailingly sensible. I am, however, a terrible patient and a bad example. I am irrationally willful and rarely heed advice, particularly when it's for my good. I have ignored high fevers, tumors, broken bones, torn muscles, and tumblers of blood. I have sliced off growths, opened sores, cauterized cuts, pulled out toenails, and sandpapered poison ivy off my arms and legs. I have discharged myself from a hospital twelve hours before a scheduled operation. I have shredded prescriptions, and although my motor is leaking have given up all additives be they vitamins, ACE inhibitors, or STP. And, of course, I have lied repeatedly to family about my health, starting with my parents when I was a small boy and continuing with Vicki now that I am an old man.

Thirty-six years have passed since the doctor advised me to have a back operation, and I am still walking. Actually, I am slightly hobbled. Five weeks ago, when I was jogging, pain suddenly lanced out from my spine and cracking across my backside splintered down my right leg. When I mutter to myself, I forswear rough language. Only when a health matter flares into disruption, do I use the f-word. Then I say, "Fuck it! I'll work through this." Five weeks ago, I used the f-word followed by "I'll run this pain into the ground." I failed. Increasing speed and mileage didn't help. Of course, I have not consulted a doctor. The only hand I trust with a scalpel is my own. I know that the disk that caused trouble years ago has come out of hibernation and is bulging. Twenty years ago, I stopped swimming because chlorine prompted me to sneeze uncontrollably and made my eyes water and burn. I realized, however, that if I didn't exercise I'd become grumpy, eat candy stores of consoling chocolate lard, and swell, to use Vicki's word, *blubbercated*. As a result, I've resumed swimming. I have, however, moved uptown and now call it practicing the natatory art. Swimming is not pain free, but the exercise doesn't hurt as much as running does, and maybe after two or three months in the pool I'll be able to jog again.

Five days a week I swim for an hour and a quarter, about the time Byron took to swim the Hellespont. I swim slightly over a mile, the distance from Sestos to Abydos. Cold water and high waves caused Byron to abandon his first attempt. On Byron's return to land, Frederick Chamier recounted, "his look was that of an angry disappointed girl, and his upper lip curled like that of a passionate woman." In contrast to its initial effect upon Byron, I hope that swimming will tighten my chest muscles and reducing the cup size of my bosom make me appear manlier. William Ekenhead, a lieutenant in the Royal Marines, accompanied Byron on the swim. Not long afterward Ekenhead was promoted to captain, and later while celebrating his promotion fell off a bridge in Malta and was killed. No one accompanies me on my swims, thereby reducing the likelihood of marine history repeating itself. Although currents made crossing the Hellespont difficult transforming one mile into four, I don't think Byron could master the challenges I face. He swam naked, and I doubt he could cope with a saggy bathing suit, chlorine, goggles, a nose clip, and a school of aged women in nearby lanes waving their fins in unison, exercising to the music of Chubby Checker.

Browning began "Rabbi Ben Ezra," writing, "Grow

old along with me! / The best is yet to be, / The last of life, for which the first was made." If Homer can nod, so can fine poets, but to all except readers whose goggles are fogged over, Browning's lines are claptrap. As one ages, faces lose name tags, familiar roads become unfamiliar, stories leak from storied urns, and animated verse falls flat. As a person floats downstream, his body changes. In *A Traveller in Little Things*, W. H. Hudson recounted meeting a ploughman in his seventies who did not realize that his senses had "faded" but instead believed that the world had deteriorated and grown darker. When he was a boy, the man recounted, he used to hear larks and see yellow hammers. "I never told him," Hudson wrote, "that yellow hammers could be seen and heard all day long anywhere on the common beyond the green wall of elms, and that a lark was singing loudly high up over our heads while he was talking of the larks he had listened to sixty-five years ago in the Vale of Aylesbury."

For years my friend David and I have competed against each other in "The Great Coin Game." We keep eighteen-day score cards on which we record the number of coins found each day. All coins count the same. A quarter is not an eagle, and a dime isn't a birdie. Until recently the rules have been constant, and we played as equals. But time has forced me to grant David a handicap. He has gone blind in one eye, and although my world has darkened like that of Hudson's ploughman, I still see out of both eyes. As a result, to be fair and stay on par with my cycloptic friend, for every coin he finds, I must now find two. Despite the handicap, I thought that I could still get the better of David. Before agreeing to assume the burden of extra coins, I noticed a bank bag of coins scattered across the bottom of the pool at the Community Center. One morning when the pool was empty, I went treasure hunting. Alas, not one coin was a silver cob. They were all corn plasters.

Would that I swam like Byron unhampered and free, only spray trailing behind me, or that a lifeguard-gatherer followed me and scooped up my belongings. When a person enters the age of forgetfulness, life ought to become simpler. Instead it becomes more complex. Once I dashed through my taxes like members of Polar Bear clubs racing into cold ponds laughing and splashing, celebrating the coming of spring. Now the forms almost drown me. My blood pressure soars, and I gasp and splutter and grind my fists into my eyes in hopes of rubbing away the swirling plankton of figures. Before and after swimming I wend though untold snags. All are barbed and because I am forgetful not until later do I notice that one of my things is missing, left at home, at poolside, or in the locker room.

The number of items seems countless. I ride my bicycle to the Community Center. In the basket I carry a lock and chain. Before leaving the driveway, I put on a helmet and clip the right leg of my trousers tightly to my leg. I do this last to prevent the gears from grabbing my pants, jerking me sideways, and dumping me on the street like road kill. At the Center I lock the bicycle to a rack, thread my left arm through the straps on the helmet, and so I won't lose or forget it, as I have done in the past, I attach the clip to the handlebar. To help me remember to put the clip on before I set out for home, I wrap it around the gear shift on the righthand side of the bar. I also carry a small sports bag in the bicycle basket. In the bag are a towel, shampoo, a swimming suit, and a cloth eyeglass case with three pockets, two sealed with Velcro, the other with a zipper. I put my goggles and nose clip in the Velcro pockets. On being given a locker key at the Center, I put the key in the zipper pocket. Despite the zipper the key wanders unconscionably. It has invisible legs and escapes supervision after I open my locker. It is diabolically addicted to vanishing when I change from street clothes into my bathing suit then after swimming when I remove the bathing suit and don street clothes again. Sometimes it hides under the bench in front of my locker, other times in my sports bag. Thrice it has remained in the cubicle in which I showered after swimming. Before drying I removed it from the eyeglass case and in preparation for opening my locker laid it on a shelf. I then forgot about it. A considerate key would call or at least whistle when I leave the cubicle, but my key is fond of hide-and-go-seek and remains silent. As any oldster will know, I carry other things. Under my coat I wear a fleece with zipper pockets. In the pocket on the right side I put a house key and a small metal strip that allows me to use the pool at the Center. In the pocket on the left side of the fleece I store my wrist watch. These items are better behaved than the key, but, they, too, bear close observation. Zipping up rather than down closes the pockets on the fleece, an engineering matter that confuses me. Despite being wet and heavy my bathing suit and towel manage the occasional disappearance. The suit is not bold, and it doesn't roam from the shower cubicle. In contrast the towel is an adventuresome traveler. One morning as I left the Center I noticed that the sports bag was light. I looked inside and discovering that my towel was missing, I returned to the Center. I searched by the pool, in and around the locker room, and in the lounge and lobby. I was thorough. I even explored halls, some of which I had never walked. I was mystified until a kindly, younger swimmer pointed at my neck and said, "Maybe, that's it." Following swimming, I had put on my shirt then sat down on a bench to pull up my underpants and trousers. So that I would not forget the towel, I wrapped it around my neck. Promptly I forgot it and left it around my neck while I put on my fleece and jacket, zipping both up to my Adam's Apple. So far my bicycle helmet has behaved well. I attribute this comportment to confidence resulting from size. The helmet does not have to misbehave to be noticed.

Younger people might not think my watery adventures as exciting as those experienced by Odysseus as he sailed back to Ithaca. But, quite frankly, seasoned old guys will testify that Odysseus's troubles with Polyphemus,

Scylla, Charybdis, and the omophagic Laestrygonians were kid stuff in comparison to my aqueous struggles. By the by breaking down has some positive consequences. Generally only exhaustion results from practice. But an endless litany of ailments enables the elderly to perfect the art of complaint. Moreover, a regimen of complaints teaches a person how to control conversation. A pleasing conversation depends upon not listening. Whenever an experienced complainer meets an acquaintance, he should immediately ask, "How are you doing?" Almost always the person will begin to describe his afflictions. Before he disconnects the ankle bone from the shin bone, however, his inquisitor should tremble spasmodically then cough violently sounding like a loose agitator inside a washing machine. "Oh, Lord! What in the world is wrong with you?" the acquaintance will exclaim thus handing the reins of conversation over to the master complainer.

In discussing autobiography in *Hours in a Library*, Leslie Stephen said that distorting a neighbor's character didn't provoke wonder. But, he continued, "it is always curious to see how a man contrives to present a false testimonial to himself." Autobiography is not an Anabaptist genre in which chroniclers depict absolute truths. If a man lives long, he is not simply one person but a group of people most of whom have faded leaving behind hazy anecdotes. In crafting his autobiography, a man does not so much present a false picture to himself and others as he gathers bits of the past and present, and often of expectations that he imagines he will have in the future. These he cobbles together producing a being that has and has not existed and whose depiction is both accurate and inaccurate. Memory does not recall clearly. It fabricates, and if the goal is impossible, that is, to produce marmoreal truth, it does not serve the autobiographer well.

Stephen's caveat about the autobiographical kindles flawed criticism and distorts reality, the truth of which must necessarily be partly false. With age, chroniclers generally become more honest. Life narrows. Ambition smolders, and possibilities turn to ash. Writers accept their unimportance and realize how calmly friends and family members will bear their departure. Their deaths and the deaths of their books will be passings—quick and pro forma. In their breakdown years, aging writers, however, often become liable to accusations of academic dishonesty. Aware of ends, they grow impatient with the prescriptions of writerly propriety. They stop worrying about plagiarism and quote unhampered by quotation marks, a sensible, time-saving practice not appreciated by immature censors. For my part I generally cite sources but not always. Quotation marks resemble dog tails and break the flow of an elegant page transforming it into a visual kennel. As justification I quote H. G. Wells and for the ironic Hell of it studiously identify him. Wells urged pen-pushers to consider the feelings of the dead. He disliked grave robbers. No decent person scavenged through the winding sheets of other people's books. Wells thought it poor form to glue the words of the dead next to statements made by people with whom they'd never have associated in life. "The only artistic, the only kindly, and the only honest method of quotation is plagiary." If you cannot plagiarize, Wells advised, "surely it were better not to quote."

In one's breakdown years, the most effective literary jump-starter is autobiography. "Do we all become garrulous and confidential as we approach the gates of old age?" Mrs. Humphrey Ward speculated. "Is it that we instinctively feel, and cannot help asserting our one advantage over the younger generation, which has so many over us?—the one advantage of time!" The answer to both questions is "yes." "The garrulity of old age, and the aptitude of a man's mind to recur to the passages of his own life," Anthony Trollope explained, prompted his writing autobiography. In introducing his account of his life, Alfred Austin wrote, "The garden that I love—the society of days gone by is the most friendly and congenial of all forms of companionship, for one peoples and composes it according to the humor of one's imagination." The writer tells stories to delight himself, not to impose sense on or elucidate the nonsensical. He plants flowers in his garden, the blooms of which only he appreciates. Last Christmas did a former Governor of Mississippi approach the cashier's counter at the Designer Show Warehouse in Manchester and address the clerk, saying, "I'm here to purchase shoes for my feet. I have been told that you sell such things. Is that correct?" "Yes," the clerk replied, "We have thousands of shoes for sale. Just look around." "Yes, I see lots of shoes," the Governor answered, "but do you sell them for feet?" Is it true that Milton composed the famous stanza that reads, "A flea and a fly in a flue / Were imprisoned, now what could they do? / Said the fly, 'Let us flee.' / 'Let us fly,' said the flea. / And they flew through a flaw in the flue." I suspect that lead article in the most recent number of the *Ophthalmologists' Review* did not focus solely on displaced eyes. In one of the cases, a practitioner described the problems endured by a patient whose eyes were far apart and so near the edges of her face that when she cried tears trickled down her back, not her cheeks. On being asked by the editor of the *Review* how he was treating the woman, the doctor replied, "With antibiotics to combat the bacteria."

Such blossoms appeal primarily to oldsters. They have time enough to imagine and appreciate while others are so busy shearing days into meaningful scraps they only see wilt. "Ignorance appraises a book by its exterior," Richard Garnett judged in *Essays on Librarianship*. What I or my friends look like is inconsequential. Of course, my friends are old. They are crumbling. Binding them in Moroccan goatskin leather and decorating them with gilt lettering won't preserve their pages. But if forced to write honestly and be true to my time of life, then let me admit that appearance determines my perception of others, excepting the elderly. "You might not be able to tell a book by its cover," my friend Josh said recently, "but a tattoo reveals all you need to know about a person." As the pool at the Community Center is only twelve feet at its deepest, so my feelings are sane and shallow. I am too old to splash around over my head in indignation. When I was young and naïve, I believed most politicians public-spirited. The despicable behavior of some officials seemed aberrant and so upset me that if I had not been stunningly healthy I might have suffered a premature breakdown. I have since learned worse. Now about the only things that rile me are bad manners and garbled prose, this last the literary equivalent of bad manners — an attitude that reflects the ancient notion that rituals matter more than beliefs. Unlike belief, ritual builds and supports community for better and for worse.

In writing about Milton, Macauley said that generalization was "necessary to the advancement of knowledge" while particularity was "indispensable to the creations of the imagination." "In proportion as men know more and think more, they look less at individuals and more at classes," Macauley elaborated. "They therefore make better theories and worse poems. They give us vague phrases instead of images, and personified qualities instead of man. They may be better able to analyze human nature than their predecessors. But analysis is not the business of the poet. His office is to portray, not to dissect." Writers who have lived beyond their allotted seventy years understand that theories resemble dust devils. They swirl and howl, kick up dirt and confuse, but then they vanish so quickly that a person has difficulty believing they existed. What matters to the anecdotal aged writer are details, not personified qualities, classes and vague phrases, but particularity, the fact that my bicycle helmet and bathing suit are blue although chlorine has caused color to begin leaching out of the suit or that Mississippi Brethren of The Whole Cloth call the male Gallus Gallus Domesticus a Gentlemen Chicken.

My days are Post-It notes of details. On a tripod beside

the registration desk at the University of Connecticut's Outpatient Medical Center in Farmington is a poster measuring two feet by three feet. Printed along the top of the poster is "We Are The Faces Of The Possible." Below are one hundred photographs arranged in ten columns of ten pictures each. All the people look pleasant, and most are smiling. While ninety-eight of the people are women, only two are men. Because he wore a blue and yellow bow tie, one of the men was easily categorized. The other man rolled his hair high up over his forehead forming a wave. At first, I thought the hairdo trendily hermaphroditic, suitable for an aspiring performer on *America Idol*. Not until a nurse drawing blood assured me that the person in the photograph was male was I certain about his gender. "Why do you care about such things?" Vicki asked later. "I don't give a hoot about biological appurtenances. I don't care that the newly-appointed dean of men at a well-known small college in New England is a woman." I responded. "But in high school mathematics courses were my favorites. I'm a counter and have always enjoyed tinkering with numbers. Although my eyesight is now blurry allowing digits to waver and wander and live independent lives, I am still addicted to trying to get figures right."

In his *Village Sermons*, Charles Kingsley asked, "Why is it that neither angels, nor saints, nor evil spirits, appear to men now to speak to them as they did of old?" "Why," he replied answering rhetorically, "because we have *books*, by which Christ's messengers and the devil's messengers, too, can tell what they will to thousands of human beings at the same moment, year after year, all the world over!" "I say, we ought to reverence books, to look at them as awful and mighty things," Kingsley continued. "Consider! except a living man there is nothing more wonderful than a book! a message to us from the dead — from human souls whom we never saw, who lived perhaps thousands of miles away." Kingsley's sermon was heterodox. Books are not codices. Scribes do not copy them on papyrus. Still, his enthusiasm is infectious. I read the *Sermons* recently and immediately started thinking about writing a diary. Although I am momentarily alive, I intend to declare that my diary was written in the 18ᵗʰ century thus transforming its pages into messages from the dead. The diary will be my intellectual coffin. In it my ruminations will be immortalized in adipociric prose. The book's binding will be leather. Tooled around the borders of the covers and along the spine will be spikes of asphodel bright with white and yellow flowers. I chose asphodels because their seeds nourish the dead. The diary will open to a frontispiece, a full-page hand-painted print. On it will appear the ruin of a red brick classical Georgian country house, a symbol which for astute readers will evoke awareness of my last years.

The roof has collapsed. In doing so it shattered the house's walls and scattered its bricks making pilfering inviting and easy for plagiaristic scavengers. One of the house's two chimneys still stands. Dreadlocks of ivy wrap the chimney turning it into a high-rise aviary with apartments. Jenny Wren, Little Robin Redbreast, Poll Parrot, and some of the four and twenty blackbirds of dainty pie fame will certainly be among the tenants. Maybe the wise old owl who the more he saw the less he spoke will also roost there although I am garrulous and not naturally inclined to discretion. Rummaging around the grounds will probably be Dapple Gray the pony, Betty Pringle's medium-sized pig, and three or four of Bo-Peep's lost sheep. According to A. C. Benson, Edward Fitzgerald said that modern writing tried to compress "too many good things into a page." I will scatter a few bulbs of daffy-down-dillies in the grass then follow Fitzgerald's advice and store my pencil in the toolshed.

No, no—let the young practice moderation. Beneath its shadow respectable mediocrity thrives lulling people to sleep and protecting them from thought. The old should live intemperately. Contrary Mary gave me a flat of silver bells and cockle-shells. I'm going to plant them.

They'll look good surrounded by a ring-a-ring o' roses. A nurseryman assured me that Aphrodite's flower will thrive if the gardener fills his pockets with a mix of posies rather than a blend of straw and manure. Still, in the throes of creation a diarist should not forget that it is not always better to receive than to give. Mary's gift may be a Trojan Holstein if the old poem "Her Dairy" accurately depicts her horticultural tendencies. "'A milkmaid, and a buttercup, and cowslip,' said sweet Mary, / 'Are growing in my garden plot, and this I call my dairy.'"

In *The Sanity of Art*, George Bernard Shaw said, "The man who writes about himself and his own time is the only man who writes about all people and all time. The other sort of man, who believes that he and his period are so distinct from all other men and periods that it would be immodest and irrelevant to attend to them or assume that they should interest anyone but himself and his contemporaries, is the most infatuated of all egotists, and consequently the most unreadable and negligible of all the authors." When a scribbler's immune system causes him to be allergic to the new, self is his only subject. If Shaw is correct, and it is nice to think so, the writer's focus on self smacks of the sublime by appealing out of time to all people. I and my car are deep into our breakdown years, the car because while I drove home from Farmington recently through a blinding snow, a light on the dashboard never stopped flashing Check Engine, and I because parts of my motor are permanently out of whack, the oil pressure heating and rising, the crankshaft racked with pain, and the gaskets around the water pump swollen and clogged.

Because I am heading for the garage, I am prefacing my diary with what is nearest to me, not memories of beginning, but, concerns about ending, that is, my will. Apportioning bubbles—money and property—is easy and can be accomplished in half a paragraph. In the attic, however, is a sugar chest of curios. At first glance the contents seem a miscellany of the odd. In fact, they are keys to my identity. I'd like them to be left to sympathetic descendants or maybe to the reading public itself. Perhaps they could be housed in a special room attached to the Library of Congress. Last night I opened the chest and pulled out a handful of things. Among them were a Singing Bone, the sheet music to "Launch the Lifeboat," two squirrel eggs, a glimpse of Beulah Land, a pair of Mrs. Wiggs' rose-colored spectacles, skin shucked from a Chunk Head snake, and the craw of the Great Speckled Bird. Finding a small nest of ninnies pleased me as did a set of studs and cuff links decorated with rainbow scarab beetles. At the bottom of a thimble sealed with wax lay the integrity of personal injury lawyers. In a pink bon-bon box were dried ice crystals harvested from a cirrus streamer as it crossed Cloud Land, the index and thumb fingers sliced from a yellow kid glove, and a lock of curly hair the wife of a tobacco farmer cut from the corpse of her Bible-Headed baby. My favorite discovery was splinters from a broomstick that crashed when the witch piloting it ran low on bile and neglected to stop at a haunted house and refill the handle.

Compendiums of wisdom gleaned from age and experience will constitute the diary's initial pages. I anticipate that the I who appears in the text will learn from the aged Gentleman of Letters who composed the diary. As *the I* becomes younger, he will imbibe wisdom and as he approaches the book's final pages will be an astonishingly learned and judicious infant prodigy. In the book I won't dwell on the days before the root of my colt's tooth was poisoned by virtue and had to be extracted. Neither will I weep through paragraphs describing sorrow. Readers experience enough unhappiness of their own and turn to books to be distracted from life as it is. Scattered throughout the diary will be blank pages. I expect that thumbprints, hunks of peanut butter, and coffee stains will eventually mark these pages. Emptiness frightens people, and as they look at the blank pages, they will unconsciously begin to imagine. They will linger over the absence of print, pausing to mull and nibble. Unlike pages pregnant with forgettable prose, emptiness always gives birth. And let me assure potential readers that not until I reach babyhood will there be nudity or any tedious descriptions of salacious doings.

Since the first page of the diary must focus on the last of me, I am not sure how to begin. Traditionally aspiring goners hear birds twittering and see flashes of seraphic light. Some practically roller-skate through tunnels to reach the light while others beg bystanders for mirrors so they can gaze at the lovely appearance of death. Harriet Paine imagined a sea shining in front of her and her elderly friends "with the white-winged bark ready to carry us to lands of undreamed-of beauty." At the Community Center a person can rent a kayak. For my part I can manage the J-stroke and paddle a wooden canoe on the Willimantic River. But I am not comfortable in kayaks. No one taught me the Juju-stroke that Paine believed would propel her through the everlasting weir onto diamond sands and golden shores.

In any case the initial pages pose a narrative dilemma. If I am roast meat for worms, I probably won't be able to write about dying. If I'm dying, writing definitively about the land across the river will also be difficult. On the other hand, I may not write the diary. When people are young and limitless choices lie temptingly before them, they generally act decisively. In contrast as people age and choices decrease and eventually disappear, they grow indecisive, in my case starting a diary one day then abandoning it before cataloging events of the preceding day. Maybe, though, I will compose a graphic diary, the autobiographical equivalent of the graphic novel. And excitingly, since the diary will focus on my existence in the 18th century, it will be the first graphic autobiography published and consequently will attract much literary and popular attention.

The decision to write or not to write aside, I have already collected sheaves of encomiums. The accolades are so astonishing that critics are bound to be jealous and spitefully accuse me of choreographing alleluias. Consequently, I won't quote more than a few. Their words are ambrosial, but for modesty's sake most of the composers must remain the choir invisible. "What a blessing it is that Robert Hitchens is now burning in furnace number 10," a poetaster wrote typically. "How distraught Hitchens would be if compelled to acknowledge that Pickering's prose reduces the acclaimed inception of *After To-Morrow* to dry sticks, sapless and too cankered to support a single anorexic titmouse." To ease the understanding of those whose studies have been restricted to the entrepreneurial, let me quote Hitchens' celebrated initial sentence: "In his gilded cage, that hung between pale-green curtains over the window-boxes that were full of white daisies, the canary chirped with a desultory vivacity."

The most moving tribute appears in James Boswell's *The Life of Samuel Johnson*. It is, however, extraordinarily long and appreciative, and I won't reprint it because I'd have to cut it and cutting would diminish Johnson's grandiloquence. One simply does not revise The Master. To pluck a lower literary chord, according to Holcroft Manly Ames, "Pickering, Esquire" is a scribe for the centuries: 18th, 19th, 20th, and 21st. "He embodies and enspirits G.K. Chesterton's admirable definition of a sentimentalist as 'a man who has feelings and does not trouble to invent a new way of expressing them.'" One tribute is an acrostic, the first letters of each line combining to spell my Christian name, Samuel. Although meant to celebrate, the poem is doggerel, and I include it only because it appeared in 1802 in the initial issue of the *Edinburgh Review*. "Sweet, sweet, happy, honey-luted diarist, / At the cry of reason's pleas, your pages fly bewinged and doth inspire / Matchless wisdom that thumbs the harp's angelic silver strings. / Unto you Athena bows and sweeps the sacred olive. / Even bold envy laps the ground and shrinks before your feet. / Long may your diary stand, a rock unmoved amid the tempest's roar." Gratifying the sentiment is, but no rational man could wish the verse more extensive. Imagine an acrostic of my last name. The first line would cause a hitch in the iambic gait of the most rhapsodic odist: "Philoctetes — you — Lemnian-man, arrow-wielder, snake-defiler, eye of the Great Horse."

Vicki opposes the decision not to print all the tributes to the diary and accuses me of vainglorious modesty. "How," she demanded, "can a person be diffident who writes only about himself? No matter how many literary tricks Harlequin teaches him, it is impossible for an over-educated, country-club jitterbugger emeritus to transform himself into Everyman." Happy men rigorously avoid knowing themselves. They are, as St. John Adcock explained, a little blind. "We lose more than we gain whose sight is so painfully keen," he wrote, "that we cannot help seeing through each pleasant fancy and detecting the bare fact that lies at the back of it." Vicki assumes she understands me better than I understand myself. Maybe she does. To be exclusively himself an Old Gentleman, Leigh Hunt wrote, "must be either a widower or a bachelor." I am neither. According to the mathematical truism, Vicki is my better half. To avoid the erasing inherent in solving linear equations, I concede that Vicki understands me better than I do. For the Holiness record, however, let me say that I enjoyed my worse half greatly and regret that it was not worser.

At the beginning of *What I Remember*, Anthony Trollope's brother Thomas said he never intended to write autobiography. "There has been nothing in my life which could justify such a pretension," he explained. However, in the next sentence he twisted through a literary volta and testified, "But I have lived a long time." After this evangelical declaration he wrote a full-bodied two-volume autobiography. A year later a third volume entitled *Further Reminiscences* appeared. I don't resemble Tom Trollope. The gestation period of a cumbersome autobiography is longer than that of an elephant. In contrast, only recently did I conceive of writing my "lofty Bibliotheca" (a critic's panegyric). Moreover, I will limit my reflections to a single volume. Certainly, the length will acquit me of being vainglorious. Additionally, it will forestall snoring and garner praise as less is inevitably more, as the great Longinus attests. Of course, since dullness defines the days of most people, I intend to include arid longueurs. The banality will be familiar to readers. Not only will the descriptions contribute to an appealing homey timbre, but they will draw readers into the text and make them feel cousinly toward me. Some will pat the book on the cover and stroke the spine as if it were my back. Others will exclaim, "Goodness, Pickering really understands my life." For example, last Tuesday morning after taking off my pajamas, putting on my clothes, and eating breakfast, I rode my bicycle to the Community Center. Once there I removed my clothes and put on my bathing suit. After swimming a mile, I took off my bathing suit and showered. After showering I put my clothes back on. I then biked to the university gymnasium where I took off my clothes in the locker room and donned running togs. After jogging for five miles, I returned to the locker room and peeled off my running outfit. I showered. I then put on my clothes and cycled home arriving at my back door at 11:56. Thus before noon, I changed dress ten times, transforming unobserved tedium into recognizable, sartorial, almost literary, boredom, the stuff of everyone's every day.

Vicki continued in the interrogative mode when I did not answer her question, asking, "how could two-hundred-year-old praise tumefy?" "You have kept no reviews of your books, no tapes of interviews, no pictures from newspapers, none of the hundreds of articles you have written, no medal, no citation, no laurel, and not a single laudatory letter from a student. Ten years after the breakdown has become permanent, you will have rusted into a granular heap of unidentifiable parts." "How then will our children discover who you were and who they are?" "They won't know anything about me, and they will be free to shape themselves," I said. "Freedom," Vicki scoffed, quoting Janis Joplin, "is just another word for nothing else to lose." "I do not want our children to be postscripts to me," I said emending a statement made by Anne Thackeray Ritchie in *From the Porch*. Actually, *plagiarized* is more accurate than *emended*. When Vicki asked if my assertion about being a footnote was original, I immediately said, "Of course. I'm a respectable textual scholar. I'm not a sentence thief, and I'm not a dumbbell." "You may be old," Vicki said, "and although your eyes blink, your back creaks, and your heart has forsaken the anapestic for an unrecognizable beat, you are still the smartest man I've ever met." "Damn straight, Pippin," I said then slipped on my coat, picked up my swimming bag, unlocked my bicycle, and rode off headed for the pool.

Sam Pickering with his daughter, Eliza, shucking peas.

About the Author

Sam Pickering grew up in Nashville, Tennessee. He spent 67 years in classrooms reading and teaching and has long been a rummager and writer wandering New England and the South, the Mid-East, Britain, Australia, and Canada. He has written some thirty books and is a member of the Fellowship of Southern Writers.